ANF          23 . 1 . 46
Gaston.
   5/8 + 2d postage
      less 5%

*Non est potestas Super Terram quae Comparetur ei Iob. 41. 24*

# LEVIATHAN
## Or
### THE MATTER, FORME and Power of A COMMON-WEALTH ECCLESIASTICALL and CIVIL

By THOMAS HOBBES of MALMESBVRY.

London
Printed for Andrew Crooke
1651

THEY (the U.S.A. and U.K.) respect the right of all peoples to choose the form of government under which they will live, and they wish to see sovereign rights and self-government restored to those who have been forcibly deprived of them.

*Atlantic Charter, Article III.*

THEY recognize the necessity of establishing as soon as possible a general international organization, based on the principle of the sovereign equality of all peace-loving States and open to the membership of all such States, great or small, for the maintenance of peace and security.

*The Moscow Declaration, Article 4.*

THE Organization is based on the principle of the sovereign equality of all peace-loving States.

*Dumbarton Oaks Tentative Proposals, Chapter II, Article (1).*

# WORLD WAR
## Its Cause and Cure

*By* LIONEL CURTIS

'To-day an anarchy of sovereign States cannot escape chronic war or preserve individual liberty or create the conditions of prosperity and employment within their own boundaries unless, in some way, they can bring themselves collectively under the reign of a single constitutional law.'

*Speech to the House of Delegates and Senate of Virginia, 17 February 1940, by the* MARQUIS OF LOTHIAN, *as British Ambassador to the United States of America.*

OXFORD UNIVERSITY PRESS
*London : Humphrey Milford*
1945

OXFORD UNIVERSITY PRESS
AMEN HOUSE, E.C. 4
London Edinburgh Glasgow New York
Toronto Melbourne Capetown Bombay
Calcutta Madras

HUMPHREY MILFORD
PUBLISHER TO THE UNIVERSITY

327

S 1492

PRINTED IN GREAT BRITAIN

# FOREWORD[1]

*By* SIR WILLIAM BEVERIDGE

THE Atlantic Charter defines the peace for whose establishment its signatories fight as a 'peace which will afford to all nations the means of dwelling in safety within their own boundaries and which will afford assurance that all men in all lands may live out their lives in freedom from fear and want'.

These are noble and simple words. They have been accepted by the leaders of all the United Nations as representing the common aspirations of their peoples. There is no doubt that they do so. How can realization of these aspirations be made secure? How can these leading words of the Atlantic Charter be turned into deeds? Mr. Lionel Curtis's pamphlet on *Faith and Works*, following its predecessors entitled *Decision* and *Action*, sets out to answer this question.

Before discussing the answer, it is well to examine a little more closely what is implied in the question, that is to say, in the words of the Atlantic Charter. Those words provide for continuance of separate nations with their own Governments; they contemplate a world of nations of many sizes, large and small, all of whom are to be able to dwell in safety within their own boundaries. At the end of the last war the aim of the victors was phrased by some of them as making the world safe for democracy. But democracy is a means, not an end. The aim for the next peace can be put better: we should decide to make the world safe for small nations.

### Freedom from Fear

That phrase implies all that is essential. If the world is safe for small nations, it will be safe for all nations. If the world is safe for small nations, it will be an ordered world in which the rights of each nation are determined by justice and not by relative strength, as in an ordered community the unarmed citizen is safe beneath the protection of the law. If

[1] These introductory pages were published as a review of *Faith and Works* in the *Observer* on the 2nd May 1943. I have to thank Sir William Beveridge and the *Observer* for their kind permission to reprint them here.

the world is safe for small nations, it will be a world in which the human spirit can blossom in all its infinite variety of national cultures and not be beaten flat into a totalitarian mould.

How can the world be made safe for small nations? Not by their dependence on a larger neighbour, for that destroys nationhood. Not by their own arms, and not by grouping themselves with other small nations; not even the largest single nation in the world to-day can be safe by its own arms, for safety does not mean living always on the brink of war, even if one survives war. It means security—being without the fact or the constant fear of war. Security for all nations, small and great, can come only through the enthronement of impartial justice between nations and the arming of justice with decisive force for her decrees. 'The scales of justice', as Mr. Winston Churchill once said, 'are vain without her sword.' Who is to supply international justice with her sword and wield it for her?

The answer to that question is given by Mr. Curtis in two propositions. First, force adequate to maintain justice and peace and prevent wars cannot be supplied by any one nation. The British Commonwealth, on whose control of the seas in the nineteenth century the *Pax Britannica* was based, 'has twice in this century failed of its major purpose'. Second, the force on which international justice rests must itself be international. It cannot be composed of men owing their whole personal allegiance to one particular nation. They must owe allegiance to a Government which itself is directly responsible to the citizens of many nations. There must, in other words, be both national Governments and an international Government.

This double theme is developed by Mr. Curtis with a combination of eloquence, practicality, and historical illustration which make, between them, an argument of compelling force.

### Liberty at Home

In contrast to some advocates of federation across national boundaries, Mr. Curtis does not suggest removing from the sphere of national Government any functions other than those which are essential to external security. His proposal is 'that the powers of the international Government should be limited to defence, foreign policy, colonies, civil aviation, and effective means of making the cost of these services a first charge on the nations united, leaving all internal and social affairs, including the incidence of taxation between one taxpayer and another, to the national Governments where they now rest'. Mr. Curtis keeps the sphere of national Government large; it would be the only Government of which most ordinary citizens in their daily lives would be aware. This proposal has three advantages over more ambitious schemes of federation.

First, it keeps down to the indispensable minimum the sacrifice of national powers and thus makes more likely the acceptance of this sacrifice.

Second, it gives the best practical guarantee that the armed force developed by the nations that combine will not be used for any purely national purpose. For everything except the common good of external security each nation will preserve its individuality. The international Government will not itself have any national purpose.

Third, it makes it possible to give equal opportunity to all men in all lands to live out their individual lives in freedom from fear and want, while not leaving it free to all nations to develop armed force of their own or to take an equal share in arming international justice. When the present conflict ends in the destruction of Nazi tyranny and its satellites and apes, the hope of lasting peace will depend on the extent to which it is possible to establish and enforce the principle that armed force for use in war against other nations is not an appanage of nationhood. This principle can and no doubt will be enforced against the defeated tyrannies, by disarmament, adequate inspection, and instant action to stop rearmament. It will need to be applied also to all other nations, so far as the power of the United Nations extends. It can be applied, most convincingly and most effectively, to themselves by the United Nations or some of them.

Mr. Curtis, of course, does not assume establishment of a world-wide international Government at once, if ever. He assumes only that a sufficient number of separate nations, knowing that war between themselves is unthinkable, decide, while keeping independence for all other purposes, to pool their strength for armed conflict formally and finally, as the best means of achieving external security for themselves and as the support of international justice between all nations. A sufficient number for this purpose means more—much more—than the States of the British Commonwealth; that is the lesson of two wars and of the League of Nations. It does not mean of necessity all the United Nations; a close, permanent union of some of these nations for external security would not imply any difficulty in their co-operating in a looser bond with all others who were like-minded.

Can such a union of nations for peace arise out of the present war? The answer is 'yes', for it needs no more than the recognition of plain facts. There is infinitely less possibility of future war to-day between any of the great English-speaking nations of the world than there was between the States which came together in the American Confederation, and later in the American Union. There is none of these nations which for all practical purposes of communication is not closer to all the rest than were those early American States.

### These things shall be

Can such a union of nations for peace arise from this war? The answer is that it must. To deride as Utopian plans for international Government and abolition of war is the idlest form of bad dreaming. The shadow of total war has lain over the world long enough to let all men see what it means. The choice is no longer between Utopia and the world our fathers knew. If lasting peace be Utopian, the choice is between Utopia and Hell.

To win wars is not enough. We must prevent them. We must make the world safe for small nations, and so for all nations. We cannot do so by having no force at all in the world, for that makes it a paradise for criminals. We cannot do so by any combination of forces which owe their first allegiance to any single nation; in the words forming the title of a famous lecture by Lord Lothian, 'Pacifism is not enough, nor Patriotism either.'[1] We can do so by placing international security in the hands of an international authority, by setting the Government of each nation free for its national tasks, free to build for all its citizens, in accord with their national ways of life, an ordered opportunity for service and freedom from fear and want.

[1] Burge Memorial Lecture, 1935.    Republished by Oxford University Press, 1941.  1s.

# PREFACE

A<small>T</small> the Conference of Paris in 1919 American and British delegates agreed to create laboratories for the scientific study of international questions, that is to say of questions which determine the issues of peace and war. For this purpose our American colleagues organized the Council on Foreign Relations in New York. The British delegates established the Royal Institute of International Affairs, which is now commonly known as Chatham House. When this war was pending the Foreign Office asked Chatham House to detail some of its experts to assist it by doing long-distance research. Arrangements were made to send these experts, when war broke out, to do their work in Balliol College. I was asked, as a member of the Council of Chatham House resident in Oxford, to act as liaison officer between the Council and its group of experts serving the Foreign Office, who were afterwards known as the Foreign Research and Press Service. These experts were under agreement to abstain from publishing any opinion on political questions whilst serving the F.R.P.S. I felt myself bound by the same restriction.

At the close of 1940 Lord Lothian suddenly died in the British Embassy at Washington. Ever since he and I had worked together in South Africa on the movement which led to the Union, we had been the closest of friends. In 1935 he delivered the Burge Lecture, under the title *Pacifism is not enough nor Patriotism either*. In this lecture he propounded the doctrine that international gangsters like Mussolini and Hitler are not the real cause of world wars, but only a symptom of that cause. He dwelt on the fact that mechanization has knit the widely scattered families of mankind into one society, so far as important social and material needs are concerned. Politically the world remains divided into more than sixty sovereign states. Within each of those states is established (more or less) the rule of law, a system that seeks to make right, and not the will of the stronger, the determining factor. The people in each of these states are controlled by government in the real sense of that word. Between these sovereign states there is anarchy, a Greek word which means the negation of government. And where there is anarchy (no government) there no rule of law can exist, and the will of the stronger remains the decisive factor. He saw in this state of anarchy which exists between sovereign states the real cause of world wars. He predicted that world wars would continue until national states began to merge their sovereignties into one international sovereignty.

The day after Lothian died Lord Astor, the Chairman of Chatham House, asked me to arrange for publication by the Oxford University Press of the speeches that Lord Lothian had made as British Ambassador to the United States. I had thus to read his speeches from beginning to end and was startled to find that though he was then speaking in an official capacity, he had none the less reasserted the doctrine set forth when he gave his Burge Lecture in 1935. Speaking to the alumni of Swarthmore College on the 11th November 1939 he had said: 'Neither pacifism nor militarism will end war. The unity of the nations under a single constitution, with a representative governmental authority possessed of the powers necessary to enforce that constitution and prohibit and prevent resort to violence, will do this.'

Had Lothian lived, he would, I believe, have tried to show the successive steps required to give effect to this doctrine, so I felt that, now he was gone, I must do whatever an obscure survivor could to keep alight the flame he had kindled. To do this I must try to show what practical steps would have to be taken to apply his doctrine to the world-crisis with which we are faced. I must try to say, in the light of his teaching, what changes would have to be made after this second war to save the world from moving towards a third and even greater catastrophe. In my spare time I worked out the answer to this question in a pamphlet entitled *Decision*. My friend the University Printer agreed to get it into type whenever compositors were available between the important jobs which the Press was doing. In my position I was not at liberty to publish such a pamphlet; but I meant to have it in print, ready to publish the moment the end of hostilities had set me free to do so. I happened to show the proofs, however, to one whose experience and judgement I trusted, because I wanted his comments on what I had said before revising the proofs. On reading them he remarked that this was the first attempt he had seen to work out a coherent policy of post-war settlement. 'But', he added, 'public opinion is by no means prepared for the changes which you think are necessary to save us from a third catastrophe in the next generation. To give public opinion time to mature, you must publish at once.' In the end he convinced me that I ought to resign my post in the F.R.P.S., and so become free to say what I thought must be done, if we were not again to lose the peace after winning the war.

*Decision* was published in the summer of 1941. From reviews in the Press and from private letters I received valuable comments, to which I saw that effect should be given in developing the policy outlined. So I presently published a second pamphlet entitled *Action*. This second pamphlet was the subject of further constructive comment, in the light of which I decided to state my case in a more comprehensive and final form. I therefore drafted a third pamphlet entitled *Faith and Works* and circulated the proofs to some 150 friends. From these I received more than sixty replies. After soaking my mind in their comments and criticism, I redrafted the proofs. The pamphlet so revised was published in the spring of 1943.

In 1942 arrangements were made by the University of Oxford, and approved by the War Office, for men and women serving in the forces of all the United Nations to spend a week's leave in Oxford and go through a course of lectures. Expenses were met by the Westminster Fund. Every week a fresh group arrived to go through the course. At one of them, in September 1943, I was asked to outline the policy for giving effect to our pledges under the Atlantic Charter which I had worked out in my pamphlets.

I found myself talking to some eighty people in uniform, mostly men with a few women. The men were of all ranks from generals to privates. They were drawn from the Allied forces, the majority from those of this country, the Dominions, India, and the U.S.A.

The interest taken by the group in the subject of post-war settlement was such that I was asked to repeat the talk to others who came week after week to spend their leave in Balliol. This interest was clearly due to a state of mind natural to people who had fought in battle or were now in training to carry this fight to a finish. 'How are our children to be saved from facing the horrors of war, which we are now facing and our parents faced in the last war?' is the question uppermost in the minds of the combatant forces. From week to week one could read that question in all their faces. It lay in the background of the questions they put. The time allotted for these talks and the questions which followed them was 11.30 to 1 p.m. on Fridays. Demands were made for further discussion, and these the management met by asking me to attend the final meeting at 9.30 a.m. on Saturday mornings, held for a general discussion of the lectures delivered during the week. To me these further discussions have been of the utmost value, for at them I was able to see what the attitude of men and women in uniform was after thinking over the talk of the previous day and reading the pamphlets.

The fact must be held in mind that every week I was meeting another and different audience. People who choose to spend their leave attending lectures in an Oxford college are drawn no doubt from a high educational level of the millions in uniform. But no one group I addressed could have had contact with any other. Yet in certain respects all were alike. The question foremost in all their minds was, as noted above, whether measures could really be taken, when victory was won, to prevent the recurrence of wars like these, and to secure social reform.

How widely their feeling on questions like these differed from that which their own political leaders were expressing was apparent. This difference was specially marked among American soldiers, the largest national factor in some of the audiences. Let me give two examples. The thesis I advanced in these talks was this, that no single democracy, not even the U.S.A., could now hope to protect its freedom and prevent attacks on it, as Britain had done in the nineteenth century. Democracies could now establish security for themselves only by combining their plans and powers of defence in one common authority or union. Such a common authority or union would only secure complete and final immunity from war when it had grown to include the people of the American Commonwealth with those of smaller democracies. I added the caution that I myself had no expectation of living to see an international union of defence which included the people of the U.S.A. I believed that would only happen if and when, as a preliminary, an international union had been made to include the democracies of western Europe as well as the British democracies. I further argued that such a union could only include nations which were democratic, i.e. those whose governments were based on elections and a constitutional system. My view was that no international union which was organic could ever include dictatorships with democracies.

To my utter astonishment both those positions were sharply criticized by the American officers. They took the strongest exception to my view that the U.S.A. would not enter such an international union at the outset or until the American people had time to see how it worked. All I could say was that I hoped and prayed they might prove right in actual practice. My own opinion had been based on insistence by both American parties that the U.S.A. must never enter into any international arrangement which would in any degree impair its own external autonomy.

More curious still was their strong insistence that Russia should be included from the outset in the international union I proposed; for just at that time American dispatches in the Press were showing a strong reserve with regard to post-war commitments with Russia. The view I had taken was that, if and when an international union had come to include the people of America with other democracies, it would then be strong enough to include countries like Russia and China, and even Germany and Japan provided that their own governments had then become answerable to their peoples on an electoral basis. But so great was the enthusiasm of these American soldiers for Russia, and their insistence that she should be included in the union from the outset, that I felt that my argument had failed to convince them.

This impression that a gap divides public opinion in America from the views expressed by the politicians is confirmed by a broadcast called 'The grass-roots and the elephant' by Raymond Gram Swing, which was printed in the *Listener* of the 7th November 1943. These meetings have given me the impression that a similar gap exists in the Allied countries and especially in Canada and in the United Kingdom. While politicans continue to insist that all constructive proposals must be framed to preserve national sovereignties intact, even in their external relations, members of the forces are prepared to consider and discuss any change which may be required to ensure that their children will not be called upon to face another and perhaps more terrible holocaust.

To these discussions I should owe a great deal had they only raised the difficulties in the way of the policy I proposed. But that was not so; for they often produced constructive suggestions. To take one instance—an American sergeant, in civil life a lawyer, who had studied the history of his own constitution, drew my attention to the fact that the federal government in America had taken over the war-debts of the states which entered the Union. He suggested that Allied democracies might be readier to join an international union for defence, if the union Government assumed their war-debts. A merger of war-debts in the hands of one government might also provide a solution to the tangled problems of Allied debts which will have to be faced after the war. My answer was that I know too little of finance to say how far this might be possible; but I pointed out that such a constitution as I was suggesting could only be framed by an

International Congress like the Congress of Philadelphia, or
those which framed the Australian and South African Con-
stitutions. A proposal to consolidate war-debts could properly be tackled by such a Congress.

I learned so much from these discussions with men and
women in the forces that I decided to bring my case up to
date in another pamphlet, *The Way to Peace*, which was
published in 1944. The opening chapter was the outline of
the policy I gave in these talks. The chapters which followed
this outline were based on impressions left by the questions
put by my listeners after the talk, and also by the comments
they made at their closing meetings held on the following
day. Some observations I made at various times when I was
saying good-bye to successive leave courses at their final
meetings are thrown together in the last chapter.

In the view of my publisher, Sir Humphrey Milford, the
time has arrived for the writer to digest the matter worked
out in these four pamphlets into one book, under a title
which correctly describes its contents, *World War, its Cause
and Cure*. When writing the second, third, and fourth pamphlets I could not assume that readers had seen the previous
papers. I had therefore to restate some of the facts and
arguments, though in different language. These unavoidable
repetitions would have made the four papers insufferably
tedious if merely printed together in the same cover. I had
therefore to reconstruct my case, to present the argument in
its proper order, and to avoid repetition.

To this, however, I have made one exception. Several
readers of *The Way to Peace* have told me that they found
the policy I am trying to outline more clearly expressed in
the record of my talks to the Leave Groups than elsewhere.
This is natural, as this talk was repeated a number of times
before it was written and printed. I am, therefore, leaving
most of this talk to stand as it appeared in print. In this
book it appears as Chapter XXXVII. Readers too busy to
go through the book and study the data on which these
proposals are based, by reading this one chapter and those
which follow in which I am trying to answer the questions

put to me after the talk, will find the proposals explained in the simplest words I can find.

A good deal of the matter which appeared in *The Way to Peace* has now been transferred to the Preface and the earlier chapters. A certain amount of new matter on the history of national sovereignty has been introduced into these chapters. This new matter I owe to my friend Mr. Bowle, who allowed me to read the typescript of his work on the growth of political thought, an invaluable book which will, I hope, be published as soon as possible.

I must in conclusion acknowledge the debt I owe to readers to whom I was quite unknown—staff officers, men of experience in public administration, finance, commerce, and industry who have sought me out to give me their help and advice. The development of this policy to its present form from the first crude outline presented in 1941 is largely due to these experienced and informed collaborators. With one exception, the posts they now fill forbid me to thank them by name. The debt which this book owes to the knowledge, experience, and intuitive wisdom of Sir Malcolm Stewart is beyond measure, as also to the Clarendon Press and its incomparable staff.

LIONEL CURTIS

ALL SOULS COLLEGE,
    OXFORD
*1 December 1944*

# CONTENTS

O LORD GOD, when thou givest to Thy servants to endeavour any great matter, grant us also to know that it is not the beginning, but the continuing of the same until it be thoroughly finished, which yieldeth the true glory.

## CHAPTER I

# PREVENTION OF WAR

THE South African War was on both sides fought with greater humanity than the wars which spread to the world at large in the present century. It none the less left in my mind a lasting impression of how evil a thing war always is. When it ended in 1902 I remained in the Transvaal with some friends of a like age to serve Lord Milner in the work of restoring order.

In 1906 Sir Henry Campbell-Bannerman came into power and announced his intention of granting responsible government to the conquered republics. We officials who handled the conflicting interests of the inland and coast colonies had no doubt in our minds that, if this and no further step were taken, we should all in a few years be shooting each other again. Lord Selborne, who had now succeeded Milner, commissioned me privately to visit the governments of the three neighbouring colonies and frame a report on the situation.

I was thus brought into close personal touch with the members of all four governments. They impressed me as able, upright, and public-spirited men. On the other hand, I was shocked to find that the members of each government seriously questioned the public spirit and indeed the good faith of all the three others. There must, I felt, be something wrong with a system which had led perfectly decent men to think so meanly one of another. This youthful experience accounts for the strong conviction that runs through these pages that political thinkers who attribute wars to the shortcoming of statesmen, and see no remedy except to provide an unbroken succession of heaven-born rulers, are declaring their own intellectual bankruptcy. Wars can be stopped from breaking out if we see the defects in political systems and cure them in time, but not if we wait for faultless men to direct them. It is in our power to change what is wrong in a system. It is not in our power to ensure an unbroken succession of statesmen great enough to work any system however defective. Though political systems cannot be perfect, they may be fool-proof.

B

The report to Lord Selborne was on these lines. The way to prevent a conflict between the four colonies was to merge their governments and electorates into one. Lord Selborne agreed and published that view on his own authority. It was backed by Generals Botha and Smuts in the Transvaal, and by Francis Malan and Dr. Jameson in the Cape. By 1909 the Union of South Africa was an accomplished fact. My own conviction is that had it not been accomplished by 1914, we should have had on our hands a second South African war, which might well have turned the scale in the great struggle with Germany which began in that year.

In 1909 that coming struggle was visibly casting its shadow before it. The German Empire was demanding 'a place in the sun', and was building a fleet to challenge the sea power by which alone the widely scattered communities of the British Empire could be held together. We were thus impelled to ask ourselves what the nature and purpose of this so-called Empire are. So in 1909 I undertook to give my whole time to the study of this question, in collaboration with friends prepared to devote what time they could spare from their ordinary duties.

Except when I had to devote some years to the Montagu-Chelmsford reforms in India, and to the establishment of the Irish Free State, my life has been given to political research detached from party affiliations. After many years the results were given in a book too long for all but a few to read.[1] I am now trying to see how conclusions reached in the course of long years apply to the present crisis in world affairs. What practical answer do they suggest to the questions raised by the Atlantic Charter? How when this second war is ended are we to prevent a third breaking out in the next generation? I will try to state my answer to this question in clear and unmistakable terms, and also in a space short enough for busy people to read. Before doing so, however, I think I should say what kind of answer a writer with my limitations is entitled to make.

[1] *Civitas Dei*. Macmillan.

CHAPTER II

# POLITICAL EXPERTS AND THEIR FUNCTION

DEMOCRACIES are, from their nature, ruled by people who have to seek re-election. They are therefore disposed to tell their electors what they like to hear and to promise them what they want to get. But the problems of life cannot in fact be solved by action based upon wishful thinking. They can only be solved in so far as those concerned are prepared to face unpleasant facts and distasteful exertion. If democracy is to work, there must be people, like Walter Lippman and Dorothy Thompson in America, who study political problems on their merits, without seeking election. Such thinkers, standing somewhat apart from political machinery, are at least as essential to its working as the politicians themselves.

In the course of long years I have come to think that political experts fall into two schools. One school, and by far the larger, refuse to waste time on 'Utopian' discussions. They are chary of projects which the politicians decline to consider. I know one distinguished professor who declines to discuss the idea of an international state, because he believes that no democracy will ever consent to relinquish its national sovereignty. He will not waste time and thought on a project which, as he believes, can never be realized. That attitude will, I suspect, appeal to most of my fellow-countrymen as the practical view, the essentially British view. I must, therefore, try to explain the attitude of that very small number of political thinkers to which I belong.

The duty of a political thinker is, as I see it, closely analogous to that of a consulting physician. Suppose that a lady calls on a specialist in Harley Street, tells him that her husband is ill and describes his symptoms, but adds 'Doctor, I must ask you not to advise a surgical operation, for my husband will not hear of it.' There are some consultants who would answer the lady as follows: 'I should guess, from what you have told me, that your husband is suffering from incipient cancer. If on examining him I think that is so, it will then be my duty to tell him that a surgical operation alone will relieve his pain and prolong his life. If you forbid me in advance to give him that opinion in clear unmistakable terms, I must then decline to see him. I must ask you to find some other consultant.'

That is my own position. After years of study I have come to the same conclusion that Lothian had reached in the Burge Lecture he gave in 1935.[1] He there propounded the view that the cause of world wars is not dictators on the one hand, nor Baldwins, Chamberlains, Simons, Hoares, or Lavals on the other. The essential cause is the fragmentation of human society, now integrated by mechanization, into more than sixty sovereign states. The relation between those states is anarchy, which leads to periodic wars. That was his diagnosis, and if it is correct, as I myself believe it is, we can only remove the recurring threat of world wars if we are prepared to face a political reconstruction, which corresponds to a surgical operation. If I am then told that this view is Utopian because democracies will not consent to this operation, then I can only reply that, if so, democracies can never avert the threat of war, and that freedom, the principle of their life, is doomed. The promise of a better world held out by Roosevelt and Churchill in their Atlantic Charter would, in that case, be a sheer illusion. If Leviathan is the idol democracies worship, they are dooming their children to pass through the fires of war. They are dooming themselves. That is my own opinion, based on a lifetime of study. I can no other.

This opinion means that the promise of the Atlantic Charter cannot be realized without some constitutional change, which amounts to a surgical operation. A consultant who advises an operation must be prepared to tell his patient what, in his view, is the most limited operation that is required to save his life. No trustworthy specialist would seize the opportunity of having his patient on the operating-table to attempt such a reconstruction of his organs as might, in theory, improve his health, should he survive it. He would limit the operation to what is required to save his life. That is what I am trying to do in these pages. Having said that some con-

[1] Oxford University Press. Price 1s.

stitutional change is needed to stop the recurrence of world wars, I try to show how that change can be confined to the narrowest possible limits.

I have now modified and developed the proposals outlined in a series of pamphlets in the light of the useful comment they evoked. These comments have also convinced me that I must restate in the fewest and simplest words I can find the principles upon which these proposals are based. If readers should think that the following chapters are out of place in a work on political construction, I will ask them to reflect on some words addressed by Sir Stafford Cripps on the 25th July 1942 to a Conference on Mineral Resources and the Atlantic Charter arranged by the British Association.

'We are fighting for a moral and not merely for a material issue. Though our plans must be scientifically prepared, there must be behind them the inspiration of our most deeply religious convictions.'

So before discussing plans let me state the convictions that inspire them and say how and why they were reached.

## CHAPTER III

# ULTIMATE VERITIES AND HOW WE KNOW THEM

THE question I was asked to examine in 1910 was 'What is the purpose and justification of the so-called British Empire?' I began the inquiry by noting the primary facts. This Empire already included nearly one-fourth of mankind, and sections of all its leading races, religions, and levels of civilization. One could not say what was the nature and purpose of this cross-section of human society without saying what was the purpose of life on this earth. I found myself forced to consider what the essential truths which lie at the roots of our life are, and also what kind of answer we can hope to give to such questions. Do our lives end with physical death, or do they persist beyond time and space? To such questions the Church replies that the answers can only be known through supernatural means; and that God has revealed them to man in Scriptures divinely inspired. From the time of Saint Paul onwards the Church has said that if Christ did not rise from His grave, then is our hope vain.

Just before I had started this work of research a writer, who called himself Guy Thorne, had published a novel called *When it was Dark*, which commanded widespread attention and ran through many editions. In this story a malignant Jew bribes a great archaeologist to go out to Palestine and there forge in a rock tomb an inscription in which Joseph of Arimathea is made to say that he himself removed the body of our Lord before the women came to the tomb. The Jew then arranges for another and innocent archaeologist to discover and publish the inscription. The instant result is that morality, government, and order everywhere collapse, and the whole civilized world is plunged into chaos. But the fraud is exposed, and at once moral standards, government, and order are everywhere restored. Now was this ridiculous novel right?

The essential truths which our Lord propounded were belief in God, a God of the living and not of the dead, and that men have an infinite duty to Him and to their brethren. Would faith in these doctrines really be shattered if some archaeologist found unanswerable proof that the body of Jesus was removed from the tomb and had not returned to life? Did not Lessing utter an evident truth when he said:

'The ultimate verities can neither be proved nor disproved by anything which happens in the world of phenomena'?

If one who had died appeared and spoke to us it might prove that his personality continued to exist after physical death. But would it prove that his personality and ours would exist beyond time and space when this planet has reverted to gas and flame? It would certainly prove no such thing. The answer to questions like this, whether our souls are indestructible, cannot be a matter of proof. It must be a matter of faith. For if immortality could be proved by anything which happens in the world of phenomena, there would be no room for faith in the proper sense of that word.

I was thus led to conclude that when we come to ultimate verities, to ask what they are, the best we can do is to decide on an answer, and then act on it. From its nature a genuine faith cannot be proved. The important thing is to act on our answer when we have made it. The test of faith is in works.

Some knowledge we have; enough to discern the alternative faiths, and to guide us in choosing between them. We all know we exist and are conscious of our own personalities. From our senses, sight, hearing, and touch, we each infer that in the bodies of others are personalities akin to our own. Each is aware of a moral sense, of some instinct which tells him that whether he does right or wrong is a matter of infinite importance. While each desires to please himself, he constantly feels that he ought to do something else in the interests of others. And this, in fact, is the supreme question, the answer to which is the ultimate verity. Is this instinct valid or not? Or is it an illusion? The materialist answers that this distinction between right and wrong has no validity and that matter, desire, our own sense of pleasure, are the final realities. The idea of virtue is a figment. To this Aristotle replied that 'without virtue man is merely the most dangerous of the animals'. It is not intelligence so much as this moral sense that distinguishes men from the brutes. The ethical man asserts its validity: the materialist denies it; but neither can prove his assertion or denial; yet each must sooner or later decide upon which of these two possible faiths he will act.

This test of action does not leave us at the mercy of guess-work. If the instinct which tells us to regard the good of others as indispensable to our own is illusion, and were felt to be such by all, then the stronger must dominate the weaker, till, in the end, all men have perished from the earth. On the materialist basis no human society is possible.

On the other hand, in so far as each can identify the good of others with his own, an ordered society develops in which men enjoy happiness to an ever-increasing degree.

The materialist creed was aptly stated in the words 'eat and drink, for to-morrow we die', and then cease to exist. Should I so lead my life, and then find that this view is wrong, I have made the greatest of all mistakes. Should I live and die in the faith that to seek the good of others is to attain my own, and should this prove to be wrong, then my mistake has no lasting result and is not serious. When I have ceased to exist, the pleasures I have missed will have ceased to matter. We now know that a time will come when this planet will no longer support any form of life. Then nothing will matter, if the materialist faith is right.

I am saying this at the outset as shortly and plainly as I can to save the reader's time. For those who honestly hold the materialist creed, the rest of these pages have neither sense nor value. They are based on a postulate that cannot be proved, a faith that our sense of duty is valid, and that for each to put the good of others before his own is a matter of infinite importance.

This postulate leads me to further conclusions. Whether we act rightly or wrongly to-day is not of infinite importance unless we continue to exist beyond physical death, and indeed, when this planet has reverted to gas and flame. But if those personalities of ours are eternal, indestructible, and independent of our corporal frames, what then is the final reality behind the universe? It cannot be matter. It must be of the nature of personality—spirit. By spirit I mean that invisible intangible essence, our personalities. To talk of 'impersonal immortality' does not make sense. The reality behind the visible universe must be a supreme personality, freed from all limitations, the Holy Spirit of God. To talk of an 'impersonal god' does not make sense. He must be a God infinitely more of a person than you or I.

Personality, in the highest form that we know it, is described as genius, the quality in men like Plato, Shakespeare, Washington, or Lenin, a quality we only attribute to minds which have brought into being things which did not exist before. I, therefore, think of God as a being so creative that He must create other creators, endow them with free-will like His own, and call them to create in partnership with Himself. He has given us a definite task to create what our Lord described as the Kingdom of God upon earth. By that He meant a system of society based on the law of God, which is the duty of men to Himself and each other. Such a system must be a commonwealth, by which I mean the Sermon on the Mount translated into political terms. The British, American, Swiss, Dutch, Scandinavian, and other self-governing nations are political expressions of the Sermon on the Mount, though imperfect expressions.

Aristotle said that the State exists 'for the sake of goodness'—in plain words, to make better men of its citizens. The Greek mind had realized that schools, teaching, and preaching are not the only means by which character is shaped. More decisive, indeed, is the structure of society in which we grow up. A British or American reader will see this, if he thinks how different his character and outlook on life would have been had he been bred in Germany or Russia, in India or Japan. The social and political structures in which we grow up are moulds into which our plastic natures are run. If the end and object of life is to make men better, an essential means to that end is to see that the moulds into which their natures are run are properly shaped. What men in the mass become will mainly depend on the kind of polity in which they are bred. The structure of the State is therefore of cardinal importance, as the Greeks had seen.

In the view of our Lord, the end and object of life is to perfect the nature of men. 'Be ye perfect, as your Father also is perfect.' He was bred at Nazareth, a day's walk from the Greek settlements which bordered the Lake of Gennesareth. As one of His own race has said, 'A greater than Aristotle was there.'[1] One cannot believe that a Jew 'greater than Aristotle' could have lived within one day's walk of these Greek communities, without getting some grasp of the central idea for which their civilization stood. Can we doubt that a mind so profound had seen that to perfect men you must perfect the social structure which shapes their characters? This cannot be done merely by teaching and preaching, by calling on men to be better. The political structure in which they grow up must be also improved, must be made to conform with realities—that is to say with the laws of God. To our Lord the final reality in human nature was not self-interest, but a faculty in men, however imperfect, of putting the interests of others before their own—the virtue that distinguishes men from beasts. To develop this faculty is to perfect mankind. But a faculty, like a muscle, is developed by exercise. The right kind of polity is one which depends for its working on the sense of duty in men to each other, and so develops that sense by its operation. The essential idea which Jesus taught is set forth in his prayer, 'Thy Kingdom come, Thy will be done, as in Heaven *so on earth*'. The task which He left to His followers was to create on earth a polity ordered in accordance with the will of God, a polity based, that is, on the infinite duty of each to God and his fellow men.

It is this sense of duty which alone enables men to unite in an ordered and civilized polity, as that force of mutual attraction called gravity serves to unite innumerable particles and hold them together in the planet we live on. The idea that self-interest can bind men together, which inspired the teaching of the Manchester School, absurd from the outset, has

[1] Vladimir G. Simkhovitch, *Toward the Understanding of Jesus*. New York: The Macmillan Co., 1923.

now been disproved by its failure in practice. The mysteries, in which philosophers have clouded political theory, dissolve when the obvious truth is admitted that the only force that unites men in a state is conscience, a varying capacity in most of them to put the interests of other people before their own.

The philosophies of this age set out to exhibit 'wishful thinking' as the cardinal error of the human mind. In a broadcast Mr. A. P. Herbert remarked: 'We are all warned against wishful thinking, but told to have faith. For myself I find it hard to decide where wishful thinking ends and faith begins.' Another word for 'faith' is 'vision'. 'Where there is no vision the people perish'[1] is one of the best-known and most quoted texts in the Bible. The reader who turns up this text in the Revised Version will find that what the author of Proverbs really wrote was something incomparably truer and more profound. 'Where there is no vision, the people cast off restraint.' I have now been given an even better translation: 'Where there is no vision the people become a mob.' The verse continues, 'but he that keepeth the law, happy is he'. The rule of law only results from a vision of spirit, of personality, 'of things unseen' as the final reality. The conditions in which we are now living exactly illustrate the truth recorded in this proverb. In the twentieth century, philosophies that deny all moral and spiritual values, and also the lack of any sort of philosophy, have plunged the world into anarchy. It is for that reason that I find it necessary to assert the faith that inspires these pages as expressed in the words: 'We look not at the things which are seen, but at the things which are not seen: for the things which are seen are temporal; but the things which are not seen are eternal'[2]—words which contrast in the simplest terms the materialist and spiritual answers to the question 'What is the final reality?'

[1] Prov. xxix. 18.       [2] 2 Cor. iv. 18.

CHAPTER IV

# FORCE AS A NECESSARY INSTRUMENT OF CONSCIENCE

M Y thesis is that the practical problems of life can only be solved in the light of a faith; but that faiths are worthless except in so far as those who hold them express them in works, and test them in practice. The immediate task before us when hostilities cease has now been expressed in outline in the Atlantic Charter, which has met with acceptance by the United Nations. So, in view of current philosophies, I find it necessary to note at the outset that all that I have to say on practical politics is based on faith that our sense of duty is valid, that for each to put the interest of others before his own is of infinite importance. Those who confess the opposite faith, that the pleasure of each is and can be the only real motive of human conduct, must show how any system of society based on that creed can enable men to obtain pleasure, or indeed continue to exist. For me, the state is the organization without which it is not possible for men to obey and also to develop their moral sense. It alone enables the general conscience of its members to restrain the power of the strong to override the interests of the weak. Such restraint is expressed in laws which are not effective unless, in the last resort, force in the shape of the prison and gallows can be used to exact obedience. But force is an instrument only. The essential power behind it is something spiritual, the general conscience of those who compose the state. The rule of law can exist within the state and nowhere else. Outside the state there is anarchy, a condition in which, not conscience, but the power of the strong, is decisive.

For the 2,000,000,000 people who now inhabit this planet there is no common state, no government through which the general conscience of mankind can be made effective. They are grouped into upwards of sixty sovereign states. Within the limits of each state the rule of law prevails, more or less, according to the quality of each. The relation between these states is exactly expressed in the word 'anarchy', a condition in which the power of the stronger state must be in the final outcome decisive.

It is time to consider how far this view of relations between separate states squares with the facts.

In his able book *The Twenty Years' Crisis*, Professor E. H. Carr, who was trained in our Foreign Office, has closely examined what happens in practice. The facts as he cites them point to the conclusion that the relations of sovereign states are in the long run determined by their relative power. To some extent, so he thinks, the factor of power will, in the case of democracies, be modified by a sense of right and wrong in its use. 'Belief', he says, 'in the uses of conciliation even in dealing with those against whom it would have been easy to use force has in the past played a larger part in British and American than in German and Japanese foreign policy.'[1] But even so his conclusion is that the position in which sovereign states, even commonwealths, are to stand to each other will in the end be settled by their relative power.

My own view is, that as between the citizens of a commonwealth, where the rule of law prevails, force is an instrument only. The general conscience is the decisive factor, the rule of right over might, to an ever-increasing degree. The relations between sovereign states is a field of anarchy, where the will of the stronger must in the end prevail. And this must always be so until nations have ceased to be sovereign, and have brought themselves under the rule of one international state. That day will come and with it unbroken peace upon earth, but not in this era. Men will see it, but not now. They shall behold it, but not nigh.

The final decision which each of us must take, in public as well as in private matters, must rest with his own conscience. That follows from the faith upon which these pages are based, the faith that each man's good consists in his putting the good of others before his own. To do good to our fellow men we must in a wide range of matters act in common; we must all do the same thing together, and this we cannot do if we are each to act on our own judgement.

[1] *The Twenty Years' Crisis*, p. 303.

Honest opinions will often differ, because our human minds are limited. We must therefore accept the direction of some common authority and obey it until we are convinced that this authority has become 'the negation of God'. It is then our duty to destroy it. Rebellion is never a right until it is also a duty. But unless we are ready to accept under normal conditions the direction of some common authority, we cannot in fact discharge our duty of creating a better life for our fellow men. As there must be some rule of law, there must be some paramount authority to make the law and tell us what it means.

But that is not all. As the knowledge of men is imperfect, so is their sense of duty. In all societies are people too idle or selfish to obey the law of their own accord. Unless the authority which makes and declares the law is also able to impose it, by physical force if necessary, it presently becomes, not a living law, but a dead letter. Where undutiful people cannot be made to pay their taxes, and criminals cannot be arrested or punished, a state of chaos or anarchy supervenes, which makes it impossible for dutiful people to promote a better life for their fellow citizens. They could not, for instance, provide the social services that poorer citizens need unless taxes were enforced. The authority which makes the law must therefore claim an unlimited right to call upon all dutiful citizens to enforce it, even at the cost of their own lives and property. In the British and American Commonwealths this is so, not only in theory, but even in positive law. That a public officer has the right to call upon ordinary men in the street to aid him by using force to arrest a criminal or quell a disturbance is a rule firmly established by decisions in the Courts. Whether the law is to run, and an ordered society is to exist, thus depends upon whether there are citizens enough with sufficient sense of duty to obey the common authority and enforce the law. If our sense of right and wrong is valid it follows that the use of force to compel obedience to law, so far from being wrong, is a positive duty.

The opposite doctrine that to use force is always wrong, even to stop wickedness, is of ancient lineage, expressed in the Sanscrit formula *Ahiṁsā paramo dharma*.[1] The saintly character of some who have spread it abroad in our own time has given it all the prestige of a higher morality. Let us borrow the words which Cromwell addressed to the Ulster divines: 'I beseech you, in the bowels of Christ, think it possible you may be mistaken.' For should they be wrong the doctrine they teach is immoral—by one degree only less immoral than the doctrine that might is right, which is the negation of all morality. These are times when false coin should be nailed to the counter.

In Aylmer Maude's life of Tolstoy I was startled to find how much the conclusions I reached in Chapter III have in common with those that Tolstoy reached in his *Confession*. On the other hand, his argument in vol. ii, chap. II, that it is always wrong to use force, even to restrain wickedness, reasoned with all the vigour of that powerful mind, leaves me unconvinced. I would urge pacifists to read this chapter, and indeed the whole of this great biography conveniently printed in 'The World's Classics' by the Oxford University Press.

The claim which a Commonwealth makes to exercise force is exclusive. It cannot allow any of its members to use force except at its own command. The community as a whole claims an unlimited right to dispose of the lives and property of its members in the general interest. Commonwealths struggling to exist are at this moment making and also enforcing this claim. No greater or more exclusive right could be claimed over individual men than this country claims when under its laws it sends millions of its citizens to face death in all the terrible forms which modern mechanized war presents. It claims a right without limit to take the property of us all, so far as that may be found necessary to save the existence or even promote the well-being of all. That is what sovereignty means, the exclusive claim of the State, of its citizens as a whole, to over-ride the authority of Churches, corporations, professions, trade-unions or any other form of association. Of its nature this paramount claim is exclusive.

Sovereignty vests in the citizens as a whole, and not in their

[1] Never to use force is the highest morality.

government, to which they delegate powers to express their sovereignty in laws and also to enforce them. A sovereign people can delegate powers to several governments. Powers can be shared by a number of governments within one commonwealth as in the U.S.A., but not sovereignty. That is the truth which Lincoln realized. The right which states like Maine or Virginia have to enforce their laws does not proceed from their own sovereignty, but from the sovereignty of the whole American Commonwealth as expressed in its constitution. And the same is true of the federal government at Washington. Sovereignty is from its nature indivisible, and can be shared by two or more commonwealths only when they have ceased to be two or more and have merged themselves into one commonwealth. They may keep the machinery of their several national governments, but the powers of those governments then derive from the larger community into which those two or more commonwealths have merged and in which one indivisible sovereignty vests.

In a commonwealth, at any rate, there is no such thing as a sovereign government for the plain reason that the government derives its authority from the people. The loose habit of speaking of sovereign governments has dangerous results in practice.

That the peace of the world cannot be kept unless national governments surrender 'some part of their sovereignty to an international body', has become almost a common form in schemes for post-war settlement. With rare exceptions the people who use this formula mean that the international body is to represent and be created by the national governments or legislatures. They oppose any suggestion that an international body should be made answerable to the peoples themselves and derive its authority from their votes. They condemn the necessary means to the end they propose. I go so far as to say that no transfer of sovereignty to an international body by two or more national commonwealths can be effected unless the international body is directly elected by the peoples of these commonwealths.

## CHAPTER V

# BIRTH OF THE COMMONWEALTH

THE history of civilization begins with a war between freedom and despotism: we are now fighting its latest campaign, and our task is to make it the last.

The issue behind this secular conflict, as I see it, is that set out in the previous chapters, the issue whether our sense that right differs from wrong is valid, or whether the will of the stronger must be the decisive factor in human affairs. Are men to dwell on this planet as slaves of a despot or as beings able to shape their lives for themselves and therefore responsible one to another for shaping them rightly?

The system whereby all questions at issue are to be decided by one master, whom all his subjects are to obey, and may not remove, is simple and therefore easy to work. How a number of people, however small, are to decide questions for themselves, including the supreme question who is to rule them, is difficult from the outset. The vital issue, at every stage in the history of free institutions, has been how an ever-increasing number of people can succeed in making effective decisions.

For aeons before recorded history men were living in caves, on the flesh of wild animals, and the fruits, foliage, or roots of natural plants. In course of time they learned to tame and breed animals like sheep and cattle, and to live in the main on their flesh and their milk. A tribe, possessing their flocks and herds in common, would wander about over large areas in search of grazing. The next stage was reached when people in regions favoured by soil and climate began to discover how to cultivate plants which yielded edible seed, leaves, or roots, trees which yielded fruit, and how to increase the natural yield. Cultivators were obliged to lead a more settled life than pastoralists, and tended to gather in villages for mutual protection. It was in such villages that a manner of life, deserving the name of civilization, began to take root.

In village communities tillers of the soil formed the habit of gathering to discuss questions at issue between themselves

C

and interests common to the village as a whole. In all parts of the world these village communities for long ages assumed that nothing could be settled until all the members of the village assembly were agreed. This was true in Europe, Asia, Africa, and America. We all know by experience how difficult it is for a dozen or more people to reach decision by unanimous consent. The result was that village communities were seldom able to reach decisions in time to resist attacks by nomadic pastoral tribes led by a chief, who was free to make his own decisions and to make them quickly. Such leaders were able to conquer and tax the helpless village communities, and include them as subjects in kingdoms and empires.

In the epics of Homer we have a contemporary picture of village communities which had not as yet suffered this fate. As we see from the *Odyssey*, the people of Ithaca, some 1,000 years B.C., had their village assembly, which their head man Odysseus was bound to consult. But all the evidence goes to show that these village assemblies in Greece were still observing the practice followed by other village assemblies throughout the world, that no decision could be reached until all the members saw eye to eye. Their independence, however, was still secured against foreign conquest by the mountains which guarded their valleys and the seas which surrounded the Greek peninsula.

Some five centuries later we find in Herodotus a widely different picture. Some village communities had grown to be cities like Athens. The citizens are now able to pass laws, to elect officers to carry them out, generals and admirals to command their armies and fleets, to vote the supplies to create and maintain these forces, and to tax themselves to meet the expense. And all this was possible because, somehow or other, the assemblies had acquired the power to reach decisions. They no longer waited to secure unanimity. After ample discussion the talk was stopped and decisions were reached by the simple expedient of counting heads and allowing the majority to settle the issue at stake. At times, of course, the expedient failed, and decisions were voted which minorities refused to accept and resisted by force. The result was a 'stasis' or revolution. But in general the system worked, because, in debate, majorities learned how minorities felt, and did not press their decisions beyond the point which minorities could bear. It worked in cities where enough citizens had learned to regard their own desires and interests as of less importance than the interests of the city as a whole. It was this which led them to obey laws against which they had voted, rather than resist them by force, and even to force others where necessary to obey the law. This feeling of devotion to the city, this habit of obedience to its laws, made them ready to suffer and die that the city they loved might continue to flourish. Such cities, however small, as compared with modern communities, had learned how to reach decisions, and therefore to govern themselves. They began to produce not only statesmen and merchants but poets, artists, thinkers, and men of science. Their weapons, their ships, and the tactics by which they used them were all better than those of the subjects of great empires in Asia. They had laid the foundations of the freedom for which we are fighting to-day.

Two concepts which sprung from their manner of life must be noted. As one of their greatest philosophers said, 'Without virtue, man is merely the most dangerous of the animals.' In the Greek view it was not intellect but the moral sense which distinguished man from the brutes. The end and object of life was to perfect this manhood, which men might achieve in so far as they learned to put the interests of others before their own. But how was this to be done? They observed that the major factor in moulding the characters of men was not teaching or preaching, important as they saw those to be, but the social framework in which a man lives.

This point is of such importance and yet so often ignored that a modern illustration may help the reader to grasp it. A future historian might well select the late Mr. Wendell Willkie and General Eisenhower as types of the character which American civilization produces. Both these Americans are German by race. Let the reader compare these men as he knows them from their deeds and words with what they would have become had their forebears remained in Germany and had they themselves grown up in the social framework of the German Reich. He will thus realize how much more potent social environment is in shaping the characters of men, than race.

The Greeks saw that it followed from this fact that to perfect men you must perfect the polity in which they grow up. This led to their other great concept that 'The State exists for the sake of goodness.' For them their city-state was not an end in itself, but a mould in which to shape the most excellent type of citizen.

## CHAPTER VI

# RISE AND FALL OF THE GREEK COMMONWEALTH

IN the sixth century B.C. Cyrus, a chief of nomadic tribes, had created by conquest an empire which centred in Persia. His successor Darius extended those conquests to the shores of Asia opposite the Greek peninsula. To conquer the Greeks he and his son Xerxes prepared the largest armies and fleets that the world had yet seen. These Persian forces were defeated by the better weapons, armour, ships, tactics, and leadership of the Greeks. It was Athens for the most part that met the brunt of the Persian invasion. Their victories were the greatest example of how quality can defeat quantity. For the time being they saved for Greece and the world their essential manner of life, the practice whereby in some measure numbers of people can reach decisions and so govern themselves.

One merit of this system lay in its power of developing in men a supreme devotion to the good of others. Its defect lay in the fact that this supreme devotion was limited to those others who dwelt in the same city. In Athens, the greatest of these cities, the number of citizens was somewhere about 10,000. That was the largest number who could meet in one place, listen to debates, and reach decisions by majority vote. That a commonwealth larger than that could ever exist was to them inconceivable. With their common language and culture they felt themselves superior to the rest of the world, a people apart. None the less the supreme devotion of a Greek citizen was to his city, and not to Greece as a whole. The laws he obeyed were those of his city, and she alone was entitled to ask him to give his life for her sake. For Greek civilization, for Hellas, as they called it, no government came into being which could bring the citizens of her numerous cities under one general law. Between these cities was anarchy, and anarchy leads to war. Despite their common language and culture the cities of Greece were always at war with each other, thereby weakening Greece as a whole.

Meanwhile a powerful king, Philip of Macedon, was carefully studying the strength and weakness of Greece to the south of him. Unlike the Persians he adopted and improved on their weapons, armour, and tactics. For the free institutions from which the material progress of Greece had sprung he had no sympathy, and indeed feared them as tending by example to undermine the loyalty of his own subjects to his rule. Had the Greek cities been able to unite they could have preserved their liberties; but Philip kept them divided by using exactly those tactics which Hitler has used in dividing the nations of Europe. By threats and cajolery he hypnotized most of the cities, each of them hoping to remain neutral, and so to preserve their freedom. Athens and Thebes were thus isolated, and in 338 B.C. he destroyed their forces at Chaeronea. Thereafter the cities throughout Greece lay at his mercy, obedient satellites of the Macedonian Empire.

In 197 B.C. the Macedonian Empire, including Greece, was conquered at Cynoscephale by the Roman Republic, which was fast becoming a military empire. The brilliant but transitory freedom realized in the Greek Commonwealth was thus quenched for more than a thousand years.

CHAPTER VII

# IMPACT OF ISRAEL ON GREECE AND ROME

GREECE was but one of the roots from which our civilization has grown, and by no means the oldest. In Palestine was a small people wedged in between the great monarchies of Egypt, Syria, Assyria, and Babylon. Their tribal god was called Yahwe. Amongst them appeared prophets who taught that Yahwe or Jehovah (as our version spells his name) is the one true God, and that the gods worshipped by neighbouring peoples were no gods at all. Some of these prophets like Ezechiel taught that Israel was Jehovah's chosen race; but others like Jeremiah taught that all nations and kindreds and tongues who recognized Jehovah as the one true God were alike his subjects and children. Jehovah's favour was not to be sought by the sacrifice of victims, the burning of incense and pagan rites, but rather by the righteous dealing of men one with another. But the Hebrews themselves were constantly falling away from this teaching. They adopted pagan rites from the Gentiles around them, rites performed by professional priests, to whom they became a vested interest. These naturally looked on the prophets as enemies to be destroyed when possible. The first chapter of the prophet Isaiah might have been issued as a Protestant manifesto by Wycliffe, Huss, Luther, Knox, or the English Puritans.

When Philip had mastered Greece his son Alexander set out to subdue the Persian Empire. On his march to Babylon he conquered Palestine and Egypt and founded a number of Greek cities, some round the lake of Galilee, others in Egypt, the largest of which was Alexandria, where he settled a number of Greeks and Jews. The Empire founded by Alexander was presently conquered and annexed by Rome. It thus fell out that Jesus of Nazareth was born, lived, and died under Roman rule.

At the age of 30 He began to preach that Jehovah was the God of the whole earth, the God of the living and not of the dead. In His mind God was the loving Father of all men, to whom they owed an infinite duty, and also as brethren, one to another. The will of God could not be performed by the sacrifice of beasts, and such pagan rites, but only by service rendered by men one to another. 'Be ye perfect, as your Father also is perfect.' For men to perfect their sense of duty was the end and object of human life, which was inde-structible.

His home in Nazareth was only a day's walk from some of the Greek colonies on the shores of Galilee. This contact with Greek civilization explains why all His teaching centres round what He called the 'Kingdom of God'. He had grasped the idea that men to perfect themselves must per-fect the framework of society in which they grow up. Their sense of duty could best be developed by exercise. The social system must thus be made to depend for its operation on the principle that those who worked it must learn to put the interests of others before their own. Such a system would not be a 'kingdom' but a 'commonwealth'. He used the word kingdom because in the Aramaic language He spoke there was no other word than *malkūtha*, or kingdom, to denote a polity. When His followers came to record His teaching in Greek they translated *malkūtha* into the Greek for kingdom which is *basileia*. To express what Jesus meant by the Kingdom of God, they should rather have used the word *polis* which the Greeks had applied to their city common-wealths. If we analyse what kind of society Jesus meant by the Kingdom of God, as defined in the Gospels and especi-ally in the parables, we shall see that the polity He describes could not be a monarchy. A commonwealth is, in fine, the Sermon on the Mount translated into political terms. The task which He left to His followers was step by step to realize for the whole of human society a world polity based on the infinite duty of men to their Father and brethren. The Divine Polity, as conceived by Christ, was a human common-wealth, not a catholic church.

This vast conception was in mortal antagonism with the Roman Empire, and also with the semi-pagan system of ritual administered to their own advantage by the Jewish priests.

The civil combined with the ecclesiastical power to destroy Jesus, after a mission which covered less than three years.

His Jewish disciples, simple fishermen, had in that time been unable to grasp the full content of His teaching or of the task which He left them. They saw that to serve their Father they must serve each other, and not by performing rites. But even so, the pagan idea of sacrifice began to creep back in a subtle form. The idea grew up that Christ had once for all superseded the sacrifice of beasts in the temple by the sacrifice of His own death on the cross. On the eve of His crucifixion He had broken bread and passed round the cup of wine and had bade His disciples 'Do this in memory of me.' They obeyed Him from the first; but in ages to come 'The Lord's Supper' came to be regarded as a sacrament which superseded the sacrifice of bulls and goats. The performance of this sacrament was essential to the worship and service of God. These rites became the necessary means for the saving of souls. As with all rites, its performance required a priesthood to administer it. In the course of centuries that priesthood acquired a power and authority in the Christian Church greater than was ever achieved by the priesthood of the Jewish temple.

A few years after the Crucifixion the Conversion of St. Paul gave a sudden impetus to the spread of doctrines which Christ had preached. A Pharisee of the Pharisees, Paul had grown to manhood in Tarsus in touch with Graeco-Roman civilization. He at once arrested the dangerous tendency of some apostles to narrow Christianity to a sect of Judaism. He established the principle that a gentile need not become a circumcised Jew to become a follower of Christ. He then set out on a mission to convert the whole Roman Empire to the new religion.

The Roman Empire, like that of Japan, was based on belief that the Emperor was a god, to whom his subjects were bound to do sacrifice. When Christians refused, they were thrown to the beasts. Their doctrine continued to spread in spite of, or rather because of, their persecution by the state. Meanwhile the Empire was decaying as all autocracies must, and was threatened with destruction by barbarians from the north.

In A.D. 313 Constantine, to heal the internal schism, proclaimed the principle of religious liberty and legalized the Church. To defend the north-eastern frontier of the Empire he moved its capital from Rome to Constantinople. From that moment onwards the Jewish idea that the Church is something separate from the state combined with the model of the Roman Empire to transform the character of the Church. The Bishop of Rome rapidly acquired the prestige and authority which had clothed the Emperor in Rome. The Church and its priesthood acquired an authoritarian character, which rivalled the Empire itself, now centred in Constantinople.

As the Empire waned, so the Church waxed, extending its influence over the barbarians who were fast destroying the Empire, and reducing Europe to chaos. Islam was threatening the very existence of Christendom till in 717 Leo the Isaurian broke their attack on Constantinople by land and sea and in 732 Charles Martel destroyed their armies at Tours. When Charles Martel died in 741 the Pope sanctioned the coronation of his son Pepin as king of the Franks. Pepin's son Charles the Great established the temporal power of the Pope in Italy, and extended the Frankish Empire to the Ebro and the Elbe.

The Church had now realized that it lacked the power of the sword to enforce its spiritual authority on the barbarians. So the Pope conceived the idea of exerting that authority to reconstitute the Empire of Rome, and of vesting Charles with the office of Emperor. When Charles entered the Basilica of St. Peter on Christmas Day A.D. 800, and knelt on the altar steps, the Pope unexpectedly placed the imperial crown on his head and proclaimed him as Emperor of the Romans. This act was tantamount to assertion that the Pope had the right to confer sovereignty on the Emperor. Charles, however, asserted his right to rule the Church. The conflict of Emperor and Pope was thus inherent in Western Christendom from A.D. 800.

In the long struggle which followed, the Emperor's power was fatally weakened by his having to bargain with German princes for the forces he needed to assert his authority in Italy. In A.D. 1279 Boniface VIII received the envoys of the Emperor, Albert I, seated on a throne, crowned with the diadem of Constantine, holding a sceptre and girt with a sword. 'Am I not', he said to them, 'the supreme Pontiff? Is not this the throne of Peter? Is it not mine to guard the laws of the Empire? I, I am the Emperor.'

In the upshot neither Pope nor Emperor had the physical power to maintain the *Pax Romana*. Throughout the Middle Ages Christendom was torn by internecine wars which neither Emperor nor Pope was able to control.

CHAPTER VIII

# THE COMMONWEALTH RAISED TO THE NATIONAL SCALE

As we saw at the end of Chapter VI, the brilliant but transitory freedom of the Greek commonwealths was quenched by subjection to Macedon and Rome. In the Middle Ages the principle of the Commonwealth began to emerge in England 'without observation' and on the national scale.

In 1066 the Norman Conquest united the people of England under a monarch with few restraints to his power, until in 1215 King John was forced by his barons to sign a charter defining their privileges. In terms of Magna Carta the King undertook to discuss and settle with the barons and bishops the revenues they should pay him. His grandson Edward I, who came to the throne in 1272, had the wisdom to extend this practice to merchants and owners of land. At once he was faced with a practical difficulty. The barons and bishops, in number short of two hundred, could be gathered to meet the King at Westminster. The merchants and squires were too many to meet in one place, to bargain with Edward and to settle a bargain. So Edward issued writs instructing the county courts and borough councils to elect representatives few enough to meet him at Westminster. But in these writs he was careful to specify that the settlements made with him by these elected squires and burghers were to be final and binding. They were not to be subject to further confirmation by the county courts and borough councils which had sent them to bargain on their behalf. The elected squires and burghers must have power to decide. For this reason the assembly gathered by Edward I has been known as the Model Parliament. By the representative principle a whole nation, including all its cities and counties, achieved a machinery for controlling their own taxation. In course of time this power of decision was extended to govern all other public questions at issue.

By the close of the Middle Ages Parliament had asserted its right to decide which branch of the Royal House was entitled to inherit the Crown. Sovereignty in fact had passed to the people, and England emerged as a sovereign nation. Parliament, however, had always supported the Crown in contesting the claim of the Pope to temporal power over the realm, including the right to exact a tribute. In 1366 Parliament commissioned Wycliffe, an Oxford scholar and afterwards Master of Balliol, to draft a paper asserting its right to tax the Church itself in case of need. Wycliffe went on to challenge the spiritual as well as the temporal claims of the Church. As the teaching of Moses and the prophets had been overlaid in Palestine by paganism and its rites, so now the teaching of Christ had been overlaid by pagan beliefs in Europe. Wycliffe saw that the power of the Church was founded in belief that priests could change bread and wine into the body and blood of Christ and that by giving or withholding the sacraments they could determine the eternal future of laymen for weal or woe. He denied that these claims to supernatural powers had any authority in Scripture. His doctrines spread by the Lollards made headway in England. Czech scholars who came to Oxford returned with the writings of Wycliffe. They were read by John Huss, a teacher in Prague, who started a revolt against Rome in Bohemia. A later result of the Hussite movement was the Reformation started by Luther which led part of Germany and later England to renounce their obedience to Rome.

With the Reformation two other movements, the one cultural, the other economic, combined to end the Middle Ages and to open the era of modern history.

## CHAPTER IX

# NATIONAL SOVEREIGNTY

THE fall of Constantinople to the Turks in 1453 had spread Greek scholars and their books to teach their language throughout Europe. These classical writers were eagerly read, and their works multiplied by the art of printing on paper which Jesuit missionaries had brought to Europe from China in the course of the fifteenth century.

The fall of Constantinople had also cut the routes by which silk from China and spices from the Indies had reached Europe. In 1492 Christopher Columbus seeking a route to China by sea discovered America. In 1498 Vasco da Gama rounded the Cape and opened a sea route to India.

The Reformation led to a Counter-reformation which revived the spiritual zeal of the Church. The Papacy still claimed authority to divide between Spain and Portugal the western and eastern hemispheres they had opened. Protestant countries like England and Holland denied that authority. But even the kings of a Catholic country like France claimed to derive their sovereignty direct from God. The era of national sovereignties rapidly superseded the medieval idea of Christendom as a single state. The idea, never reached in practice, that the spiritual authority of the Pope or the sword of the Holy Roman Emperor could restrain nations from war vanished like the dream that it was. War was accepted as part of the natural order of things.

In 1625 Huig van Groot, better known as Grotius, a Dutch lawyer and civil servant, published his great book *De jure belli et pacis*. He sought to found the relations of sovereign states on natural law, which in his view was as unchangeable, even by God, as the laws of geometry. In this work sovereign states and the outbreak of wars between them were accepted as part of the order of nature, and inevitable as such.

The modern conception of international law derives from the work of Grotius. The word 'law' like the word 'right' stands for different ideas. It is used to denote the customs observed by a people, as in Iceland, where in the Middle Ages there were courts to interpret the customary law, but no executive to enforce their decisions, and no legislature to alter the customary law. In a stricter sense it is used to denote law in states where a government exists to enforce the decisions of courts. In such states it can truly be said that a rule of law is established.

International law, as propounded by Grotius, is law only in the sense that was recognized in Iceland. In the international field there are international courts, but no executive to enforce their decisions and no legislature to change the law as declared by the courts. None the less, international jurists are wont to speak of the rule of law as existing under a system where sovereign governments jealously guard their right to accept or reject the findings of international courts. We have here a typical case of the abuse of political terms, upon which theories are based which lead to disaster when reduced to practice. In his *Use and Abuse of Political Terms*, Sir George Cornwall Lewis has shown by quotations from the speeches of Cabinet Ministers and from leaders in *The Times* how the speakers and writers have passed from one meaning of words like 'right' or 'law' to a totally different meaning, in the process misleading themselves as well as their hearers and readers.

The conception of sovereign states as propounded by Grotius was accentuated by the English philosopher Thomas Hobbes. As a royalist refugee in France he accepted the position of tutor to the future Charles II. His book was published in 1651, under the title of *Leviathan, or the Matter, Form and Power of a Commonwealth, ecclesiastical and civil* 'with a frontispiece depicting a newly planned town with a background of open country. Towering above the scene, there stands the crowned figure of a huge man shown from the waist upwards, with the arms outstretched protectively, grasping in his right hand a great sword and in his left a crozier. The body of the figure is made up of a swarm of little people, with their backs to the reader and their eyes fixed on the figure's expressionless face.'[1]

---

[1] Bowle's *History of Western Political Theory*, chapter xvii. In this chapter I am deeply indebted to Mr. Bowle, who has allowed me to read his work in typescript. It will, I hope, be published as soon as possible.

'The state', according to Hobbes, 'might be regarded as a great artificial man or monster (Leviathan) composed of men.'[1] Men, he conceived, in a state of nature had lived a life no better than that of the beasts, a life in which the strongest did as he pleased. Hobbes had translated Thucydides, and had doubtless taken to heart words that historian imputes to Athenian envoys when demanding a tribute from the people of Melos: 'You know as well as we do that right, as the world goes, is only a question between equals in power, while the strong do what they can and the weak suffer what they must.'[2]

The result is 'a condition which is called Warre' . . .

'whatsoever therefore is consequent to a time of warre where every man is enemy to every man; the same is consequent to the time wherein men live without other security than what their own strength and their own invention shall furnish them withall. In such condition there is no place for Industry; because the fruit thereof is uncertain: and consequently no Culture of the Earth; no Navigation, nor use of the commodities that may be imported by sea; no Commodius Building; no instruments of moving and removing such things as require much force; no knowledge of the Face of the Earth; no account of Time; no Arts, no Letters; no Society; and which is worst of all, Continual Feare, and danger of violent death; and the life of man solitary, poore, nasty, brutish and short.'[3]

In the theory of Hobbes, men to escape from this bestial anarchy bound themselves by an indissoluble compact to obey one sovereign authority, whether a monarch or an assembly. He lived in an age when Protestants read in the Hebrew Scriptures how Jehovah had made a covenant with the chosen people of Israel. The current belief that the Hebrew polity was based on a covenant prepared the public mind to swallow the idea that the state was based on social contract, which has no support in historical fact. Hobbes was one of a few in that age who did not accept the Hebrew Scriptures as literal truth; but he did not scruple to avail

[1] Bowle's *History of Western Political Theory*, chapter xvii.
[2] Thucydides, v. 85–116.        [3] *Leviathan*, Part I, chap. 13.

himself of current beliefs, to introduce and support his theory that sovereignty is based on social contract.

Hobbes anticipates several ideas finally realized in Nazism —a subordinate Church, control of the press, a doctrinaire education of youth, and the transfer of populations. In the view of Hobbes the rule of law could only exist within the limits of a sovereign state. That between such states no rule existed, but a state of anarchy which was always liable to lead to war, was a consequence of his view which Hobbes accepted.

A different view was taken by Baruch Spinoza, a Jewish philosopher born in Amsterdam in 1632. Spinoza saw that wars between sovereign states were inevitable, and that international law could not be law in any real sense of that word so long as no rule existed competent to enforce it on states and their subjects. In his great work *The Political Treatise* he agrees with Hobbes to this extent that he justifies sovereign power as the price of order, but, unlike Hobbes, regards government as an expression of the impulse to mutual aid instinctive to mankind.

'The ultimate aim of government is not to rule by fear, not to exact obedience, but to free men from fear, that they may live in all possible security. No, the object of government is not to change men from rational beings into beasts or puppets, but to enable them to develop their minds and bodies in security and to employ their reason unshackled. In fact the true aim of government is Liberty.'[1]

'It follows', says Bowle,[2] 'that the aim of men is, in the words of Jesus, "to have life, and to have it more abundantly", and the state must be directed to this end.'

Spinoza's view met with little attention from political thinkers, and none whatever from practical statesmen, till the nineteenth century. In 1926 Lowes Dickinson published *The International Anarchy 1904–1914*, in which he argued that war was the inevitable result of the sovereignty claimed by national states. At that time a number of secret documents and treaties had been published by Governments in Berlin

---

[1] Bowle, chapter xx.  [2] Ibid., chap. xxi.

D

and Moscow. The British Government had not as yet published the documents which Dr. Gooch and Professor Temperley were commissioned to edit. German propaganda to prove that Germany had not been responsible for the war was in full flood. One has only to read the pages of Mr. Lowes Dickinson, who did not wait till he could read the British documents, to see how effective the German propaganda was. The German and Russian documents had convinced him that of all the governments involved in the war, the German Government was the least to blame for its outbreak. He failed to see how in seeking to whitewash German policy he weakened his case that war was the product of national sovereignties, of international anarchy, a point cogently argued in his preface and closing pages. After his death a popular edition was republished in 1937 with a foreword by Sir Arthur Salter, closing with the words: 'International anarchy is the cause of war; and international government, therefore, the indispensable condition of preventing it. That is Lowes Dickinson's theme, the truth of which is confirmed not only by the events which he narrates, but by all that has happened since.'

In 1935 the Marquis of Lothian gave the Burge Memorial Lecture, which was published by the Oxford University Press under the title: *Pacifism is not enough nor Patriotism either*. On pp. 55-6 his conclusion was summarized in the following words:

'The League, the Kellogg Pact, and all the expedients of pacifism cannot end war or the evils which spring from the anarchy of statehoods. It is quite right that we should use the League and the Pact for what they are worth, for they are the crude beginnings of the new world order, and because the nations are not likely to take the next and vital step until they have substituted co-operation for unrestricted self-centredness and have discovered in practice that co-operation is not enough. But none of these methods can end war or create the conditions in which it is possible for mankind to live a free and civilized life. These will only be established when enough citizens of national states, while retaining their full autonomy in national affairs, are willing to form themselves into a world nation for common purposes, to enter into that organic and indissoluble bond which is the foundation not of a League but of a Commonwealth of Nations.'

After his death the lecture was reprinted with a preface by Sir William Beveridge, in which he said:

'The fundamental cause of war is neither unjust treaties, nor racial or religious or cultural differences, nor maltreatment of minorities, nor need of raw materials and markets, nor imperialist ambition, nor strategic considerations, nor those broad-shouldered scape-goats, capitalism or nationalism. The cause of war is the anarchy of sovereign states. The end of war throughout the world can only come through world federation. That is the theme of this remarkable lecture: "Pacifism is not Enough, Nor Patriotism, Either". There is only one way of ending wars and of establishing peace in the political sense of the word, and that is by introducing into the international sphere the principle of the state, that is, by creating a federation of nations with a government which can wield the taxing, executive, legislative and judicial power, and command the exclusive allegiance of the individual in the super-national sphere. Pacifism is not enough, because justice in the international sphere, as elsewhere, is futile without force to back it. Patriotism is not enough, because selfish force, force except as the servant of justice, is self-destructive in the international sphere, as elsewhere.

'That is the theme expounded in this lecture with a force and reasonableness and economy of words, making it better worth reading than almost anything else that has been said about international problems.'

In 1939 Lothian was appointed British Ambassador at Washington, where he died of overwork in December 1940. In the speeches he made in his public capacity he did not hesitate to repeat the warning he had given at length in his Burge Lecture. Addressing the House of Delegates and Senate of Virginia in February 1940 he said:

'As Mr. Elihu Root said a few years ago, mankind is confronted with almost the same fundamental problems as confronted the fathers of the American Constitution. If they are to be solved they must be diagnosed and answered as convincingly as were the problems of 1776 in the Federalist papers and the American Constitution. To-day as then an anarchy of sovereign States cannot escape chronic war or preserve individual liberty or create the conditions of prosperity and employment within their own boundaries unless, in some way, they can bring themselves collectively under the reign of a single constitutional law.'

Since the time of Washington, Lincoln, Root, Lothian, Beveridge, and Salter are the only men in public life who have not bowed the knee to Leviathan, and have warned the world that wars will continue to destroy freedom and civilization till national states begin to merge their sovereignties into one international sovereignty. Apart from these exceptions, political leaders continue to worship Leviathan, regardless of the claim which their idol makes, that the sons and daughters of men must be passed by millions through the fire in his honour.

## CHAPTER X

# THE COMMONWEALTH RAISED TO THE CONTINENTAL SCALE

IN Chapter VIII we traced the steps whereby Parliament came to control supply, the making of laws, and even to decide who was entitled to inherit the Crown. But what was to happen when King and Parliament failed to agree, as they so often did? This question was finally settled at the end of the eighteenth century by transferring the substance of the King's power to the Prime Minister who could for the time being command a majority in Parliament, or, failing that, a majority of the electors willing to return a new Parliament to support him. Since then the power of 'the Crown in Parliament' to decide everything has become absolute. When the King declares that he wishes it so (*Le Roy le veult*) he is really declaring that Parliament has reached a decision.

The discovery and colonization of America had ere this been raising a further problem. By the middle of the eighteenth century there had come into being some thirteen colonies in North America, each with a parliament of its own, if only for the reason that representatives could not then be sent across the Atlantic to sit at Westminster. The colonists were thus represented in their own assemblies but not in the British Parliament, which none the less essayed to tax them for the common defence. The thirteen colonies proceeded to assert their independence of Great Britain. As so many sovereign states they made a compact with each other to supply the men and money necessary for the struggle. In spite of repeated and conspicuous failures to discharge the compact, their independence was won, partly through the incompetence of George III and his ministers, partly by the aid of foreign powers hostile to Britain, but first and foremost by the greatness of Washington.

In 1783 their independence was recognized by Great Britain. In order to fight the mother country the colonies had established a Congress of delegates sent from their thirteen assemblies. It was given no power to tax the colonists, except by virtue of laws to be passed by the assemblies. Funds needed to meet the cost of the war had been raised by loans, and when peace was declared Congress was liable for the interest and sinking fund on 42,000,000 dollars. In response to four requisitions made by Congress for 15,870,987 dollars no more than 2,450,803 dollars were remitted by the State assemblies. By 1786 Congress was in open and acknowledged default. Moreover, when Congress requested the States to execute the treaties it had made with Britain and Spain, a number neglected to take the necessary action. In New England the spirit of anarchy spread to the taxpayers, who began to refuse to pay taxes due to the States. The situation became so alarming that the state governments agreed to appoint delegates to revise the articles of confederation. They met at Philadelphia in 1787, under the leadership of Washington. Experience in war and peace had taught him that no real system of government could be based on compacts between sovereign governments, and that Congress was powerless so long as its authority was derived from a number of states which, because they were sovereign, could always ignore the compact, and frequently did so. Congress could only make decisions if it derived its authority from the citizens themselves, and was able to enforce those decisions on every citizen. Congress must therefore be able to raise the money required to meet the duties imposed on it by taxing the individual citizens, without waiting for thirteen legislatures to impose the taxation. The principle at stake was the same as that which inspired the writs issued by Edward I when he summoned the Model Parliament.

This principle was embodied in a new constitution framed by the Congress of Philadelphia. Under its terms all duties and powers not specifically given to the central government were reserved to the state legislatures which remained in being. By virtue of this constitution the Government of the United States was henceforward able to make effective decisions. Since 1788, when it was adopted, there has come into being a commonwealth large in area as the whole of Europe west of Russia, which maintains its diverse communities in a state of peace.

This peace has, none the less, been attained at the cost of a civil war. The Southern States were alarmed by a movement in the North to abolish the system of slavery upon which their social structure was based. Desiring to part from the North they argued that the Union ratified in 1788 was based on a compact between sovereign states, which, because they were sovereign, their governments were free to cancel at will. This doctrine was challenged by President Lincoln, who denied that the Union was based on compact at all. The constitution, he held, had its root in the 'dedication' of each American citizen to the welfare of all. The Government of the United States was entitled to call on every citizen to give his property, and if necessary his life, to compel every other citizen to obey the law of the United States as enacted under the constitution. The Southerners resisted this claim by arms, and Lincoln, supported by Congress, called on every citizen of the United States qualified to bear arms to force the Southerners to obey the law. Enough of them responded to secure this result, though a million men lost their lives in the struggle. Since this decision no threat of war has seriously menaced the internal peace of the United States. Had Lincoln failed, and had the Union dissolved into a number of sovereign states, its territory would have become the scene of wars, perhaps as frequent as those which have ravaged Europe and South America.

CHAPTER XI

# NAPOLEON TO HITLER

WE must now return to the eighteenth century, to see how the creation of a commonwealth in America reacted on Europe. In France the monarchy was utterly destroyed, and replaced by republican institutions. But unlike the American colonists the French were inexperienced in the practice of translating public opinion into effective decisions. The country swiftly lapsed into anarchy. Faced with starvation, the expedient was tried of massacring everyone charged with the crime of thwarting the government, till order was restored and effective government established by a general whose soldiers had found that he always led them to victory. Napoleon displayed a supreme capacity for those effective decisions which for the moment hungry, distracted France needed. He quickly perverted her passion for liberty into his own passion for power, till under his leadership the French had conquered Europe and were hoping to conquer the world. These hopes were frustrated by British sea power, which alone prevented Napoleon from bringing the world beyond Europe under his despotism.

Till the end of the nineteenth century the unquestioned control of the ocean routes by British sea power gave the human race such a sense of security from world wars as they had not known since Columbus and Vasco da Gama opened those routes. If you wish to charge that vague and over-worked term 'security' with definite meaning, it is well to recall the comparative freedom from constant anxiety which prevailed in the latter half of the nineteenth century, and then contrast it with the growing fear of impending disaster which descended upon us with the twentieth century.

From 1815 to the close of that century the menace of war on a world-wide scale was banished by British sea power. Behind a shield outstretched on the arm of the parent commonwealth self-government flourished and deepened its roots in North America, whilst south of the Line in the African and Australasian continents, younger commonwealths sprang into being. The system appeared as so firmly established in English-speaking communities that its rapid extension in western Europe and even in Russia was assumed to be merely a question of time. The system of freedom will extend its influence in the world so long as its strength is too great for governments opposed to it to think of destroying it, and no longer than that. **The safety of free systems is always to look to their own strength and not to measures for weakening their enemies.**

How was it that Britain, a mere speck on the map of the globe, was able to keep so long an unchallenged control of the oceans that cover the greater part of its surface? The answer is that British inventors like James Watt had given these islands a flying start in the art of harnessing physical power. For several generations Great Britain was able to beat all her competitors in producing goods. It was this flying start which enabled her taxpayers to sustain a burden of world power out of all proportion to the relative size of her people and area.

A further question remains to be answered. How came it that nations in Europe, Asia, and America were in the nineteenth century willing to tolerate control of the seas by British sea power? It will here suffice to mention the most important and least noticed of several reasons. The traditions and habits of the British people were such that any attempt to create or maintain conscript armies like France, Germany, or Russia was out of the question. For this reason, if for no other, there was no serious danger that England would use her sea power to embark on Napoleonic conquests. The world was content to see England forbidding the Grand Alliance to conquer South American states, because England herself was devoid of the armies necessary for such conquests. For lack of such land forces, if for no other reason, England never attempted to challenge the hegemony of Europe which Bismarck achieved by merging the German states into one empire all-powerful on land.

The German people, or at least their rulers, were not content with a European hegemony. Political union quickly enabled a disciplined, intelligent, and highly industrious people to exploit to the full the arts of harnessing physical power which Britain had first developed and applied. The British were rapidly losing their flying start in the field of production. When trouble began to brew in South Africa, the German Emperor was disposed to exercise the same kind of decisive voice in world affairs that his government was now used to exercise in European affairs, by virtue of his paramount army. He found himself powerless to transport that army across the seas. But a time was already in sight when the rapidly growing resources of German industry would enable the German Empire to build and maintain fleets strong enough to challenge the power of Britain to control the sea routes. If once those fleets could escort German armies across the seas, the German Empire would then be able to speak with the same decisive voice in world affairs as in European affairs, since Austria and France had been humbled to the dust.

For the moment the arrogance and impatience of the German rulers themselves frustrated those schemes. In 1914 they blundered into a premature war, which presently united the maritime powers throughout the world, including the U.S.A., to support the British. In the spring of 1918 a last desperate effort to sweep the Allies from Europe almost succeeded. Then hunger began to sap the morale of the German people. By November the military power of Germany had utterly collapsed. The victorious Allies dictated an armistice, and then assembled in Paris to construct the framework of a new order.

The problem they had to solve had been set by the Industrial Revolution, which, starting in England, spread to the world at large. A rapid increase in power to produce the means of living was quickly followed by an increase in the number of human beings to live on them. While the growing power to control the forces of nature increased the size of human society, it was rendering its structure far more complex, and fresh complexities were developed by each new discovery or invention. The growth of trade cycles is a case in point. There were gluts of goods which could not be sold, and millions of people were unemployed, unable to purchase the goods, and wasting their bodies and souls in idleness.

The political mechanism required to translate the needs and desires of ordinary men into action, that is to say, to reach decisions, failed to keep pace with the march of invention. Decisions could not be taken in time to cope with the growth of social evils. Inside the national states social reform was in grave arrears, and the feeling began to develop, fostered by thinkers like Marx, that the growing evils could only be met by entrusting all powers to one dictator, on the pattern of Napoleon, to a superman armed with the force to cut Gordian knots by rapid decisions.

The evil was not confined to social affairs. The relations of states one to another were also complicated by the march of invention; for greatly improved systems of transport by sea and land had made every growing community closely dependent on other and often distant communities for their means of life. While every year was laying an increasing burden of social and international questions on every national government, there was, and could be, no increase in the time available to statesmen for solving them, nor in the fund of nervous energy required to grasp the issues at stake and reach the decisions required.

All this reinforced a willingness to accept the rule of dictators. At the same time, the progress of physical invention was providing dictators with means for controlling the bodies and souls of men. Machine-guns, war-planes, high explosive, and especially broadcasting would have made the mouth of Napoleon water, had he foreseen them.

Freedom is the food which nourishes the growth of men and society. Power has the properties of a strong drink. The taste for it grows upon men the more that they take of it. Dictators are seldom content with the mastery of their own people. They presently aspire to use it for conquering others. In a world bedevilled by despots, commonwealths must always live under threats of impending war. They must always divert a great part of their national wealth, which might have been used for social reform, to paying for armaments, beating their ploughshares into swords. More important still, the time and thought of their rulers, which might have been given to social reform, is absorbed in ceaseless efforts to avert war, or else to win it when those efforts have failed. The power of governments to effect social reform will always remain dangerously shackled in a world overshadowed by the constant menace of war. In this age of mechanization we have reached a stage when human welfare cannot increase until we have found how to restore that degree of security from world wars which was felt to exist in the century which followed the Battle of Waterloo.

**The problem to be solved is this: how rulers can be given the power to make the decisions required to effect this object, and still remain answerable, in fact as well as in theory, to the people they rule.**

## CHAPTER XII

# WAR TO END WAR

IN the war of 1914–18, as now, we gave out to the world that this was 'a war to end war, and to make the world safe for democracy'. In 1916 I published a book called *The Problem of the Commonwealth* in which I pointed out that in the nineteenth century we, the people of the British Isles, had maintained a navy so strong that no foreign aggressor had attempted to attack the British Commonwealth which included nearly a quarter of mankind, scattered all over the globe. I argued that the outbreak of war in 1914 had proved that the Government of the United Kingdom no longer commanded resources sufficient to prevent any attack on the Commonwealth. In this age of mechanization no Imperial Government could hope to maintain forces too strong for any aggressor to attack so long as it commanded resources limited to the British Isles. To prevent further attempts to destroy the Commonwealth there must be a government empowered to command the resources of the Commonwealth as a whole.

This book passed through several editions, but no one in authority appeared to support my thesis that a second world war would take place unless we made ourselves too strong to prevent it. I never expected, indeed, to live as I have done, to see my forecast verified as it now is.

At the close of 1918 came the sudden and unexpected collapse of Germany. In January 1919 the victorious Allies assembled in Paris to frame the peace: but the object for which the war had been fought and won—to prevent further wars and make the world safe for democracy—was at once treated as secondary to another, which President Woodrow Wilson propounded in his formula 'self-determination'. The concept of personal sovereignty, which prevailed in the previous centuries, was foremost in the minds of the statesmen who met at the Congress of Vienna, and we know the result. In the course of the nineteenth century the work of that Congress was torn to pieces by another concept, by the idea that sovereign peoples enjoyed an unlimited right to settle their own affairs each for themselves. The idea of freedom and democracy was identified with the concept of national sovereignty, and this concept was foremost in the minds of the statesmen who met in Paris in 1919. Their business, as they conceived it, was not merely to safeguard national sovereignties, but also to increase their number. Several states were created to take the place of the Austrian Empire and others along the Baltic coast.

So much had been said, however, of the war as a war to end war and to make the world safe for democracy that some provision for that end had to be made. The sovereign states old and new were to sign a covenant pledging them all to unite their forces to restrain any aggressor who might try to challenge their sovereignty. We know the result. When China was threatened by Japan, when Abyssinia was threatened by Italy, and Czechoslovakia by Germany, the States Members of the League thought first and foremost how to keep out of war. When Germany attacked Poland the only states which drew the sword to prevent her were the British democracies and France. They declared war as the allies of Poland. Except by the British Dominions, no semblance of collective action was attempted by States as Members of the League to offer security to Czechoslovakia and Poland when threatened with destruction. The Covenant was, in effect, no more than a paper pledge, with no organic backing of a common authority planning for defence.

## CHAPTER XIII

# THE STATUTE OF WESTMINSTER

WITH the single exception of Eire, the Dominions in both these wars sprang to arms when the British Government declared war. Neither then nor at any time have they ever been asked by the British Government to commit themselves to action of this kind in advance. Such proposals, when made by writers of books or in the Press, have found no support from Dominion Governments. No British Government would ever have thought of asking an Imperial Conference to adopt such commitments as those assumed by the governments that signed the Covenant of the League. The reason why Dominion Governments signed the Covenant so readily was because membership of the League would give them an international recognition of their status as sovereign and independent states. Their minds, with those of the other governments assembled in Paris, were preoccupied with the question of national sovereignty.

In 1923 the Imperial Conference met to consider the problem of defence. Its decisions were as follows (Cmd. 1987, p. 16):

(1) The Conference affirms that it is necessary to provide for the adequate defence of the territories and trade of the several countries comprising the British Empire.

(2) In this connexion the Conference expressly recognizes that it is for the Parliaments of the several parts of the Empire, upon the recommendations of their respective governments, to decide the nature and extent of any action which should be taken by them.

(3) Subject to this provision, the Conference suggests the following as guiding principles:

   (a) The primary responsibility of each portion of the Empire represented at the Conference for its own local defence.

   (b) Adequate provision for safeguarding the maritime communications of the several parts of the Empire and the routes and waterways along and through which their armed forces and trade pass.

   (c) The provision of Naval bases and facilities for repair and fuel so as to ensure the mobility of the fleets.

(*d*) The desirability of the maintenance of a minimum standard of Naval strength, namely, equality with the Naval strength of any foreign power, in accordance with the provisions of the Washington Treaty on Limitation of Armaments as approved by Great Britain, all the self-governing Dominions, and India.

(*e*) The desirability of the development of the Air Forces in the several countries of the Empire upon such lines as will make it possible, by means of the adoption, as far as practicable, of a common system of organization and training and the use of uniform manuals, patterns of arms, equipment, and stores (with the exception of the type of aircraft), for each part of the Empire as it may determine to co-operate with other parts with the least possible delay and the greatest efficiency.

(4) In the application of these principles to the several parts of the Empire concerned the Conference takes note of:

(*a*) The deep interest of the Commonwealth of Australia, the Dominion of New Zealand, and India, in the provision of a Naval Base at Singapore, as essential for ensuring the mobility necessary to provide for the security of the territories and trade of the Empire in Eastern waters.

(*b*) The necessity for the maintenance of safe passage along the great route to the East through the Mediterranean and the Red Sea.

(*c*) The necessity for the maintenance by Great Britain of a Home Defence Air Force of sufficient strength to give adequate protection against air attack by the strongest air force within striking distance of her shores.

(5) The Conference, while deeply concerned for the paramount importance of providing for the safety and integrity of all parts of the Empire, earnestly desires, so far as it is consistent with this consideration, the further limitation of armaments, and trusts that no opportunity may be lost to promote this object.

By resolution (3) (*a*) the Imperial Conference recognized that each part of the Commonwealth bears the primary responsibility for defending its own shores from invasion. By those that follow it is made clear that any such defence will be futile unless adequate provision is made for controlling the maritime routes which connect these widely separated countries, the most vital of which is the route through the

Suez Canal and past Singapore. It was recognized that defence of the various parts of the Commonwealth must depend on provision for defence of the Commonwealth as a whole. That was the vital responsibility; but why was the Conference silent on the question as to what authority was to be held responsible for making that all-important provision? The only possible answer is that in 1923 every member of the Imperial Conference assumed that this vital responsibility would continue to rest, where it had always rested, with the government and people of the United Kingdom.

When these governments reassembled in 1926 the minds of all were centred on the task of affirming and completing the independent sovereignty of the self-governing Dominions. Its resolutions were crystallized in the famous words of the Balfour Report defining the status of the United Kingdom and of the Dominions as 'autonomous communities within the British Empire, equal in status, in no way subordinate one to another in any respect of their domestic and external affairs, though united by a common allegiance to the crown, and freely associated as members of the British Commonwealth of Nations' (Cmd. 2768, p. 14).

On the question of Defence, 'The Resolutions on Defence adopted at the last session of the Conference were re-affirmed' (Cmd. 2768, p. 25) and also reprinted (Ibid., pp. 35 and 36).

When recording their official recognition of the Dominions as separate sovereignties, and interpreting that sovereignty to mean that each Dominion was entitled to a separate and final control of its foreign relations, the question whether any authority was still responsible for the vital function of defending the Commonwealth as a whole could no longer be evaded. This embarrassing question was briefly dealt with as follows in the Balfour Report.

'We went on to examinethe possibility of applying the principles underlying the Treaty Resolution of the 1923 Conference to matters arising in the conduct of foreign affairs generally. It was frankly recognized that in this sphere, as in the sphere of defence, the major share of responsibility rests now, and must for

E

some time continue to rest, with His Majesty's Government in Great Britain (Cmd. p. 25).

'Equality of status, so far as Britain and the Dominions are concerned, is thus the root principle governing our Inter-Imperial Relations. But the principles of equality and similarity appropriate to *status*, do not universally extend to function. Here we require something more than immutable dogmas' (Cmd. p. 14).

The reader must hold in mind that the words 'foreign affairs' are constantly used to cover such matters as the Halibut Treaty which Canada negotiated with the U.S.A. as well as the issue of peace and war, which is, to use the words of the report, 'the major share of responsibility covered by the words "foreign affairs" '. This major responsibility is, as the report records, inseparable from the function of defence. The Imperial Conference of 1926 thus recorded that whilst the self-governing states of the Commonwealth recognize each other as separate and independent sovereignties, each responsible for their own local defence, the major responsibility for the defence of the Commonwealth as a whole still rests where it has always rested—on the government responsible only to the voters and taxpayers of the United Kingdom of Great Britain and Northern Ireland. The Government of the United Kingdom accepted that position, which meant that it accepted in advance an obligation to go to war with any aggressor who attacks any self-governing Dominion. The Dominions also accepted that position, subject to this, that a Dominion is in no way committed to war if the United Kingdom is attacked, until it has seen fit to declare war. And this is what happened in the case of Eire. Incapable of any local defence and dependent on British sea power to prevent any landing of enemy forces on her shores, the Government of Eire maintained a position of neutrality, which gravely imperilled the whole Commonwealth and the Allied cause, helped to prolong the war, and cost the British Commonwealth and her allies the lives of thousands of seamen and numbers of ships with their cargoes.

These resolutions, recorded by the Imperial Conference of 1926, impose on the United Kingdom of Great Britain and

Northern Ireland a responsibility for defending a quarter of mankind scattered all over the globe. They also in terms restrict the resources that its government commands for that purpose to the human and material resources of Great Britain and Northern Ireland. They remain on its minutes and govern the situation to-day. Industrious students will find the subject treated at length in Chap. V of Prof. Hancock's *Survey of British Commonwealth Affairs*. The only reference I have seen in any popular book to the fact that the British Government accepted responsibility for defending the Commonwealth as a whole is on p. 27 of *The British Commonwealth* by Sir Edward Grigg. Can anyone point to any reference in the Parliament or the Press of the British Commonwealth to this resolution? The silence of publicists on the fact which governs the security of the Commonwealth, and therefore the future peace of the world, is another ominous fact.

The upshot is that Dominion Governments have never signed or been asked by the British Government to sign any pledge to go to war when the United Kingdom is attacked. The Government of the United Kingdom has signed a written agreement to defend the Commonwealth as a whole and therefore to go to war with any Power which attacks any self-governing Dominion. The inevitable consequence is that, whatever the Statute of Westminster may say, the issues of peace and war are controlled as before by the British Government. I can recall only one case in which a political leader has mentioned this obvious fact. In the summer of 1939 the Foreign Secretary, Lord Halifax, made an important speech on foreign policy at the annual dinner of the Royal Institute of International Affairs. He was followed by Mr. Menzies, a member of the Australian Cabinet, who made the following observation:

'In spite of the theorists—and there are many theorists in the world—the foreign policy of the British Commonwealth is to a large extent in the hands of the Foreign Secretary of this country. We may, as indeed some of our predecessors did, claim that we are equal in all things in point of foreign policy, but the fact will remain that the great issues of peace and war will be much more determined by the gentleman who sits in a room looking across the Horse Guards Parade than it will by my colleagues in Canberra or one of our colleagues in Ottawa or Pretoria. The nations of the world will not be prepared to sit down for a few weeks or months while the members of the Commonwealth have an intimate chat as to what they are to do.'

The fact which governs this whole situation is that political responsibility cannot be divorced from financial responsibility.

Our rulers combine to present this Commonwealth to our Allies as the model of a system whereby the United Nations can accomplish the aims they are pledged to accomplish under the Atlantic Charter.

Addressing the Pilgrims' Club in New York on the 25th March 1941 Lord Halifax said:

'In the British Commonwealth of Nations our experience has taught us that nations differing greatly in numbers and wealth, in race and social structure, can yet freely associate together. What has been possible for them is not impossible for others, and the British Commonwealth which, by the quality of its resolution, is the bastion of the world defence to-day, may well by its geographical dispersion become the bridge of greater world unity to-morrow. In many respects the world must be treated in future as a single whole.'

So our leaders always repeat with emphasis that twice in this century the Dominions have rallied their forces in defence of the Commonwealth when attacked. Thank God they did, and unless they had done so in time, we must all have gone down to destruction. But Lord Halifax alone[1] has mentioned the obvious fact that the British Commonwealth failed to prevent these two attempts to destroy it—attempts which involved, as they must always involve, the world in war; and he was taken to task for doing so. The fact is ignored that the object for which we have fought these wars, to which all Allies are pledged in terms by the Atlantic Charter, is to prevent such wars happening again. The system our

---

[1] In his speech at Toronto.

Allies are asked to copy has twice failed to achieve that object.

The thesis advanced in 1919, and now again, may be stated as follows:

'The voluntary co-operation of the British Democracies as equal and sovereign states enabled the war to be won in 1918. In 1941 it has so far prevented a decision in favour of Germany and will, we believe, again be effective in winning this war. As victors our peace-aim will then be to create such a world order as will once for all render the recurrence of wars like these impossible. The example of the British Commonwealth points to the principle upon which this new world order should be based.'

**This thesis, however, ignores two shattering facts. In 1914 the British Commonwealth had failed to prevent the outbreak of world war. In 1919 a League was constructed on the model of the British Commonwealth, into which that Commonwealth was incorporated. By 1939 the two together had completely failed to prevent the outbreak of an even more terrible world war.**

CHAPTER XIV

# BRITISH HEGEMONY

THE League of Nations has fallen in ruins, whilst the British Commonwealth still stands, and this no doubt is the reason why statesmen are once more pointing to the Commonwealth as the model upon which to construct international relations after the war. It is worth considering, therefore, why the Commonwealth remains in being whilst the League, supposed to be based on its principles, is in ruins. The reason, as I see it, was stated in some remarks which I made to the Conference on British Commonwealth Relations, which met in Australia on the 3rd September 1938, exactly one year before the war we are now fighting broke out.

'The official theory is that the foreign policy which may involve all of us in war is controlled by the governments of Great Britain, Ireland, Canada, Australia, New Zealand, and South Africa, in co-operation. I ask the Conference to examine this theory, and especially those delegates who come from countries which, unlike Great Britain, have practical experience of the working of federal institutions.

'Professor Scott, in his book submitted by Canada, explains that the Privy Council has ruled that the Federal Government and Parliament cannot implement Canadian treaties dealing with industrial conditions, except in co-operation with the governments and legislatures of all the provinces. This, he argues with unanswerable force, means that Ottawa can only negotiate such treaties in co-operation with the nine provincial governments, which is impossible. He does not pause to argue that this is impossible, because he, and all his readers who have lived under federal institutions, know that any attempt to negotiate a treaty where ten governments in Canada are parties to the negotiation, is, and must be, abortive. How, then, can anyone with federal experience argue that the policy required to preserve the peace of the world can, in fact, be conducted in co-operation between six governments answerable to six legislatures and electorates, separated by all the width of the world?

'The peace of the Commonwealth has so far been preserved because the British Government has since 1926 from hour to hour and day to day made decisions which it could not have made had it waited to secure the assent of five Dominion Governments to the steps proposed. Such an attempt would have meant paralysis, would have ended in no foreign policy at all, and would quickly have plunged the world into war.

'My conclusion is that the official and universally accepted doctrine that the Balfour Declaration and the Statute of Westminster have, in fact as well as in law, given Dominion governments, legislatures, and electorates control of the issues of peace and war, is a dangerous illusion.

.    .    .    .    .    .    .

'One word as to what I mean by responsibility for peace and war. I have no doubt that if the British Commonwealth is attacked, all the Dominions will rush to arms as in 1914. But a prior responsibility to making war is a continuous responsibility in peace for averting war.'

In plain words, the British Commonwealth had continued to function since 1919 by virtue of a British hegemony. The Government answerable to the electorate of Great Britain and Northern Ireland continued, and still continues, to make the decisions on peace and war, which unless they are made in time must involve any political system in the fate which has overtaken the League of Nations.

A system of hegemony is always exposed to two opposite dangers, of becoming too strong, or becoming too weak. One or other of these tendencies will sooner or later compass its downfall. The first of these dangers can be seen in the case of Athens in the Delian League, in the active or latent hegemony of the German Reich from 1870 till the present hour, and in the transient hegemony of France after 1918 till 1933. There is not now the slightest risk that the British Government will ever attempt to reduce the self-governing Dominions to the kind of servitude which Athens imposed on her allies in the fifth century B.C., which France imposed on Germany when she occupied the Ruhr, or which Germany in 1940 succeeded in imposing on most of the nations of Europe. The British hegemony, on the other hand, is a typical example of the weakness which may undermine such a system. A smoke-screen of rhetoric from British as well as

Dominion ministers, extolling the Statute of Westminster, and from constitutional writers, has obscured the realities from the eyes of their peoples.

The primary task of civilized governments is the maintenance of peace. It is only when they have failed in this task and war is upon them that the task of winning the war for the moment becomes primary. And even so, as Thucydides said, it is only to attain a higher state of peace that governments go to war. In spite of all that Imperial Conferences, statesmen, lawyers, and statutes may say, no government is sovereign in fact which is not treating prevention of war as its primary task. The United Kingdom has always regarded that task as primary, not merely for the British Isles, but for the Commonwealth as a whole. The Dominions which attained self-government within that Commonwealth naturally came to regard that position as part of a natural order, and their own domestic affairs as their primary task. The Covenant of the League, the Imperial Conference of 1926, and the Statute of Westminster made no substantial change in this ingrained habit of mind. The task of maintaining peace not merely for its own people but for those of all the Dominions continued to rest on the Government of the United Kingdom. In one solitary instance the truth was blurted out by one responsible minister, Mr. Menzies.

In exactly a year from the Sydney Conference the self-governing Dominions, except Eire, were at war with Germany, a result directly due to the weakness inherent in British hegemony. For reasons already explained Great Britain in the nineteenth century was able to maintain for the whole Commonwealth forces too strong for its enemies to think of challenging. With the close of the century that day had passed, never to return. The German Empire had come to think that British control of the high seas was no longer beyond her power to challenge. By 1914 a war had begun which quickly involved the greater part of the world. When British and French financial resources were exhausted, the tide was turned, just in time, by the entry of America, whose great potential force the German Government had underrated.

Then, as now, the cry went up for 'a peace which would make the world safe for democracy'. There were two ways of securing this end. One was to keep Germany too weak to think once more of destroying the democracies. The other was to make the democracies so strong that Germany would never try to attack them. The victors relied on the first of these policies rather than the second; and this was their cardinal error, if only because when the time came they had not the power to enforce the provisions they had made for keeping Germany weak. So far as democracies look for security to measures for keeping their enemies weak, instead of to measures for making democracy strong, they will fail, and will always fail. So long as a system of democracy is too strong to be attacked, its example will influence its potential enemies, the peoples who accept despotic rule, to demand for themselves responsible government. It will slowly but surely transmute potential enemies into friends. In the nineteenth century this process was at work in countries like Germany and even in Russia and Japan. It ceased to operate as soon as the power which sheltered the growth of democracy was felt to be open to challenge.

The U.S.A. as well as the Dominions have grown to nation-hood under conditions which have led them to regard the task of their own domestic development as primary, and the task of preventing world wars as one which by nature rested on Great Britain. That attitude persists even in the light of our present catastrophes. In an able and thoughtful article dated January 1941, and printed in the March issue of *The Round Table*, its Canadian correspondent writes:

'Canada's continuance in the British connection may therefore depend on the capacity of British statesmen to build a new Europe with a reasonable chance of peace ahead of it. The burden rests squarely on British statesmen, for victory will mean a sufficient renewal of isolationist sentiment in the United States to postpone the day of vigorous American leadership throughout the world, and the Dominions will also be inclined to retreat to their own regions. Moreover, they are politically too immature and in-experienced to help in a major way. European reconstruction will be Great Britain's task.'

Behind this doctrine lies the fallacy that problems of European construction are local to Europe. It is for Europe, and for England as part of Europe, to decide between freedom or slavery for countries like Serbia, Czechoslovakia, or Poland. But problems like these are only the occasion and not the essential cause of the vital issue at stake. The vital issue behind the murder at Serajevo, the rape of Czechoslovakia, or the conquest of Poland is whether a similar fate is to overtake the United Kingdom itself—and this is an issue which involves the fate of the whole British Commonwealth, and, indeed, the whole overseas world.[1] From the moment that happens, or shortly after, the whole resources of Europe, Asia, and Africa will be available to the cause of despotism, for attacking the last outposts of freedom in America, South Africa, Australia, and New Zealand. They will presently find themselves learning to black out their cities and to excavate bomb-proof shelters. In the three older continents the cities will blaze once more with light, and their people no longer sleep in cellars. For the field of battle will have left the Old World and passed to the New.

To be fair it must be admitted that the view quoted above is by no means confined to American and Dominion writers and thinkers. The majority of men in public life, and especially officials, speak, write, or think as though Great Britain could for ever sustain the burden of world peace as she sustained it in the last century. The most cogent answer to this view is a glance at the map of the world. Will any realist with his eye on this map argue that Great Britain and a fragment of Ireland can, in this century or ever again, sustain the cost of armaments, by sea and air, to give the sense of

[1] At a private gathering on the 7th April 1941 the project of a Balkan Federation was discussed by M. Tilea, the former Minister of Rumania. M. Tilea used these words, which I have his written permission to quote: 'Peace is indivisible. We must realize that the real aim of any aggression in the Balkans or elsewhere is the British Empire; an attack on small provinces like Bessarabia or Thrace really means an attack on Cyprus, Gibraltar, or Africa. Similarly, war between Japan and Australia would affect the Balkan Federation.'

security which her navy gave to the free communities from 1815 to the close of that century?

The realist, forced to face this question, takes shelter behind the formula that in future the burden will be borne by England 'in co-operation' with the Dominions and also with the United States. He will ask us to put our trust in methods which have always failed to prevent the recurrence of war—methods, the weakness of which the despots have grasped and exploited to the full.

## CHAPTER XV

# STABILITY

IN the course of this war Hitler has proclaimed the new order he intended to impose on this world. It is in effect a reversion to despotism enlarged to a world-wide scale, enforced by the German race in their own interests, with himself, or a man like himself, as the despot. In the countries struggling to prevent this despotism a demand has been raised for a counter-statement of the peace aims for which we are fighting. As to this Churchill has said that in England a detailed statement would at once impair that union of parties, Conservative, Labour, and Liberal, which must be maintained for winning the war. His decision has met with widespread approval. As a matter of fact the essential objective has already been stated in unequivocal terms not only by Churchill himself and his colleagues to the Right and Left, but also by the President of the U.S.A. In his final address before the election, given at Cleveland on the 2nd November 1940, Mr. Roosevelt had said:

'If the human race as a whole is to survive, the world must find a way by which men and nations can live together in peace. We cannot accept the doctrine that war must be for ever a part of man's destiny.'

In his speech to the Pilgrims' Club at New York on the 25th March 1941 Lord Halifax quoted Churchill as saying:

'Will our children bleed and gasp again in devastated lands?'

On the 14th January 1941 *The Times* had published a letter by Mr. Ernest Bevin to the Transport and General Workers' Union, saying:

'I sincerely trust that this year will bring us victory, the opportunity to begin the great work of reconstruction, and the building of a peace of such a character that this time we shall be able to feel that future generations will never have to face a holocaust such as this.'

On the 27th January 1941 Lord Halifax himself had said in Washington:

'Our first war aim is to win the war, and our main peace aim is, with others, to reconstruct the world so as not to have another war.'

His opposite number, Mr. Winant, closed his first speech as American ambassador to Great Britain, on the 18th March 1941, with the following words:

'Those who now suffer and die in this effort do so for the common good of the free peoples of the earth who shall follow after them, and who with the help of God shall build from these sacrifices a citadel of freedom so strong that force may never again seek its destruction.'

Such quotations from the lips of statesmen reflect the profoundest desire of the peoples for whom they speak. Now, as in 1919, it is clearly recognized by statesmen and people alike that hopes for secure employment and social betterment in general can only be realized in a world order freed from the constant menace of recurring wars.

From statements like these it is clear that when hostilities cease the British and American Governments are committed to the task of trying to establish some world order designed to prevent the recurrence of war. Stability, so far as the maintenance of peace is concerned, is the key-note of these declarations. It is time, therefore, to consider what minimum conditions have to be realized before a political system can begin to acquire stability. What political systems have been found to be stable in actual experience?

Political systems are of two kinds, organic and inorganic. The organic systems are sovereign states such as Great Britain, France, the U.S.A., Germany, Italy, Russia, and Japan. Examples of inorganic systems are the Holy Roman Empire, the American Confederation, the Grand Alliance, the German Confederation, the Austrian Empire, Scandinavia before the partition, the Alliances which lost and won the World War, and the League of Nations.

That these inorganic unions are unstable systems is the lesson of history, that is to say, of practical experience. On the latest and most carefully planned of these systems we now have the recorded verdict of His Majesty's Government. On the 7th September 1939 Sir Alexander Cadogan, dating his letter from the Foreign Office, wrote to the Secretary-General of the League a note containing the following words:

'The position to-day shows clearly that the Covenant has, in the present instance, completely broken down in practice, that the whole machinery for the preservation of peace has collapsed.' (Cmd. 3452.)

That all these composite systems are highly unstable as compared with sovereign states is a fact. This fact is explained by the nature of the bond which unites people in a sovereign state, as distinguished from the bond which attempts to unite sovereign states in a composite structure.

A state exists wherever the people living in a definite area are organized under a government which claims a right to demand an unlimited sacrifice from each individual in the interests of all the others in that area, and when also that claim is sufficiently recognized and obeyed by enough individuals to enable it to be enforced against all in the area. When the Southern States seceded, Lincoln, by virtue of laws enacted by Congress, called on American citizens to give their lives to preserve the Union. And the Union was preserved because enough were found to obey that call and make others obey it. The bond which held the Union together was described by Lincoln as 'dedication'. This readiness of the more public-spirited citizens to obey a claim to unlimited self-sacrifice, and also to make less public-spirited citizens also obey it, is the root of sovereignty in a commonwealth. It enables one authority in the state to override all other authorities in the last resort, which is what sovereignty means by its derivation. It enables that authority to make decisions, and make them in time. Contrast decisions by a British Cabinet, or by votes in the House of Commons, with attempts to reach decisions at Geneva, and you see the difference.

The fact that men have acquired an ever-increasing control of physical forces, without acquiring a corresponding control over themselves, that is to say, over spiritual forces, is the prime cause of the chaos and anarchy which now disorders the world. Sovereignty is, in fact, the essential means whereby men can achieve control of their mutual relations.

We are constantly told that national states must now be prepared to abandon their claim to sovereignty. Plans to do this which do not also provide for merging these sovereignties in one international organ lead to paralysis and merely increase the condition of anarchy.

The doctrine that the state can be based on compact in any shape or form is the master fallacy of political thought. It is of all illusions that which has brought most suffering on civilized man. Compact is based on a balance of interests. It is bilateral or multilateral. The interests on which it is based shift and change like a bed of sand under moving water. What Lincoln called 'dedication' is unilateral, and because the claim to unlimited loyalty of each to all is not subject to change by changing events, it creates a stable system. It is bed-rock compared with the shifting sand of balanced self-interests. Attempts to create stable political systems by compacts between sovereign states must from their nature fail.

We can thus see that inorganic political systems are unstable, but also why they are so. By an inorganic system is meant a system based on compact between sovereign states. A system becomes organic when its authority is based on the loyalty of the individuals of which it is composed, and when it exercises that authority directly on those individuals.

So long as allied states are fighting for their very existence, alliances are relatively stable, though history, when it comes to be written, always shows how the inorganic bond of alliance hastened defeat or delayed victory. This war has now given us the example of the Franco-British alliance. But a greater difficulty comes in peace when the allied states try to stand together so as to render hopeless a renewed attack from their enemies, that is to say, to maintain permanent peace. And this is for two reasons. The decisions required to meet changing conditions, which will lead to recurrence of war, can seldom be made in time, because such decisions require agreement between separate sovereignties. The second reason is that, as interests change, so the basis of the compact changes. Estrangement develops first between governments and then between the peoples behind them.

Speaking at Birmingham on the 24th February 1940, Mr. Chamberlain said:

'During these six months of war our alliance with France has deepened into a friendship and an understanding so close that, as M. Daladier remarked at a recent meeting of the Supreme War Council, the two Governments to-day think and act as one.

'As with the Government, so with the peoples. . . . Every Frenchman with whom I talked laid stress on this friendship with pride and pleasure. There could be no more hopeful assurance for our common victory, and no more fruitful basis of a lasting peace because this intimate understanding which has grown up between us must not be allowed to come to an end when the war is over. It must remain to help us to work out the problems of new Europe which must come after the war in an association in which we shall gladly welcome others who share our ideals.

. . . . . . . . .

'We and France are determined to do what we can for security by the continuance of that complete identity of purpose and policy which now unites us, and which will serve after the war for the firm foundation on which the international relations between our two countries are built. Only so can we establish the authority and stability which are necessary for the security of Europe during the period of reconstruction and fresh endeavour to which we look forward after the war. But France and Britain, powerful as they are, cannot and do not want to settle the new Europe alone. Others must come in and help us, in particular, to bring about that disarmament which is an absolutely essential feature of any lasting peace.'

How far the principles stated in these pages were present to Mr. Chamberlain's mind when he spoke on the 24th February we do not know. He was then considering the post-war relations of England and France in the first instance. No Franco-British Union could have availed to prevent the recrudescence of German aggression unless the French and British peoples could have been put into a position to pursue one foreign policy, not merely for years but for generations. They could not have achieved one Franco-British policy unless it was to be backed by one Franco-British Army, Navy, and Air Force. The question of dividing the cost between the two peoples would have had to be settled on some principle. The Supreme War Council, an executive body composed of French and British Cabinet Ministers, was, at the time when Mr. Chamberlain spoke, attempting these tasks. To what extent they succeeded its members alone could say. But could such an executive body hope to succeed when peace had restored political life to normal conditions? Assuming that French and British ministers had been able to agree on policy, as they seldom agreed in the early twenties, and also on the scale of armaments required to support that policy, they would then have had to obtain the necessary votes from the French Chamber and House of Commons. It is hard to believe that an executive body which had to obtain its supplies from two legislatures elected by different nations, and therefore largely on their own domestic issues, could long have survived.

The executive body would also have had to obtain sanction for military service by the citizens of both countries. The members of the executive body themselves would have been subject to frequent changes, as governments rose and fell in Paris and London. In Paris governments had been changed on the average twice a year. Such a structure becomes fantastic if extended to more nations than two.

The conclusion is that no Franco-British executive body recruited from French and British Cabinets, and responsible to the French Chamber and House of Commons, could have long survived. In order to do its work the joint executive body must have drawn its authority from, and have been answerable to, one Franco-British representative body distinct from the French Chamber and House of Commons. Nor could that representative body be composed of delegates from the French and British legislatures; for delegates would be expected to obey instructions from the national legislatures which appointed them. The decisive discussions would then take place in two national legislatures.

For such a system to work at all there must have been a Franco-British representative body directly elected by French and British voters. The executive body responsible for

F

security must have been drawn from and responsible to that representative body. It must have had power to raise from French and British taxpayers all the money required for security as a first charge on their common resources. Then, and then only, would it have been organic, and therefore stable. An inorganic structure is like a reed, which will always break when you lean on it; but is yet strong enough to pierce your side with the broken end. So China, Abyssinia, Czechoslovakia, Albania, and Finland found when they leaned on collective security. And so we also have found, in the Franco-British alliance. Vichy is an experience we shall not forget.

On the 16th June 1940 His Majesty's Government offered to France in the hour of her agony a union which was obviously meant to become organic. The announcement which appeared in *The Times* was as follows:

'It was announced last night that, with the object of assisting France and supporting her to the utmost in the hours of stress through which she was passing, as also in the hope of encouraging the French Government to continue their resistance, the British Government had offered to conclude a solemn Act of Union between the two countries. The following draft declaration was accordingly communicated to the French Government by His Majesty's Ambassador on June 16:—

### THE DECLARATION OF UNION

'At this most fateful moment in the history of the modern world the Governments of the United Kingdom and the French Republic make this declaration of indissoluble union and unyielding resolution in their common defence of justice and freedom, against subjection to a system which reduces mankind to a life of robots and slaves.

'The two Governments declare that France and Great Britain shall no longer be two nations but one Franco-British Union. The constitution of the Union will provide for joint organs of defence, foreign, financial and economic policies. Every citizen of France will enjoy immediately citizenship of Great Britain, every British subject will become a citizen of France.

'Both countries will share responsibility for the repair of the

devastation of war, wherever it occurs in their territories,
and the resources of both shall be equally, and as one, applied
to that purpose.

'During the war there shall be a single war Cabinet, and all
the forces of Britain and France, whether on land, sea, or
in the air, will be placed under its direction. It will govern
from wherever it best can. The two Parliaments will be
formally associated.

'The nations of the British Empire are already forming new
armies. France will keep her available forces in the field, on
the sea, and in the air.

'The Union appeals to the United States to fortify the economic
resources of the Allies and to bring her powerful material aid
to the common cause.

'The Union will concentrate its whole energy against the power
of the enemy no matter where the battle may be. And thus
we shall conquer.'

By a narrow majority of 13 to 10 the French Cabinet
rejected this offer. A new Government was formed, to make
submission to Germany. Its leading members were generals
and admirals, men whose religion combined with their naval
and military training to dispose them in favour of authoritarian systems. They accepted Hitler's new order, and
showed that much as they hated their German masters they
hated still more the republican institutions which could place
in office a *front populaire*. Short of actual war on their former
allies, they did everything to oppose their efforts and those of
the French soldiers and sailors led by de Gaulle who were
struggling to save France and the world from a German
despotism.

In the offer which Churchill made at Bordeaux the second
clause is all-important. The French, in this clause, were
offered a citizenship common with that of Great Britain.
Within limits the meaning of this was made clear. The
French would enjoy free access to Great Britain, and British
subjects free access to France. The two countries were to
have 'joint organs' through which to control 'defence, foreign,
financial and economic policies'. Did Churchill realize that
this could only be done, in peace at any rate, through a

Franco-British assembly, directly responsible to French and British voters alike? He only could answer this question.

We British have a habit of speaking as though all British subjects enjoyed a common citizenship in all the highly various countries embraced by the British Commonwealth. In foreign countries Englishmen, Canadians, Australians, New Zealanders, South Africans, and Indians enjoy the status of British subjects alike. It is worth remembering, therefore, that this common citizenship of ours implies scarcely any of the things specifically offered to France as the content of a common citizenship. Any British subject has right of free access to Great Britain under its laws. But no British subject domiciled outside a self-governing Dominion has right of free access to that Dominion under its laws. Great Britain accepts responsibility for the defence and foreign policy of the Commonwealth as a whole, and because she accepts the financial burden involved thereby, her hegemony is accepted by the Dominions. Over their financial and industrial policies she has claimed and exercised no control.

This unique and historic offer to France of organic union with Great Britain which the British Government made in June 1940 is a fact to remember; but here let me state more clearly a view implicit in this chapter that **the British Democracies cannot wisely discuss organic relations with free European states until they have first discussed organic relations between themselves.**

CHAPTER XVI

# WHY CO-OPERATION BETWEEN NATIONAL COMMONWEALTHS FAILS TO PREVENT WAR

As Jesus of Nazareth saw, the divine capacity in men to put the interests of others before their own is the ultimate treasure, the pearl beyond price. To perfect this most imperfect capacity is the end and object of all rightly directed endeavour. As we increase that capacity, so will it bring in its train all secondary goods such as pleasure and happiness. 'Seek ye first the Kingdom of God, and all things else shall be added unto you.' As the law of gravity holds the physical universe together, so this sense of duty is the essential factor which makes an ordered society possible. The object of all human endeavour should be to strengthen this factor. Belief in its permanent value is the essence of faith. When this vision fails 'the people cast off restraint', the rule of law begins to lapse, and society at large falls into chaos. What the author of Proverbs wrote nearly 3,000 years ago is a true diagnosis of the vast disorder into which the world has fallen in our time. The people who still hold this essential faith, that the sense of duty in men is the thing which matters above all others, are 'the salt of the earth'—the hope of the world. Without them human society must decompose, to perish in corruption. But no faith is a genuine faith, except in so far as those who hold it exert themselves to express it in action. No vision is a true vision unless we believe that it must and can be realized in practice. That is the meaning of the prayer 'Thy Kingdom come, Thy will be done; as in Heaven, so on earth.' The paramount question for those who hold this faith is what they can do to develop the sense of duty in others as well as in themselves. First and foremost, each must look to his own duty, to seeing that he does it to others from hour to hour. Each must fearlessly teach this faith and organize its teaching. To this end the churches, universities, and schools are appropriate agencies. But as shoemakers think there is nothing like leather, so clergy and teachers are prone to think of instruction as the most important means for improving the characters of men. They are apt to forget that the social framework in which they grow up imposes its shape on their minds and souls as decisively as a mould imposes its shape upon melted wax. If we really hope to transform men into the likeness of God, we must see, first and foremost, that the moulds into which they are run are shaped in accordance with His mind. We must see that our social mechanism is such as, by its working, will develop the sense of duty in men to each other by exercise. It is only by exercise that our sense of duty becomes spontaneous, a second nature that moves us to do the right thing as a matter of course.

That love, devotion, loyalty, or whatever we choose to call our sense of duty to others is developed by demands made on it rather than by rewards offered, is one of the most neglected of psychological facts. The deepest and most enduring of all human affections is that for a child from the mother who has suffered in bearing it the utmost anguish that human flesh can endure. It is to the leaders who offer nothing but sweat, tears, and blood that the utmost devotion is rendered by followers. The supreme example is the Master who offered His disciples a cross to carry as their only reward on earth. The unbounded devotion of Jesuits to their order shows how well their founder Ignatius Loyola had read the innermost secret of human nature: and so it is with the state. The sense of loyalty which binds men together in a state and makes it operative is the slow but sure result of the claim made by the state on its citizens. By the state I mean simply all the citizens who compose the state. By loyalty to the state I mean a sense in each citizen that the best interests of all the other citizens must be put before his own desires. This sense of devotion, this instinct of duty, the state develops in its members by exercise in things small, as well as in things great, in paying taxes and in voting at elections, as well as in dying for their country when need calls. The stupendous growth of nationalism in our own time is due to the ever-increasing demands on the loyalty of its members which a state must make in this mechanized age. The state cannot develop the whole nature of man merely by asking for blind obedience. It must seek to develop by exercise his reason as well as his character. He must be made to feel that the orders he receives are framed in the interests of the citizens as a whole. This he will only feel in so far as ultimate decisions rest with the citizens as a whole, including himself. They must decide from time to time who are the people to frame the orders and hold the power for the time being. In so far as citizens feel that they themselves are the government, so will the system serve to develop the better side of their nature.

I have shown in the opening chapters of this book how the Commonwealth, the State in which the citizens themselves are the government, had its beginning in Ancient Greece, in city-states like Athens; how in the Middle Ages the principle was applied on the national scale by the English device of representation; and how in the eighteenth-century America, a commonwealth was founded on the federal principle which now embraces forty-eight states, most of them larger than England. Since then our mastery of physical forces has put all nations throughout the world in touch with and made them depend for their daily needs on each other more closely than did the thirteen states that founded the American Union. Yet human society, so united for its innumerable needs, remains split up into more than sixty sovereign states. Some of these states are genuine though still imperfect commonwealths; others the very negation of that principle. Between them is anarchy. While our power of controlling the forces of nature was increasing by leaps and bounds our power to control human forces has scarcely advanced. Our own physical inventions are crushing us to powder. As I write the steppes of Russia, the frontiers of Egypt and the Caribbean are strewn with the dead and the dying. These, perhaps, are a fraction of those that have yet to suffer and die.

So great were the sufferings wrought by the last war, even on victors, that their leaders believed that national states could henceforth be trusted to act together in time to prevent such a war if it threatened again. The procedure to be followed was set out and agreed upon in the Covenant of the League. Within twenty years peace was again in jeopardy.

Each of the national commonwealths, small and great, shut its eyes to the fact that war, if once begun, would engulf them all. Each thought first how to keep out of the war, with results as we see them to-day. And still, once more, we are now being told that sovereign commonwealths can be trusted to see that this will never happen again.

Why did this happen? How came it to pass that nations like the British, American, French, Belgian, Dutch, and Norwegian democracies each failed to see what steps were needed to avert this second world-wide calamity, and to take them in time? How was it that each in the hour of crisis thought only of how to keep out of the struggle itself, and not how to prevent a war which has now engulfed the whole of mankind?

My answer to this question is implied in what I have said in the previous pages. A commonwealth does, by its operation, evoke and develop by exercise a sense of duty in each citizen to the whole body of citizens, that is, to the state. It trains him to put the interests of that body before his own, and to treat that interest as paramount. But so long as the principle of the commonwealth is limited to sections of mankind, to particular nations, the sense of devotion it engenders in the citizen will be rendered to his own nation, his own section of mankind. In a crisis his loyalty will be limited to that nation, and will come before loyalty to other nations to which he does not belong. His very conception of the real good of his own nation will be narrowed and obscured by the fact that the system concentrates his mind on that nation alone, and not on the good of mankind as a whole. In commonwealths discussion is free. Teachers and preachers can do their work. Some of their citizens will hold and express wider views than is possible in authoritarian states which suppress public discussion. Yet, even so, the fact remains that since the last war in each crisis the commonwealths failed to take in time the action needed to forestall the impending world-calamity. When events had made it plain to England and France that their own existence was threatened, they intervened in the cause of Poland, too late to save her from the direst fate that has ever befallen one great people.

In the previous pages I have urged that, important as teaching and preaching are, the structure of the state under which men live is more decisive in shaping their minds and characters. The experience of the last twenty years has endorsed this view. The national sovereignty of the states, members of the League, was jealously preserved. The claim of each government to command the obedience of its own citizens was unquestioned. So the founders of the League were wisely concerned to establish organizations to create a public opinion in each member state strong enough to compel its government to observe and implement the Covenant. This country of ours has seldom seen a more active and widespread propaganda than that which was organized by the League of Nations Union. Yet the structure of each democratic nation, which was moulding the citizen to think of his loyalty as due first to his fellow citizens, and to put their immediate interests, as he read or misread them, before those of the world at large, and ignore the Covenant in the letter as well as its spirit whenever a crisis arose, was more potent than all the organized teaching and preaching. The net results are recorded in the letter addressed by the British Government to the Secretary-General of the League I quoted above in chapter XV:

'The position to-day shows clearly that the Covenant has, in the present instance, completely broken down in practice, that the whole machinery for the preservation of peace has collapsed.'

The national commonwealth is the most powerful agency for developing a sense of duty in its own members. That is its quality. Its effect in limiting the supreme devotion of its members to itself, to a mere minority of their fellow men, is the defect of that quality. Because it includes only a minority of human beings, it trains that minority to exalt their own interest, or rather what they misread as their own interest, above that of the rest of mankind. This defect in commonwealths cannot be finally cured until the whole of human society has been organized as one commonwealth.

That day will come, and till it comes the inevitable and temporary defect of the national commonwealth must not be allowed to obscure its essential virtue. The national com-

monwealth which England created was a notable advance
on the city commonwealths of Ancient Greece. The commonwealth that Washington created on the continental scale was a
clear advance on the national commonwealth created by the
English.

The next and most difficult step is to merge the national
and continental commonwealth in a genuine international
commonwealth, which must, to begin with, be incomplete.
This transition from national sovereignties to an international
sovereignty is the most important, as it is the most difficult,
task that the world has to face. It will, I believe, in ages to
come, rank as the Rubicon of human history. For when once
an international government has been realized, the successive
inclusion of nations outside it will be merely a question of
time, and may reach its completion more quickly than we in
this age of confusion can picture. The hope of the world rests
with those who address themselves to the task of creating an
international government, however limited and modest in
scope to begin with. One example realized in practice will
work miracles, and until that miracle is worked we must do
our best by precept to bring it to pass.

But in setting out to effect the necessary change in public
opinion let us have no illusions as to the formidable nature
of our task. By those whose voices can reach the multitude,
or whose practical experience or thought weighs with public
opinion, legislators, journalists, officials, and professors of
political science and law, the fragmentation of human society
into national states is too often regarded as the last word in
political development, as a stage beyond which mankind is
never to advance.

> And just as far as ever from the end !
> Nought in the distance but the evening, nought
> To point my footsteps further ! At the thought
> A great black bird, Apollyon's bosom-friend
> Sailed past, nor beat his wide wing dragon-penned
> That brushed my cap—perchance the guide I sought.

At the close of *The Commonwealth of Nations*, published in
1916, I quoted these lines from Browning's *Childe Roland to*

*the dark tower came.* And now I have lived to see all Europe writhing in the talons of Apollyon's friend, with his wings spread out to darken every ocean and continent beyond. In truth the guide we need.

## Appendix to Chapter XVI

In his important broadcast of the 23rd July 1942 Mr. Cordell Hull used the following words:

'To make full use of this opportunity, we must be resolved not alone to proclaim the blessings and benefits which we all alike desire for humanity, but to find the mechanisms by which they may be most fully and most speedily attained and be most effectively safe-guarded.'

In a previous passage of this broadcast Mr. Hull had said:

'In the creation of such mechanisms there would be a practical and purposeful application of sovereign powers through measures of international co-operation for purposes of safeguarding the peace. Participation by all nations in such measures would be for each its contribution toward its own future security and safety from outside attack.'

On the 5th August Lord Simon made the following comment on Mr. Hull's speech in the House of Lords:

'Mr. Cordell Hull in that speech pointed out that the Atlantic Charter does not propose to substitute international Authority for sovereign rights and self-government. The conception is that sovereign rights and self-government will be preserved and made, as far as self-government is concerned, *more authoritative and complete.*'

The Lord Chancellor, speaking from the Woolsack, was thus careful to pledge his Government and also, so far as he could, that of the United States, that in carrying out the Atlantic Charter nothing should be done to interfere with national sovereignty. Their policy would be to emphasize it.

Lord Simon said that he had read and re-read Mr. Hull's speech and I have done the same with both speeches. The impression they give me is that in Mr. Hull's mind the prevention of future wars is the paramount object, and he thinks that the maintenance of national sovereignty is not inconsistent therewith. In Lord Simon's mind the maintenance of national sovereignty is the paramount object, and he thinks that the prevention of war is not inconsistent therewith.

The reader must judge for himself whether Lord Simon was justified in telling the House of Lords that in Mr. Cordell Hull's view: 'Sovereign rights and self-government will be preserved and made, as far as self-government is concerned, *more authoritative and complete*'.

## CHAPTER XVII

# LIMITS OF INTERNATIONAL GOVERNMENT

So much for the past. But how does this all apply to the task to which we have set our hands, in 1914 and in 1939 and after this war when it is over—the task set out for us by our leaders in such telling words, 'to make the world safe for democracy', to see 'that our children do not again gasp and bleed in devastated lands', 'to reconstruct the world so as not to have another war', 'the building of a peace of such a character that this time we shall be able to feel that future generations will never have to face a holocaust such as this'?

When the war is over our leaders will doubtless tell us what changes have to be made and what sacrifices have to be faced by us, the peoples for whom they speak, if we really hope to reach the goal to which they have pointed us. Whenever that time comes it may help them if those who have no such burdens as rest on leaders whilst war is in progress set out what they think they see in unmistakable terms. It is also important that we should be told what changes in our system have got to be faced, in order to solve the one outstanding problem, to which we are now committed, how to prevent recurrence of war. I am bound to say this because the proposals I have seen which strike me as going to the root of the matter demand changes which are not in my judgement required to secure the paramount object we have in view. I say this with the utmost diffidence, for amongst the proposals I have in mind are those of Mr. Streit, Dr. Jennings, Mr. Mackay, and Sir William Beveridge, all personal friends, and writers of incomparably greater knowledge in constitutional matters than I can claim. The ground upon which I agree with them may be stated as follows:

Human society is now fragmented into about sixty sovereign states. Each of these sovereignties is so constituted that its conduct will be determined by a view of its own interests, and not by a view of the interests of human society as a whole. In the course of two centuries mechanization has made every part of human society dependent on every other.

This growing interdependence is subject to no common control. Between these sixty sovereignties a state of anarchy exists resulting in world wars, an evil which cannot be cured by any system based on compacts between the sovereign states. Stability can now be introduced into this chaotic structure little by little, and only, at the outset, by bringing two or more states into organic union, and including others as they come to see that organic union is the only basis of international stability and peace.

So far we agree; but I part company with these authorities when I urge that organic union should be limited as closely as possible to security. I believe that the power to control migration and tariffs can and should be left to the national governments of the component states.

In the view taken by these four writers, who follow more or less closely the classic model of the U.S.A., the day of national states is over. I myself take the contrary view, that national states must continue to discharge a permanent and necessary function in human affairs. What I mean can be understood by a glance at the self-governing states which grew up beyond the seas in the high degree of security ensured till the twentieth century by British sea-power—the U.S.A. and the self-governing Dominions. These states asserted the right to control and assumed the function of controlling their own composition and social structure. To these ends they control migration, including that of British subjects, both on economic and racial grounds. They enact tariffs against the mother country as well as against the rest of the world, **because a people cannot control their own social structure unless they control the distribution of taxation, and of course the development of industries.**

Man, as science has now convinced us, has aeons before him on this planet. We can surely foresee a world government and stabilized peace in course of time, without assuming a human society in which all the racial elements have been mixed into one conglomerate, following one standardized way of life. Such a human society would have acquired the uniformity of a jelly-fish, a one-celled organism, the lowest form of physical life. The highest form of physical life is the human body. Its component organs—heart, lungs, liver, brain, &c.—are all of different chemical composition, and highly different structure, all harmonized in one supreme unit. The highest form of organism is made up of highly differentiated organs, fitly joined together in one supreme unity. And so the supreme unity which human society should attain is one in which its component nations are highly differentiated in composition as well as in structure. It has been the function of national states to accomplish this. To preserve and develop this differentiation will still be their function. But the chief impediment to the discharge of this function is now the insecurity caused by the state of anarchy between them. The real clog on social reform is the cost of armaments, but still more the tax on time and attention involved by the constant menace of war. If once this material burden and spiritual menace are removed, social reform in the national states will advance by leaps and bounds. They will find themselves born to a new freedom.

Another important point is that no international government could have either the detailed knowledge or time to control conditions which determine national compositions and structures. One set of ministers cannot have the knowledge and time to deal with social questions in the component nations, and also with the question of their common security. At present, the cabinet of each nation is dangerously overburdened by having to deal with security (including foreign policy) and domestic questions as well. In any international structure it is vital that there should be two sets of ministers, one dealing with the general security and the other handling internal and domestic questions. If, in the U.S.A., the state governments were abolished, and all their functions transferred to the federal authority in Washington, it would break down from the outset. No one cabinet and legislature in Washington could transact the necessary burden of business, merely as a question of time. Constitutional authorities, who write about government without having practised it, are apt to forget the basic fact that there are only 24 hours in a day, and 365 days in a year. The handling of public business must keep sufficient time with the march of events.

A guiding principle is therefore suggested to be treated as basic, at any rate at the outset of any experiment in international construction which is to succeed.

**The control of social affairs in their widest aspect must be left to national governments, yet cannot be so left unless they continue to control the distribution of taxation and therefore tariffs within their several jurisdictions. The international government must be restricted to security and matters which are quite inseparable therefrom, for which purpose it must have effective power to make security a first charge on all the resources of the nations included.**

The crux of the whole question is, then, whether the international government can be clothed with effective powers to make security a first charge on the resources of all the nations it represents, while leaving the distribution of the burden amongst individual taxpayers to the national governments. I believe that this can be done. I am therefore bound to suggest how I think we can do it.

In 1896 the Childers Commission, which included financial experts like Lord Farrer, Lord Welby, and Sir David Barbour, agreed that the relative taxable capacities of Great Britain and Ireland were as 20 to 1, and that taxation should be readjusted on that basis. Though the economic structure of national states is now far more complicated than it was in 1896, this can still be done with sufficient accuracy for the purpose of practical government. 'Government is a rough business', said Cornwall Lewis. It cannot hope to attain perfect justice, but only such measure of justice as our limited human intelligence and knowledge of facts allow.

The suggestion, then, is that:

1. A standing commission of financial experts, equipped with adequate staff, should every five years declare the taxable capacity of the various countries in the union.

2. The revenue required for general security, as voted by

the joint representative body, should be assessed upon these various nations in the ratio so declared.

3. The quota due from each nation should constitute a first charge on its national consolidated fund, which, like the charge to meet the national debt in England, would not be required to be voted each year by the national legislature. The joint executive body would be entitled to this first charge under the constitution, the cash to become payable from the national banks into the federal bank, on a warrant signed by the treasurer of the joint executive body.

4. If the fund in a national bank were insufficient to meet the warrant, the executive body would then apply to the Federal Supreme Court (for such there must be) to transfer the control of the customs, excise, or any other revenue department, to the executive body with power to collect those revenues from the taxpayers themselves until the quota was satisfied, returning to the national exchequer any funds collected over and above that amount. If the national government still found means of avoiding a remedy so drastic, the Court should in the last resort be able to declare the joint representative body to be entitled by statute to take whatever steps were necessary. The point would then have been reached beyond which it lies not in the power of human laws to go. A constitution can make it clear, beyond the region of dispute, that the government it creates is not to be paralysed by means of the law, but only by a conscious and evident breach of it. It cannot do more; but a constitution which does less is an instrument of government which invites revolution.

5. The budget for security framed by the executive body should be for a three-year period, but should be revised every year by the representative body for the third year, so that national governments would always know what amounts would be needed to meet the quotas three years ahead. Their scheme of taxation could thus be framed in advance to enable their budgets to meet the

G

quotas, and yet leave a sufficient balance to finance their own domestic and national requirements.

There are those who hold that the high tariff walls which nations have raised against each other since the last war are the greatest menace to peace. The writers to whom I refer clearly think that this menace cannot be removed unless the power of fixing tariffs is taken away from the states and transferred to a federal government. The supreme function of such a government is to provide a common system of defence for all the component democracies, too strong for any of its enemies to think of challenging; in other words, to create a sense of security for them all. In my view, one strong reason why these tariffs have been raised to their present height is fear of war. My own conviction is that, as and when this fear is removed, a federal government will be able to influence its component states to reduce their tariffs to a lower and safer level. In so far as a greater sense of security pervades the world, Mr. Cordell Hull's policy of encouraging nations to reduce their tariffs will become increasingly operative. A guess like this can only be verified by trial. If in experience it proves to be wrong, then it is still possible to ask federated states to renounce their control of tariffs as the only alternative to a system which will end in plunging society into a new era of world wars. I suggest that this moderate course would be more likely to lead to practical results than if we assume from the outset that no international government can provide security, unless it has also the power to regulate the tariffs of all its component states.

## CHAPTER XVIII

# A BRITISH INITIATIVE PROPOSED

To found a system after this war, which will, as it grows, prevent the recurrence of these murderous catastrophes, is the task to which we are long and expressly committed. In the light of experience it is now sufficiently clear that this can only be done little by little. The question for us, the British who are fighting this war, is how to begin it. I propose to say as briefly and clearly as I can how I think this start can be made by us in the light of what has been said in the previous pages.

We must, to begin with, drop our inveterate habit of shutting our eyes to basic truths, and cease to regard their explicit statement as an indiscretion. Let us face the fact that the British Commonwealth is in jeopardy (and so is the peace of the world) until it is armed so strongly that no one thinks of attacking it. At present the task of providing such arms is a first charge on the resources of Great Britain and Northern Ireland, and on no one else. For that reason the direction of foreign policy which determines the issues of peace or war is, in fact, vested in the Government responsible to none but the taxpayers of Great Britain and Northern Ireland. No government after this war can begin to provide adequate security for the Commonwealth as a whole until the cost has become a first charge on all the resources of the self-governing Dominions, no less than on those of Great Britain and Northern Ireland. It follows as surely as day follows the night that responsibility for defence and foreign policy must rest on British citizens in the Dominions as well as in Britain, and must cease to rest, as it now rests, on the voters and taxpayers of Britain alone.

The change required to effect this object has already been outlined in the previous pages. There must be one executive body responsible for framing the estimates necessary to secure the Commonwealth as a whole from attack. That executive body must be able to secure the cash required to meet those estimates. But this it cannot do unless it is able to meet one legislative body with which to discuss foreign policy, the world situation and its dangers, and from which to obtain a decision. For it is in the light of those dangers that the estimates of the executive body must be framed. The paramount issue before this legislature would always be the amount of the first charge on all their assets which their constituents must meet in order to avert the menace of war from the Commonwealth as a whole.

Such a legislative body means that general elections would have to be held from time to time in all the self-governing countries concerned. The issue before the electors would be just that which the legislature itself was created to decide, what charge on their assets voters and taxpayers would have to face in order to avert the horrors of war. At these general elections the world situation would come under discussion; for there would, indeed, be nothing else to discuss. Dominion electors would quickly become as well-qualified judges of these issues as those of Great Britain.

If the system of finance suggested in the last chapter should prove in experience to be workable, the issues discussed at general elections and in the legislative body would not be complicated by issues domestic and local to any of the constituent nations. The most comprehensive of all these domestic issues which controls most directly their social structure is the distribution of taxes as between one taxpayer and another. Under the system here suggested that great domestic issue would rest where it now rests with the existing national government, so long as that government was observing the constitution. In so far as the system succeeded in removing the fear of war, the national governments would find themselves freed as never before to proceed with the work of internal development and social reform.

In the previous pages I have touched on the evergrowing difficulty which national governments and legislatures find in transacting the volume of business imposed upon them in a mechanized age. The system here proposed would meet that difficulty. One set of ministers and legislators would handle defence and matters inseparable therefrom. In all the component nations another set of ministers and legislators would find themselves free to handle their own domestic and social affairs.

The constitution required to effect this change would, I think, be a shorter and simpler document than those drafted by writers like Streit and Jennings. I do not here propose to enter into details, beyond one comment on the main objection to all proposals for organic union of the British Commonwealth, which is always advanced. That objection is that all the Dominions together would be outvoted by Great Britain. That objection assumes that British members of Parliament would vote as a block. When issues had to be decided in the Commonwealth Parliament, I cannot conceive English Labour members combining to vote with Conservative members against the combined vote of Labour and Capital in New Zealand and Australia. In one legislative chamber the followers of Mr. Attlee and Mr. Curtin would find themselves nearer to each other than to the followers of an English Conservative leader and those of Mr. Menzies. The most formidable argument we had to meet in the movement for South Africa Union was that the Cape would be able to outvote the Transvaal, Free State, and Natal. In practice that situation has never arisen. The voting splits in varying proportions across each of the four provinces.

Personally I think there are reasons why the Dominions should be given a more generous representation than they would have on a strict basis of population. I am also assuming an upper house in which, as in the American Senate, each nation would have equal representation. I would make it advisory, except on proposals to alter the constitution.

In the last war the situation was only saved by the timely arrival of Dominion troops, by the valour with which they fought, and the sacrifices made by the peoples behind them, till at last the U.S.A. came in and turned the scale. The Dominions supplied the margin without which the war would have been lost by 1917. And the same is obviously true in this war. My own conviction is that if the cost of defending the Commonwealth as a whole from 1919 onwards had been recognized as a first charge on Dominion resources no less than on those of Great Britain, the margin of strength supplied would have sufficed to prevent the outbreak of a second war twenty years later. The system might in time have been broadened to include European democracies and at length the U.S.A., and whenever the U.S.A. joins such a system the era of world wars will be finally over. The all-important thing for us who are now again fighting this desperate battle for freedom—freedom from fear—is to make a beginning, to make some increase in the peacetime strength behind the democracies by a margin however narrow. If this were done after the war by a union of Great Britain with some, or all, of the Dominions on the lines suggested in these pages, I believe such a union for a decade, at any rate, would be strong enough to arrest the descent of the world to a third and even more disastrous war. There would then be one government which could speak for people in the Dominions, no less than for those in the British Isles.

But what of countries like France, Belgium, Holland, Denmark, and Norway, countries whose safety has been shown by events to be closely bound up with our own? They will seek our protection, and in doing so point to the fact that in these days of air power they are all, in the hands of our enemies, pistols pointed at England, the heart of freedom in the world, no less than Belgium since the days of Marlborough. Now are we to offer the same guarantee that we gave to Belgium? Shall we promise again to go to war to protect them, and accept the Belgian condition that until an outbreak of war no conference should be held with us as to the disposition of forces required to meet war when it happens? I think our attitude should be never again to accept such conditions. I suggest that our answer should be that we offer protection on the same condition as that on which Britain and the Dominions should protect each other. Their citizens must accept the cost of defence as a first charge on all their resources, and also assume the same control of the common defence, that citizens of the Dominions have assumed. In plain words, let us offer them the chance of entering the union on the same terms that Britain and the Dominions should establish between themselves.

Does anyone doubt the ambition of Japan to conquer and colonize Australia and New Zealand? She has not as yet attempted to do so,[1] because she has known that such an invasion would mean instant war with the whole British Commonwealth, without doubt and without parley. The Scandinavian and Low Countries, if they joined for their common defence with a really united Commonwealth, would thereafter be in the same position as Australia. The German Government would then know that if one of their tanks or planes crossed the frontier of these countries to invade them, there would then be instant war with the whole Union, without doubt and without parley. The Union Government would know that also, and so long as the German menace existed would be bound to maintain forces in the Scandinavian and Low Countries strong enough to deal with any attack. In the light of mechanization as revealed in this war, that does not mean that the Union would have to maintain great standing armies in the free countries of western Europe. Success in war is no longer primarily a question of numbers of infantry, but of mechanized forces, tanks, armoured cars, and war-planes, and their bases properly equipped. The Union would have ready on the soil of Europe forces strong enough not merely to repel a German attack, but, having done so, to carry the war into German territory. The security of England, the heart of freedom, would be incomparably greater if once she were part of a union which held as a glacis the western coast of Europe, from which her very existence is now threatened. The British Commonwealth, by ceasing to be merely British, would be immeasurably strengthened as a power for preventing world war. The close contact in peace of a system of democracy too strong to challenge would begin to react on the German people themselves. Their movement towards responsible government, which started so hopefully in the nineteenth century, would be resumed. When Germany had really developed a system of government

[1] These words are left as they were written in 1941.

responsible to Germans at large, the time would be ripe to include her people in the Union. An immense step would then have been taken to remove still further the fear of impending war.

All this, I believe, might happen far sooner than men now dream if once the British democracies had shown how to construct an organic union for common defence which left to each of them their present control of their own composition and national structure. The suggestion I make is, in fact, a league of nations rendered organic for the purpose of its common defence, a league established step by step, beginning with nations already free, and broadened as its strength is proved to others less free, until it comes in course of time to include the entire world. The most difficult step to take is always the first. It is for us, the authors of freedom, to take that step, and take it in time; bracing our courage ourselves to discharge in practice and fact that prophetic resolve which the greatest of living Americans has now declared for his people. 'We will accept only a world consecrated to freedom of speech and expression, and the freedom of every person to worship God in his own way, freedom from want, and freedom from terrorism.

'Is such a world impossible of attainment? Magna Carta, the Declaration of Independence, the Constitution of the United States, the Emancipation Proclamation, and every other milestone of human progress—all were ideas which seemed impossible of attainment, **yet they were attained.**'[1]

---

[1] *The Times*, 29th May 1941, report of President Roosevelt's broadcast proclaiming a national emergency.

## CHAPTER XIX

# ACTION

'The United States and Great Britain do not now assume that there will never be any more war again. On the contrary, we intend to take ample precautions to prevent its renewal in any period we can foresee by effectively disarming the guilty nations while remaining suitably protected ourselves.'

IN these words the balance of power as the basis of world order is finally renounced by Winston Churchill. Never in history have a people been more completely committed to a policy by the words of a leader.

That this policy cannot be implemented by a government which commands resources no wider than those of Great Britain and Northern Ireland is the case submitted in these pages. They have traced the constitutional changes required to widen this command of resources. The question how to effect those changes remains to be faced.

As said in a previous chapter such changes will meet opposition from those most closely identified with the work-ing and study of things as they are. A letter which has reached me from an experienced friend who has spent most of his life in practical politics and held responsible office, illustrates the point.

'Your suggestion is that there should be separate legislatures for Defence and Foreign Policy, and for Social and Domestic questions. As the question of the "purse" will come into both I do not believe the House of Commons would agree to this, however sensible it may seem, and I think you would find the same opposition in the Dominions and the U.S.A.'

To my friend the attitude of the House of Commons is final. He ignores the fact that the purse, which the House jealously controls, is limited to the resources of Great Britain and Northern Ireland, resources now utterly inadequate for the task of defending the Commonwealth as a whole. He also ignores the fact that Dominion executives and legislatures are so constituted as to think first and foremost of their own national and domestic interests, except when war is actually upon them. In peace they have no such responsibility laid upon them as will lead them to make the prevention of future wars a first charge on their national resources.

As things now are the question what sacrifice it is necessary to make in order to prevent a recurrence of war can never be put squarely before the electorates, not even in Great Britain, where electoral issues are always complicated by social and domestic questions. Under the system suggested in these pages this paramount question of adequate insurance against war would be faced by the electorate of the union at least once in every five years. The taxpayers themselves would have to decide, and would also be able to decide, what sacrifice to make in order to obviate the catastrophes of war. They would have before them the estimate framed by the union government with all the knowledge at their disposal, knowledge of the foreign situation and otherwise. The argument of opponents who questioned that estimate would be tempered by the knowledge that if they prevailed with the electorate, they themselves would then be in office. They themselves would have to assume the tremendous responsibility of preventing a future war at a lower cost.

I submit that **a system under which the taxpayers themselves are enabled to decide what first charge on all their resources must be made in order to avert the calamities of war, must serve as the best preventive of war that human wit can devise.** But this you can only do by a system which divides external from domestic affairs, which puts them under different governments, and which also provides that issues of peace and war are dealt with at one election, while national and domestic issues are settled at other elections.

This brings us back to the question how a change can be made, which must reckon with opposition from existing cabinets and legislatures. How, in fact, can the peoples, through their electorates, be enabled to make the great decision for themselves?

The fact must be faced that members elected to a legislature tend to develop interests of their own, and points of view not quite the same ás those of their electors. To take an extreme instance: the French Constitution created for members of the legislature an interest, which certainly was not the interest of France, and more than anything led to her ruin. Under that Constitution an appeal could not be made to the electorate without the consent of the legislature. A prime minister like Briand could never appeal over the head of the Chamber to the electorate and obtain a decision. The legislature was able to block all attempts to remove this fatal and undemocratic restriction. The result was that from 1919 to 1939 the French were facing a cabinet crisis and a change of government twice a year on the average.

In one respect most politicians become more conservative than their electors. They get so used to the system they work, that, like permanent officials, they cannot see when the system itself is breaking down. Things as they are become to them sacred. They are subject to the same kind of influence which has made it so difficult for any war office to submit to reform. In plain words representative systems, like all things in human life, are imperfect, because, from the moment a man is elected, he tends to develop a point of view somewhat different from that of those who elect him.

How, then, is it possible for the people themselves, the electorate, ever to pronounce on an overdue change, if most of the people they elect unconsciously combine to prevent the need for such change being put to the electorate? The answer is that from time to time there do appear in democracies men who rise superior to the influences of their position, and who risk that position to insist that some great question at issue must be put to the electorate itself. Parkes in Australia was a case in point. It was men like Washington and Lincoln in the U.S.A., and Sir John Macdonald in Canada, who made it possible for their peoples to take those great steps they made on their march to a higher freedom.

In these pages I am trying to estimate the situation which will have to be faced whenever the totalitarian threat to the peace and freedom of the world has been broken. If that estimate is sound, then the question whether the peace is again to be lost will depend less on the conference which frames the terms of peace than on the first Imperial Conference after the war. May it not be assumed that the heads of the British democracies will need to discuss their own future relations, before they meet to discuss the future relations of the British Commonwealth with foreign governments, whether friends or foes? No gathering in history will ever have borne such responsibilities as will rest on the Prime Ministers of the United Kingdom and of the self-governing Dominions when they meet round one table in Whitehall. We cannot foretell who they will be; but, whoever they are, the blessings or curses of future generations upon them will depend upon how far they can shake themselves free from the long-established technique in Imperial Conferences of devising formulas to conceal distasteful facts and evade the real issues of peace and war which underlie them.

The first responsibility will rest on the one government which undertakes to safeguard the Commonwealth as a whole. Will the head of that government face the question clearly and boldly, whether it can keep the British Commonwealth suitably protected, so long as it commands resources no wider than those of Great Britain and Northern Ireland? Will the fact be faced that in future British forces competent to deal with mechanized divisions trained in Central Europe cannot be trained in the British Isles, but must be trained in the Dominions, in Canada especially?

When the British Prime Minister has stated and answered these questions plainly, the responsibility of Dominion Prime Ministers will begin. Their temptation will be to dwell on the indispensable part played by Dominion forces in winning this war as well as the last one. Will they face the facts that the British Commonwealth was not strong enough to prevent an outbreak of war in 1914, that the Commonwealth and the League of Nations together were too weak to prevent a second outbreak of war in 1939? Will they tell their electorates plainly whether, in their opinion, and in the light of all that happened from 1919 to 1939, the future peace of the world can be safely based on compacts between sovereign states, whether written or unwritten?

The supreme question before that Imperial Conference will be to answer the question which Mr. Churchill has now put: how are we to remain suitably protected, not this year or next, but for generations to come? The people of each British Democracy is, I submit, entitled to a clear and definite answer to that question from its own recognized leader and spokesman at the conference. I go farther and suggest that each of those electorates is entitled to give its own answer to that question, disentangled from all subsidiary questions. This in practice cannot happen unless or until the question is put to his electorate, and put with guidance, by their Prime Minister who happens to be in power at the moment. It is useless to burke the fact that **whether the electorates of the British Commonwealth can pronounce on the question which will settle whether the Atlantic Charter is valid or not, will rest with the half-dozen men who happen to be in power when hostilities cease.**

Time is important. If this change is required to prevent a recurrence of war, the great difficulties which stand in its way will never be so easy to overcome as on the morrow of war. 'There is a tide in the affairs of men, which, taken at the flood, leads on to fortune.' Two thousand years before Shakespeare wrote these words the truth they express had inspired the myth of the Sibylline books; but never was it couched with a force so awful as in those words spoken to Peter:

'Verily, verily, I say unto thee, When thou wast young, thou girdedst thyself, and walkedst whither thou wouldest: but when thou shalt be old, thou shalt stretch forth thy hands, and another shall gird thee, and carry thee whither thou wouldest not.'

If an overdue change like this is not made on the morrow of peace, it may not be made till the world has again been taught the need for it in a third welter of blood.

I am told over and over again that the British and Dominion electorates will never agree to abandon their separate sovereignties. I refuse to accept this verdict for the reason that the issue has never been put to them, in the only way in which it can be put, by their recognized leaders. In no kind of society is the call for leadership so great as in free nations, though too rarely forthcoming. By leaders I mean not men who lie with their ears to the ground, endeavouring to read a public opinion which does not always exist, in order to stay in office, but those who at critical junctures can take their political lives in their hands by telling their peoples who listen to them, if to no one else, what sacrifice they must make in order to preserve the freedom they have; which can never be done except by raising it to a higher plane.

Suppose for a moment that the next Imperial Conference after the war were to say with one voice that we cannot remain suitably protected ourselves, unless the sovereign states of the British Commonwealth begin to merge their sovereignties into one for the purpose of the common defence. I have myself no shadow of doubt as to what the effect on the British and Dominion electorates would be. I believe that the needed change would be made in a very few years. I go farther than this. If only one of those six leaders found courage to proclaim these truths, he would force them to an issue with electorates, with others as well as his own, perhaps in time to forestall the calamities which await future genera- tions or even this one. If so, the responsibility which will rest upon each of those six men, severally as well as together, is great beyond measure.

Thus, in my view, the future peace of the world will, I think, depend in the main upon how far the half-dozen statesmen who gather at the first Imperial Conference after this war are able to face the facts of the situation. They have little leisure to digest and consider these facts while the struggle continues. Till victory is won they must be mainly absorbed in executive measures necessary to win it. But in this country, at any rate, the Government has already ap- pointed expert advisers to concentrate their minds on the task of working out the measures required to implement the policy set forth in the Atlantic Charter. Dominion Govern- ments have presumably set experts of their own to work on these questions. The efficiency with which these experts are now doing their work behind the scenes will go far to determine the attitude taken by the statesmen who meet at the next Imperial Conference. The future peace of the world very largely depends upon how far these experts are now facing up to their task. But even so the final responsibility must rest with the half-dozen men who meet at the Imperial Conference after the war. Future historians will note their names, and will, I believe, say that the peace and happiness of all mankind was made or marred by what they said—or left unsaid, by what they did—or left undone, at that table in Whitehall.

## CHAPTER XX

# AMERICAN AND BRITISH EXPERIENCE COMBINED

IN January 1939 I happened to meet Streit in New York. He gave me an advance copy of *Union Now* which was not published till some months later. On reading it I saw that he proposed an immediate union of the U.S.A., the United Kingdom, Eire, Canada, Australia, New Zealand, South Africa, France, Switzerland, Belgium, Holland, Denmark, Norway, Sweden, and Finland as the one possible means of arresting the drift towards world war. Lord Lothian on reading the book said to me:

'This world crisis will go down in history as a conflict between the idea set out by Hitler in *Mein Kampf*, and the idea which Streit has proposed in *Union Now*. The essential cause of world wars is national sovereignties. World wars will continue to threaten until we begin to merge national sovereignties in one international sovereignty. The only remedy is some such union as Streit proposes. Streit has had the courage to say that the time for men to consider it is Now, and not to-morrow or the day after to-morrow. The greatest thing in this great book is the title, *Union Now*.'

Realists who find no valid answer to the reasoning advanced in this book have resorted to satire and naked appeals to national prejudice. Men who assume the pose of realism always betray their own blindness to major realities. This movement which Streit has started is more vital a step in human progress than the abolition of slavery. When realists tried to suppress William Lloyd Garrison he answered them, 'I am in earnest—I will not equivocate—I will not excuse—I will not retreat a single inch—and I will be heard.' And heard he was. Streit will be heard and remembered when the names of the realists who advised the world to ignore him are as utterly forgotten as those who were seeking to silence Garrison. His initiative will lead to a new birth of freedom as surely as Garrison's. Of such was it written:

> Thou hast great allies,
> Thy friends are exultations, agonies
> And love, and Man's unconquerable mind.

'Realists' can never defeat movements for freedom when once they are started. But they can delay their progress, and increase immeasurably the blood and tears that human beings must shed before they find and follow the road to a goal that must and will be reached.

*Union Now* appeared too late to stop the headlong drift towards war. I had written much of these pages when Streit published a sequel under the title of *Union Now With Britain* in which he urges an immediate union of the U.S.A. with Great Britain and the Dominions as the only means of ending this war quickly. For obvious reasons the European democracies are omitted for the moment. He urges his countrymen, warned by the fate of the Franco-British Alliance, to make at once to Great Britain and the Dominions the same offer of a common citizenship as Churchill made to France in her hour of anguish. While he limits this offer to countries embraced by the British Commonwealth, he does not narrow the meaning he gave to common citizenship in his first book *Union Now*. He gives it the same meaning which Churchill gave to 'Common Citizenship' in his offer to France, control of defence, foreign, financial, and economic policies.

Streit writes this book as an American speaking to Americans, and I have written these pages as a British citizen speaking to my own fellow citizens. Streit sees in American experience the key to world problems as no one else has seen it before him. His view that democracies cannot be saved and preserved until they begin to merge their national sovereignties into one international sovereignty is the root of the matter. That supreme lesson he draws from American experience, and assumes, quite naturally, that an international union should cover much the same field as the union covered by the thirteen states which first established that union. At the time they referred to themselves as 'these thirteen nations', a grandiloquence which now raises a smile. They were not nations in the sense of that word as we now use it, but rather contiguous provinces, in one territory, with a common language, institutions, and manner of life.

So much for the great lesson which America learned from

H

the Revolution and the facts that followed it. The British Commonwealth had also lessons to learn from the Revolution and the facts that followed. They were different lessons, but none the less important for that. On opposite sides of the world, in Canada, South Africa, Australia, and New Zealand, there grew into being new British colonies which could not be represented in London for reasons of distance. From the war of American Independence the British had learned a lesson they never forgot. No attempt was made to tax them by Parliament. When they claimed the right to erect tariffs against the United Kingdom, or to control the entry of migrants, including the subjects of Great Britain, that claim was conceded. They rapidly acquired to the full the rights of autonomy enjoyed by Americans. Canada, Australia, and South Africa followed the American example by merging their colonies in unions; the counterpart, on a smaller scale, of the U.S.A., and not the counterpart of American states like Virginia or New York. Like the U.S.A. they emerged as separate nations with absolute self-control of their own composition and social structure. When I use the word 'nation' or 'national state', I mean a community equipped to exercise such control. In Chapter XVII I have argued that human welfare in the long run has more to gain than to lose by this freedom for separate nations to develop their individual characters.

We are thus confronted with a new and larger problem than that which the thirteen American states were facing in 1786. The nations free to fashion their own individual characters for themselves are in imminent danger of losing that freedom to a highly mechanized despotism, which divides them and conquers them one by one. They can only save their freedom by standing together in peace no less than in war. But they cannot, in fact, hold together unless the persons of whom these free nations consist accept one citizenship which is common to all alike. That common status must mean that their common safety is recognized as a first charge on the moral and material resources of each individual. And this principle must be expressed in institutions common to all.

They must have one government to organize defences too strong for aggressors to challenge. That government must be responsible to all those persons, to all those citizens. That, as I read it, is the essential lesson of American experience. It becomes not less, but even more true, when the various nations exposed to attack are separated by oceans and the width of the world. But does it follow that nations so widely sundered, in order to secure their freedom inviolate by union for that purpose, must also renounce their present power to control their own composition and structure, because the American states, not nations but contiguous provinces, in fact found it wise to do so—a wisdom justified by results? The U.S.A. is a commonwealth of provinces. The project under discussion is a commonwealth of nations in the real sense of the term. The British Commonwealth of Nations has a common citizenship but no common government. It is thus imperfect, and its imperfection threatens it with destruction. But it has a common citizenship which has so far preserved it intact. Undoubtedly the fact that each of its nations has power to control its own composition and social structure has helped to keep it intact. The Dominions have poured out their blood to preserve a citizenship common to all.

The answer to this, I know, will be that a citizenship which does not convey the right of a citizen to live in all the countries to which it applies, and does not imply freedom of trade between all those countries, is worthless. I do not accept that answer. If it only avails to lift from all those countries the constant menace of war, it is precious indeed. But so far as domicile is concerned the argument will not hold water in principle. In national commonwealths the citizen has no right of entry and domicile in the households of his fellows. The reason for this mutual exclusion is cogent. Commonwealths have for their end and object the development of individual character, and experience has shown that this can only be done by protecting and fostering the privacy of family life. The greatest nations are not those which breed uniform types but those which produce 'distinguished' citizens. The same, I submit, will apply to human society as a whole. It ought to consist of 'distinguished' nations. No attempt should be made to assimilate one to another. The utmost scope should be given to each to develop its own individual character.

This I believe is the great contribution which British experience has to offer the world in this crisis. My case in this book is that it can be combined with the great contribution of American experience, which Streit has interpreted to this generation.

I am sure that this war would come to an end quickly, and the fear of all world wars would be ended, if by some miracle the American people could be moved to follow at once the lead which Streit has given them in his last book. But I think that this miracle would be less unlikely to happen if Americans were told that the step they are asked to take to stop this war and prevent its recurrence for all time would still preserve their control of their own immigration laws, their own tariffs, and the incidence of taxes between one American and another. Of that an American only can judge. I have no doubt how the same point would strike British citizens in the Dominions. I believe that after this war, with all its desperate hazards, they will see that no security is possible for our freedom or theirs until they decide to assume in peace the same responsibility for preventing war as that now borne by Great Britain, if once the case is presented to them with proper authority, as I said in the last chapter. I believe they will do this if they see that this can really be done without disturbing the power they now have to control their own composition and social structure.

'The British Empire', said Adam Smith, 'is not an empire, but only the project of an empire.' We now call it the British Commonwealth. But it is not a commonwealth, but only the project of a commonwealth. It has failed to make the prevention of war a first charge on all its resources. To cure this defect it must do what all Canadians, Australians, and South Africans have done for themselves, and apply American experience to its structure. My idea is that this application should be tried first in its most moderate and conservative form. I should not say this if I did not believe that the method which I have suggested in these pages would succeed. Writers of greater authority than mine believe with no less sincerity that a commonwealth of nations must control not only defence but also migration and tariffs. To attempt so much would, I fear, fail at the outset, and also be wrong in itself. No amount of argument can finally settle the point, but only trial. It is easier to try the moderate change first, for then, should it fail, it is always possible to take the further steps should experience have shown that an international government cannot prevent war unless it also controls migration and tariffs. We have reached a stage when a drop of experience is worth more than oceans of further argument.

## CHAPTER XXI

# TRUTHS FOR WANT OF WHICH WHOLE NATIONS FARE THE WORSE

IT is not given us to know how or when this war will be ended. The same is true of most future events, though here and there are things which can be foretold with practical certainty. We can, I believe, be sure that the world will not be ruled on Nazi principles for a thousand years.[1] If Hitler destroyed the last free commonwealth, his world order would presently sink in the quicksands of fraud, cruelty, and greed upon which he had raised it. The greater the house so founded, the surer and heavier its fall.

We can also have faith that in time a world society will be founded on truth and the infinite duty of each to all. Freedom will flourish again and grow as men are led by great tribulation brought on themselves to discern and obey what Milton has called those 'truths for want of which whole nations fare the worse'.[2]

In *Pacificism Is Not Enough, Nor Patriotism Either*, the Burge Memorial Lecture which Lothian gave in 1935, he ended as follows:

'The virtues which make a good citizen of a parliamentary democracy are different from those which make a good citizen of a state which is fighting for justice as against might as the ruler

[1] *The Times*, 5th May 1941, reports Hitler as saying, 'The National-Socialist state will not only survive this war, but will survive for a thousand years to come.'

[2] These forecasts were written some few hours before the following words were broadcast by Mr. Stimson from Washington:

'Hitler's régime of brutal lawlessness is merely one of those temporary reactions which have occurred at intervals during all man's long history of progress upward. Since his origin millions of years ago, ambitious men have many times attempted worldwide conquest over the liberties of their fellow men. But they have never permanently succeeded and they never will.

'. . . As has always happened before, the progress of man along the path to freedom will be taken up again and carried forward with a new spirit, and with fresh knowledge acquired by the unhappy experience of the past.'

of mankind. Brotherhood, tolerance, public spirit, a capacity for intelligent discussion are essential in the one, as self-sacrifice, discipline, dedication, a capacity to lay down one's life for one's friends are essential in the other. The peace movement of the future will consist of those who combine both these sets of virtues. Its members will see all men and nations as one brotherhood, and recognize that the troubles of the world are due not to the malignity of their neighbours but to the anarchy which perverts the policies of all nations. And they will have to be prepared, not only to pool their national sovereignties in order that a true reign of law—the only ending of war, and the only true peace—may be established on earth, but, if necessary, to use force—even war itself—to vindicate justice and the triumph of right over wrong—the road of death—until the time is ripe for peace and unity to come by the road of organic federation—the road of liberty and life. When there are enough "elect" men and women of this kind in the world, and not before, there will arise that city, foreshadowed in Revelation, in which there is no more war because the Glory of the Lord is the light thereof, and the former things have passed away.'

This greatest of all Lothian's papers passed almost unnoticed at the time.[1] Yet here, if ever, was 'truth for want of which whole nations fare the worse'. In politics as in medicine a sound diagnosis will often suggest the appropriate cure. To a world in anguish Lothian revealed the cause of its suffering. Dictators are only the symptoms, painful and visible products of a septic condition, which cannot be cured merely by plastering the sores it creates, nor even by cutting them out. Mechanical science has made the nations depend on each other for their means of living, as though they were members of one society, without creating the means to control their integral life. Our control of nature has changed our relations one to another; but we have not learned to control that change.

The future historian will see in this lecture a profound diagnosis of the real cause why millions of men in each generation are now impelled to destroy one another in a welter of fire and blood. To those who believe that here is the real

[1] The Oxford University Press have reprinted it with a preface by Sir William Beveridge, Master of University College, of which Burge was a fellow.

diagnosis it remains to think out the practical treatment to which it points, a task to which I am trying to make my own contribution in these pages. With Lothian I do not believe that the rule of law, which is freedom, can long prevail unless it is backed by an adequate power organized to enforce and defend it, a power so visibly strong that all who are minded to break the law and destroy freedom will find it too dangerous to challenge. Like him I think that the real situation in the last century was temporarily masked by British sea-power. Nor do I believe that the sovereign power of Great Britain, nor even of the United States, can ever again avail to create that sense of security which free nations enjoyed in the nineteenth century. It can only be done by making the forces required to safeguard freedom a first charge on all the people resolved to enjoy that freedom. It follows, as surely as day follows night, that control over those forces must be equally shared by all those people. But practical experience no less than theory has shown that such control cannot be based on compacts between sovereign states. The government responsible for controlling the forces must draw its authority direct from the people themselves, and exert that authority over those people direct.

I think that Streit has conclusively proved so much. In his latest book he points to the clause in the American Constitution which deals with its ratification as the most vital of all its provisions. Under that clause the people themselves in each state were asked to decide whether or no they would join the Union, and all of them decided to join. It is scarcely rash to conjecture that had the decision been left to the politicians, not one of the thirteen states would have joined. A century later Australia showed how in great matters the politicians may be thinking in one way, whilst the people who elect them think in another way. For years national conventions appointed by colonial legislatures met and always came to a deadlock. No real progress was made till Sir Henry Parkes at last demanded a national congress elected by the people themselves. That congress created the Australian Commonwealth.

The adoption of the American Constitution by the peoples of the thirteen sovereign states was, perhaps, the greatest miracle in history. How came it about that people who numbered some millions were moved to a change so fraught with blessing to those who came after them? Convincing reasons justified by events were given in the papers known as *The Federalist*. But the number of Americans who had read *The Federalist* before they voted was insignificant. What moved them to vote for this radical change was their faith in Washington who had led them to victory through years of suffering. When their recognized leader told them that the freedom won by the thirteen states was illusory unless their sovereignties were merged into one, they believed him and voted accordingly. Of a lesser miracle, the South African Union within eight years of a racial war, I can speak with some first-hand knowledge. The case for Union was explained in a memorandum which argued that unless the peoples of the Transvaal and Free State, of the Cape Colony and Natal united to form one government, responsible to a single electorate, they would soon be at war with each other again. This paper issued on the bare authority of those who had written it would have passed as a nine days' wonder and have then been forgotten. The great majority of British and Dutch supported the Union only because their recognized leaders actively led them at the critical moment. The five who worked this miracle were Selborne, Botha, and Smuts in the Transvaal, and Jameson and Francis Malan in the Cape.

Even so the first international Union will not be accomplished by books and pamphlets. It will come when some accredited leader has told his followers that no lasting peace can dawn on this earth until two or more national states have merged their sovereignty in one international commonwealth. A vessel so great, so fraught with hope for mankind, can only be launched from its berth of constructive thought into practical politics when some recognized statesman has dared to move in advance of public opinion. Then, as Emerson shrewdly said, 'The people will applaud a bold and just action even though they condemn it in advance'. A tide of opinion will gather behind him as rapidly as it did in the thirteen states of America or the four South African colonies. Such a thing may not happen for years. The suffering endured in those years will bring it about sooner or later. If it happened to-morrow, mankind would be saved from most of that suffering. The future world will remember that leader as Americans now remember Washington.

For the moment our utmost efforts are needed for saving the last stronghold of freedom, a task to which men, women, and children are giving their lives, the humblest most freely. Who, indeed, would wish to have lived in the days of Agincourt or the Armada, of Trafalgar or Waterloo rather than here in England to-day with her ruined hearths and her broken shrines? Where before have a whole people so followed a leader who promised them nothing but 'blood, tears, toil, and sweat—mistakes, shortcomings, and disappointments'? Night after night they defy the blast let loose by the powers of Hell, and thereafter gather to lay their dead in one common and glorious grave. Here, surely, free institutions are levelling society by ennobling the people. Here at least millions have realized that no great matter is ever achieved without infinite sacrifice. In this war, as in the last, victory is but a step in that greater enterprise to which free nations are committed by their nature and past, an enterprise which goes unfinished until we have brought it to pass that 'our children shall not again bleed and gasp in devastated lands'. The prayer that Sir Francis Drake wrote down for his men as he led them forth on a great adventure might well be repeated by us in this war; but, most of all, by those who outlive it:

'O Lord God, when thou givest to Thy servants to endeavour any great matter, grant us also to know that it is not the beginning, but the continuing of the same until it be thoroughly finished, which yieldeth the true glory.'

That prayer will be answered in God's own time.

## *Appendix to Chapter XXI*

AN experienced official in Whitehall told me that he had read *Decision* supposing it to be an essay on federalism, but found in it to his astonishment a frank treatment of the problem of defence. 'I have to confess', he added, 'that you have largely convinced me. On the other hand I do not feel that you have made your proposal clear.'

I then explained to him that in *Decision* I was trying to give my readers something short enough to read, and therefore confined myself to sketching my proposals in the barest outline. I foresaw that my critics would point to a number of difficulties with which I had failed to deal. My intention, therefore, had been to await these criticisms and then deal with them in a further pamphlet.

My friend then advised me to begin this second pamphlet with a summary of the proposal I had tried to set out in the first. I agreed, but said it would greatly help me if he himself would give me his draft of the summary, so far as he understood my proposals. He most kindly consented to do so, and when I received his draft found that he had perfectly stated the proposals which I had tried to convey in *Decision*. I am, therefore, printing his summary as a brief but accurate statement of the argument and scheme contained in the first pamphlet.

## ARGUMENT

### OF THE PREVIOUS PAMPHLET *DECISION*

The argument in *Decision* is directed towards the practical ways and means of securing world peace in future years, i.e. how to restore that degree of security from world wars which followed the Battle of Waterloo.

This can no longer be effected solely by the influence of Great Britain and her sea power, as it was during the nineteenth century.

The attempt to organize 'collective security' after the last war failed mainly for two reasons: (1) because the League of Nations could reach no binding decision without the consent of all its members, and (2) because of the increasing strain imposed by the ever-growing complexity of life on the time and nervous energy of national governments.

The British Commonwealth of Nations, however, still stands, whereas the League has fallen in ruins; and it is the voluntary co-operation of the British Democracies which enabled the war to be won in 1918, and in 1941 has so far prevented a decision in favour of Germany.

But this 'co-operation' of free and equal nations did *not* prevent war from breaking out in 1914 and 1939. If, therefore, we have to rely upon the strength of the United Kingdom acting 'in co-operation' with the Dominions (and even with the United States), we shall be relying on methods which have *failed* to prevent the recurrence of wars in the past.

'Co-operation' therefore is not enough. But the relative success of the British Commonwealth system contains an indication; it is due to the fact that—in foreign policy and in defence matters—it has continued to function since 1919 by virtue of a United Kingdom hegemony.

The system adumbrated by the present Commonwealth arrangements must be made so strong that its enemies will not dare to attack it and that its example will influence potential enemies themselves to demand responsible government.

The problem, therefore, is one of defence and security (and the cost thereof) for a group or union of democratic states against the danger of attack from Central Europe or in the Far East. For this group or union, a single central authority—in defence and security questions—has to be created. State unity cannot be based on compact, for the interests on which the compact is based 'shift and change like a bed of sand under moving water'.

Supposing France and the British Empire had 'won' the war, no Franco-British Union could have prevailed to prevent the recrudescence of German aggression unless the French and British peoples could have been put in a position to pursue one foreign policy, not merely for years but for generations. They could not have achieved one Franco-British policy unless it was to be backed by one Franco-British Army, Navy, and Air Force. And the question of dividing the cost between the two peoples would have had to be settled on some principle.

This was implicit in the offer of Union made by the United Kingdom Government to France on the 16th June 1940 and rejected by a majority of 13 to 10 in the French Cabinet.

The offer also included financial and economic union; but this, it is here argued, is not essential and indeed not desirable, since it would involve the joint super-national government in matters of local national particularistic concern such as control of tariffs, industrial development, migration, and social legislation.

Here also *'Decision' parts company very definitely from the 'Federal Union' proposals* of Mr. Streit, Dr. Jennings, Mr. Mackay, and Sir W. Beveridge.

In *Decision* the measure of union is *limited to the problems of defence and security*.

## PROPOSAL

The proposal therefore is that one—or more—independent countries should unite with Great Britain for purposes of defence and that this union should involve something more than the usual military alliance, and should be constituted on the following lines:

1. A joint foreign policy.
2. A joint defence policy.
3. A common budget for defence purposes.
4. One joint legislative body for defence questions only which would discuss the foreign situation, the danger of war, the necessary measures of defence; and would determine not individual taxes but the proportion of individual State revenues to be devoted to joint defence.
5. One joint executive body for defence questions only, responsible for framing the estimates necessary to secure the Union as a whole from attack, and to lay them before the legislative body.

The joint legislative and executive bodies of the Union must be given by their national States sufficient authority to make defence and security a first charge on the individual States' revenues, while leaving to the national governments the distribution of the burden amongst individual taxpayers.

The proportion of the share of total defence expenditure should be allocated to the individual States on the basis of their respective taxable capacity, on the analogy of the work of the Childers Commission (1896) in estimating the respective taxable capacities of Great Britain and Ireland.

A standing commission of financial experts should every five years declare the figures of the respective taxable capacities.

The revenue required for general security as voted by the joint representative body should be assessed in ratio according to the figures declared as above.

The quota due from each State should constitute a first charge on its national consolidated fund, and would not be required to be voted each year by the national legislature. The joint executive body would be entitled to this first charge on the national revenues, with specific allocation of security in cases of default.

The budget for security formed by the joint executive body should be for a three-year period but should be revised every year by the joint representative body, so that national governments would always know what amounts would be needed to meet the quotas three years ahead.

Elections to the legislative body would be held from time to time in all the States thus united. There is an inevitable objection that United Kingdom representation would thereby be made preponderant; but this assumes that United Kingdom members would vote as a bloc, whereas it is much more likely that they would vote on party rather than on State lines.

The Dominions might well be given a more generous representation than they would have on a strict basis of population.

There might also be an upper house in the legislative body in which, as in the American Senate, each State would have equal representation; this upper house would be advisory, except on proposals to alter the constitution.

One set of ministers and legislators would thus handle defence and matters inseparable therefrom; while in each component State another set of ministers and legislators would be free to handle their own domestic and social affairs.

This joint defence system should be initiated immediately after the war by the United Kingdom and such of the Dominions as feel that they are ready forthwith to comply with the obligations which it implies.

The system might in time be broadened to include European democracies, e.g. Belgium, Netherlands, Denmark, Norway—countries whose safety has been shown by events to be closely bound up with our own. If once the Western democracies had united with the British Commonwealth for their common defence, it should become possible to extend the same system, with the same obligations and responsibilities, to our allies in Eastern Europe—Poland, Czechoslovakia, Jugoslavia, and Greece.

If and when the United States of America were to join such a system, the era of world wars will be finally over.

All this might happen far sooner than men now dream if once the British democracies had shown how to construct an organic union for common defence which left to each of them their present control of the composition of their population and of their social structure.

## CHAPTER XXII

# REPRESENTATION: CONSTITUENCIES: INDIA: COLONIES: FRANCE

*Representation*

IN Chapter XVII I proposed that the cost of defence should be divided amongst the associated States in proportion to the taxable capacity of each. I was told at once by a friend, more qualified than I am to judge of such matters, that taxable capacity cannot in practice be assessed. I therefore submitted the proposal to a trained economist, whose reply is appended to this chapter. One expert economist, as the reader will see, thinks that the scheme could be worked. He suggests further that it might be as well if the first assessment were settled on expert advice between the States agreeing to combine for their common defence. I heartily accept that constructive suggestion.

Assuming then that taxable capacity can be made the basis on which to distribute the charge for common defence, I now go on to suggest that it might also be made the fundamental basis of representation.

This plan would have certain advantages. The average income of a citizen in Canada, Australia, and New Zealand is, I believe, higher than the average income of a citizen in the United Kingdom. If it is not so now, it certainly will be after this war. A startling statement is made by a well-informed writer in the September 1942 number of the *Round Table* on page 637: 'It is known that to the end of the financial year 1941–42 the total war expenditure of the United Kingdom was estimated at £7,300 millions, and that of Canada, Australia, New Zealand, South Africa and India together at £1,230 millions.' Now if that position continues, the average income in the Dominions will be far higher than in the United Kingdom. The taxable capacity of each will therefore be higher than it would be if the burden of common defence were to be charged on the basis of population. The proposal to base representation on taxable capacity would mean that each Dominion got a higher proportion of members in the Union legislature, than if population were taken as the basis. My suggestion that the nations smaller in population should be granted a certain weightage in voting power, is compatible with the plan of using taxable capacity as the fundamental basis of representation.

A second advantage would be that if the States discussing Union agreed to distribute the cost of defence on the basis of taxable capacity, they would also have gone most of the way towards deciding the basis of representation.

There is also a third advantage. In presenting its case to the assessment commission, each national government would naturally seek to prove that its relative taxable capacity should be reduced. This motive would be wholesomely tempered if each national government were conscious that in so far as their financial argument proved convincing, it would also have the political effect of reducing the number of members sent by their people to the Union legislature.

## *Constituencies*

The question how the electorate of each constituent nation should elect their quota of members to the Union legislature is also important. Into what constituencies if any should each of these countries be divided? Or need they be so divided?

In seeking an answer to this question it is well to hold in mind the restricted but all-important purpose for which these members would be elected, the issue, that is to say, upon which electors would be called on to decide. Under the scheme of international defence we are here considering, all domestic questions, including the incidence of taxation as between one taxpayer and another, would rest with each national legislature. The Union legislature would have merely to decide what total sum must be spent, in order to ensure the Union as a whole against the danger of future wars, and thus to give all the constituent nations that sense of security without which they cannot order their own social affairs. The total sum, when voted by the Union legislature, would then be divided automatically in proportion to the taxable capacity of each constituent nation. Under the plan we are here considering the decision how this burden would be distributed between one taxpayer and another, between one class and another, or between one locality and another, would remain with each national legislature, as at present. For this purpose each nation is divided into a number of constituencies, some urban, some rural, some poorer, some richer. The different localities and classes are thus able to elect members to champion their rival interests. The Union legislature and the elections held for it would have nothing to do with these questions at issue between various localities and classes. To divide each national territory into local constituencies would have no meaning. At elections for the Union legislature the electors and the members they elected would merely have to consider the dangers threatening the peace of the world and then decide the kind of sum required to ensure the common defence, a definite proportion of which would fall as a first charge on their national resources. The best plan might then be for each nation to elect their members as a body in one constituency on one ticket, by some system of proportional representation. This plan would eliminate canvassing by candidates, and give the greatest advantage to experienced candidates who had already proved their merits by their work in the national legislatures. The tendency would be for the Union legislature and executive to be drawn from persons trained in the work of the national legislatures, and known as such to the electorate as a whole. As local authorities are largely the training grounds for careers in the national legislatures, so those national legislatures would in turn become the training grounds for the Union legislature. This plan would also have the merit of simplicity.

## India

By the same path we are brought to the baffling problem of India. Its population is 390,000,000. The rest of the British Commonwealth contains some 110,000,000. The population of the British Commonwealth as a whole is thus

I

500,000,000. It will thus be seen that India contains over three-fourths of the people included in the British Commonwealth.

Self-government has now been recognized as the goal to which India is moving. Important steps have already been taken in that direction; but those steps have already shown how difficult it is for a people who have always lived under various forms of autocracy, and are also divided by religion and caste, to acquire the habits which make responsible government possible. They will certainly acquire those habits with practice; but the process is necessarily slow. No serious thinker would propose to entrust the safety of the British Commonwealth, and indeed the peace of the world, to any electorate of which over three-fourths would be people who have still to acquire the art of governing themselves. For that is what would happen if India were included in a Union on the basis of population. This populous country, however, is one of the poorest in the world, and if taxable capacity were accepted as the basis of representation, the problem of including India in a self-governing Union for defence becomes less difficult to solve. It suffices for the moment to say that the time when it could be solved would be brought nearer.

## Colonies

In the light of all that has happened in this war it is need-less to argue that control of the colonies is inseparable from the function of defending the commonwealth as a whole. But this does not mean that a Union Government need assume that control at once. If the German power is crushed again as it was in 1918 the Union Government can consult its own convenience and that of its member nations in assuming control. There may be cases of colonies that have no strategic importance, and these might be left indefinitely to the care of the national government which now controls them, just as the Government of India found it convenient to leave the care of some minor Indian states to the provincial govern-ments of Bombay, Bengal, and Madras. The more elastic the system the better, so long as the Union Government has undivided control of defence. And greater elasticity is possible as the nations included in the commonwealth come to feel themselves safe from attack.

For the colonies too it must be accepted that the goal of their future development must be some government responsible to the people themselves, however distant its final attainment may be for primitive tribes like those of Africa or Papua.

### France

When suggesting the early inclusion in the Union of the Netherlands and the Scandinavian countries I said nothing of France. The obvious reason was that we do not as yet know what kind of France would emerge from the present war. We may now hope for a France restored to her liberties and purged of Quislings by our gallant allies the Free French.

To any approach from a France so restored, a British Union for defence could scarcely listen less readily than it would to the Netherlands and Scandinavian democracies. The unique and historic offer of organic Union with Great Britain which we made to her in June 1940 is a fact to remember; but it may be as well to state once more a view implicit in all that was said in the previous pages. That view is **that the British Democracies cannot wisely discuss organic relations with free European states until they have first established organic relations between themselves.**

### Appendix to Chapter XXII

## THE DISTRIBUTION OF TAXATION BY A SUPER-NATIONAL AUTHORITY

THE distribution of the taxation which has to be raised for super-national Federal purposes between the states members of the Federation is not a simple matter, especially as the amounts required would be far bigger than any which have been raised hitherto for any comparable purpose, such as the budget of the League of Nations. This difficulty, like others, however, will certainly be overcome if agreement is felt to be vitally necessary, while, if this is not the general feeling, it will be only one of very many rocks upon which shipwreck is probable. Indeed, the distribution of taxation is not a difficulty which is of its nature likely to prove insurmountable, given a moderate amount of goodwill. The imposition of taxation by a super-national authority does not in itself greatly restrict the power of national governments to control the destinies of their own peoples, and since the liability to super-national taxation would replace some of the former liability to national taxation, it would not necessarily involve any increase in the burden upon the ordinary citizen.

What is really important about the basis of division of the burden between nations is that it should be agreed. Hence, it is desirable that the broad basis of division should be sketched in advance, and should be incorporated in the Federal Constitution. Nations are much more likely to accept federation if they know, roughly, what it is likely to cost them. It will probably be necessary, however, to have some body of experts to review the working of the system of division adopted either continuously or periodically with a view to detecting anomalies and recommending measures for their removal. The basis of division would have to take the form, not of the assignment of a fixed liability to each state member (since the size of the Federal budget would naturally vary), but of a set of 'taxable capacities' (or a formula for assessing taxable capacities) determining the *proportions* in which the states members would contribute to whatever total the Federal Treasurer required.

The problem of allotting equitable taxable capacities, or an equitable formula for assessing them, is essentially the same as that of formulating an equitable scale of rates and allowances for the levying of income-tax. It is therefore a problem to which a great deal of thought has been given, and it would probably be possible to secure a fair degree of agreement among experts upon the broad outline of a just solution, though in detail a considerable element of arbitrariness would be inevitable. If the countries among which the taxation had to be divided all had fairly similar standards of living, the division would be easy. There would probably be general agreement that the tax burden ought to be apportioned among them in proportion to their national incomes— i.e. to the values of the goods and services produced within them in a year. For nearly all fairly advanced countries adequate statistical sources now exist for the determination of the national income, and, still provided that standards of living are not too dissimilar, the problem of converting the different incomes into terms of one common currency is easily solved. If, however, countries with very different standards of living are included (e.g. India, where the average income per head was estimated before the war at about £10, and Britain where it was estimated at about £110), the problem would be far harder. It would be generally agreed that the poor countries ought to be let off more lightly in relation to their national incomes than the rich ones, but how much more lightly they ought to escape would clearly be a matter of controversy. Moreover, an element of arbitrariness is introduced by the fact that it is not possible to reduce the national income of a poor country to currency units similar to those used to measure the income of a rich country without a big margin of error.

When all allowance is made for the necessary arbitrariness of any solution, however, it remains true that it should be possible to agree upon some formula which taxes countries with similar standards of living in proportion to their national incomes and lets the poorer countries off relatively lightly. There are, of course, many formulae which fulfil these conditions. A very simple one is:

Taxable Capacity is proportional to Population
$$\times \text{ (Average Income per Head)}^a$$

where $a$ is bigger than one but probably less than two. Numerous alternative distributions could be secured by varying $a$ or by subtracting from average income per head some figure taken to represent the absolute minimum necessary for subsistence.

It would be best if the formula adopted could be used each year for a reassessment of taxable capacity on the basis of the previous year's national income. In this way, the distribution of the burden of super-national taxation would be continuously adjusted, not only to long-term trends in the relative wealth of nations, but to relative variations in their fortunes in the course of the trade-cycle, and a slight smoothing influence would thereby be exerted. The improvement in existing statistical sources which would be necessary to render this possible, and to render evasion very difficult, is not so great as to rule out the early introduction of such a system.

A matter which would have to receive very serious attention is the effect of a system of super-national taxation upon balances of international payments. If these were not to be disturbed, the Federal Authority would have to buy goods and services from the member states to the exact amounts of their respective contributions to its revenue. In practice, strict adherence to this principle might not be thought necessary, and it would, indeed, be possible to go a long way towards relieving, with great benefit to the whole world, countries which for any reason were especially depressed, by departing from it in their favour. There might, however, be great difficulty in fulfilling the needs of the Federal Authority without buying from some countries goods and services worth far more than their contribution to Federal taxation, and from others far less. In this case, there would be a strong tendency to create unemployment in the latter countries, while inducing high prosperity in the former. It might be practicable to adjust the matter by allowing appropriate variations in the exchange rates of the currencies of the countries concerned, and, if the amount of such adjustment required proved to be greater than was acceptable, the tax liabilities of the countries could always be modified.

## CHAPTER XXIII

# THE ATLANTIC CHARTER

IN the summer of 1941 Roosevelt and Churchill met on a British battleship and embodied the aims of peace in the following Charter:

The President of the United States and the Prime Minister, Mr. Churchill, representing his Majesty's Government in the United Kingdom, being met together, deem it right to make known certain common principles in the national policies of their respective countries on which they base their hopes for a better future for the world.

I. Their countries seek no aggrandisement, territorial or other.

II. They desire to see no territorial changes that do not accord with the freely expressed wishes of the peoples concerned.

III. They respect the right of all peoples to choose the form of government under which they will live, and they wish to see sovereign rights and self-government restored to those who have been forcibly deprived of them.

IV. They will endeavour, with due respect for their existing obligations, to further enjoyment by all States, great or small, victor or vanquished, of access on equal terms to the trade and to the raw materials of the world which are needed for their economic prosperity.

V. They desire to bring about fullest collaboration between all nations in the economic field, with the object of securing for all improved labour standards, economic advancement, and social security.

VI. After the final destruction of Nazi tyranny they hope to see established a peace which will afford to all nations the means of dwelling in safety within their own boundaries and which will afford assurance that all men in all lands may live out their lives in freedom from fear and want.

VII. Such a peace should enable all men to traverse the high seas and oceans without hindrance.

VIII. They believe all of the nations of the world, for realistic as well as spiritual reasons, must come to the abandonment of the use of force.

Since no future peace can be maintained if land, sea, or air armaments continue to be employed by nations which threaten or may threaten aggression outside of their frontiers, they believe, pending the establishment of a wider and permanent system of general security, that the disarmament of such nations is essential.

They will likewise aid and encourage all other practicable measures which will lighten for peace-loving peoples the crushing burden of armament.

This Charter was hailed with almost universal agreement throughout the British and American Commonwealths. Of equal importance are some words used by Churchill in his broadcast of the 24th August:

'There are, however, two distinct and marked differences in this joint declaration from the attitude adopted by the Allies during the latter part of the last war, and no one should overlook them.

'The United States and Great Britain do not now assume that there will never be any more war again.

'On the contrary, we intend to take ample precautions to prevent its renewal in any period we can foresee by effectively disarming the guilty nations **while remaining suitably protected ourselves.**

'The second difference is this: That instead of trying to ruin German trade by all kinds of additional trade barriers and hindrances, as was the mood of 1917, we have definitely adopted the view that it is not in the interests of the world and of our two countries that any large nation should be unprosperous or shut out from the means of making a decent living for itself and its people by its industry and enterprise.

'These are far-reaching changes of principle upon which all countries should ponder.'

The root of the whole matter, I submit, lies in those five words 'while remaining suitably protected ourselves'.

When *Decision* was printed I had not seen two other sixpenny pamphlets, the first entitled *A Real Peace*, by Lord Cecil, the second entitled *Let it Roll*, by Sir Rowland Evans, who was private secretary to Sir John Simon when in charge of the Foreign Office. Lord Cecil writes (page 15):

'We must find some way to build up the forces of peace sufficiently to make aggression by Germany or any other Power a hopeless proposition. That must be our most important purpose in the final Treaty of Peace.'

Sir Rowland Evans writes (page 10):

'It will be recalled how the words "never again", or their equivalent, occurred like a refrain in the speeches of Allied leaders in the 1914–1918 war. Here are one or two examples: "Never again shall brute force sit on the throne of justice, nor barbaric strength wield the sceptre of right." "There must be no next time." "One thing the Kaiser has made certain, and that is that no nation will ever commit that crime again." But it has happened again, and in a still more terrible form. It is plain common sense, therefore, that now steps will have to be taken, after the present struggle is over and won, to devise an effective method of preventing yet another repetition of this crime against humanity.'

On reading these two pamphlets I felt that Lord Cecil and Sir Rowland Evans had both stated the master problem which overshadows all others more clearly than I myself had been able to state it in *Decision*. Mr. Churchill raises that master-question in five words. He and the President have again announced on paper that when we are victors we are to ensure that world wars shall not happen again, and, to that end, are to see that the guilty nations shall be and remain disarmed. They have done this in response to an overwhelming public opinion, and have wisely not gone beyond that public opinion by attempting to say how it is to be done twenty or thirty years hence. I say wisely; because there is no public opinion which would justify statesmen in saying how it is to be done, how twenty or thirty years hence we are still to be strong enough to do it. Statesmen can do little or nothing to solve this problem unless there has been an adequate public opinion formed whilst hostilities are in progress, upon which they can act when hostilities cease.

When these words were first written I had seen no recognition on the part of any public man, or indeed anywhere in the public press, that this is in fact the question which governs all others, still less any suggestion as to how it could be solved. (I cannot of course foretell whether this will still be true when these words come to be printed.) To me this failure on the part of those who mould public opinion to consider or even state the question which governs the whole of our peace aims is alarming. To provide the answer to this question 'must be our most important purpose in the final Treaty of Peace', as Lord Cecil has said. But how are the statesmen to answer that question if no public opinion has been formed in the free countries behind them, before the terms of peace come to be framed; that is to say, during the war—**now?** In this connexion it is interesting to note some prescient words by Winston Churchill in his *Life of Marlborough* (vol. iv, p. 50):

'Nearly always Governments which seek peace flag in their war efforts, and Governments which make the most vigorous war preparations take little interest in peace. The two opposite moods consort with difficulty in the human mind, yet it is only by the double and, as it might seem, contradictory exertion that a good result can usually be procured.'

The Atlantic Charter calls us to work for 'a peace which will afford to all nations the means of dwelling in safety within their own boundaries and which will afford assurance that *all men in all lands* may live out their lives in freedom from fear and want'.

To those who think that the infinite duty of each to all is the principle that unites men in society, and that to develop and express it in practice is the goal of human existence, this charter erects a milestone in history. It supersedes political maxims such as 'The purpose of government is to protect life and property' or 'My country—right or wrong'. As things are now ordered the structure of society is based on the principle that the final duty of each man is owed to one of some sixty fragments of that society. Implicit in the words quoted above is the principle that each of us has a paramount duty to all his fellows, a principle denied in the structure of society as it now is. The principle of life is here propounded, not by philosophers, poets, or dreamers, but by two leaders of the greatest commonwealths in the world, and accepted by all the United Nations including Soviet Russia. It sets clearly before us the task of creating a system based on this principle, a priceless gain for those who believe in spiritual values; for without works such faith is vain.

The charter tells us that a better life for all who inhabit this planet is the object of human existence, and to that end peace is essential. Peace is not the end in itself, but the means to the end. To those who have lived through this war and the last it is scarcely necessary to argue that no better life is possible for the people who live on this planet so long as they feel that wars like these are hanging over their heads. Our first and immediate task, the moment hostilities cease, is to set in train whatever measures are needed, not only to prevent their recurrence, but slowly but surely to make men feel that such wars as these can never happen again. 'Security' is a compound of two Latin words meaning freedom from anxiety. Roosevelt is abundantly right when he sees this fear in men's minds as the obstacle blocking all roads to a better life.

The United Nations have accepted the charter: and yet one is conscious of a widespread doubt that war can ever in fact be abolished. A learned historian is constantly telling me that in every war people have always talked of making it the last, and have talked in vain.

In a recent work on Nationalism the group who produced it say:

'The necessity of conflict resides neither in Nationalism nor in the Nation, but in the nature of man. It seems Utopian to anticipate a period in which men will cease to organise themselves in groups for the purpose of conflict with other groups.'[1]

These words are significant, if only because this group discounts the idea that nations can be merged in an international state.

It is natural for those who spend their minds in studying the past to assume that where men have always failed they will always fail, and that as things have been they will remain. But physical science is a new and recent development in the long history of man. The essential evil of mechanized 'totalitarian' war is not the immeasurable suffering it imposes on countless people; for that will pass as the sufferers pass away by the process of nature. What will not pass is a rapid lowering in the spiritual quality of human material. The youths of

[1] *Nationalism*, p. 335. Oxford University Press.

vision, the spiritual leaders of their own generation, such as Rawnsley the founder of Federal Union, always too few in number, seek the posts of danger especially in air-war, and perish out of all proportion to those who need such leaders and are left without them. The airman whose letter to his mother was published by the Air Force is a case in point.[1] This letter presents so exactly the true relation of faith and works that I make no excuse for reprinting it here.

Dearest Mother,—Though I feel no premonition at all, events are moving rapidly, and I have instructed that this letter be forwarded to you should I fail to return from one of the raids which we shall shortly be called upon to undertake. You must hope on for a month, but at the end of that time you must accept the fact that I have handed my task over to the extremely capable hands of my comrades of the Royal Air Force, as so many splendid fellows have already done.

First, it will comfort you to know that my role in this war has been of the greatest importance. Our patrols far out over the North Sea have helped to keep the trade routes clear for our convoys and supply ships, and on one occasion our information was instrumental in saving the lives of the men in a crippled lighthouse relief ship. Though it will be difficult for you, you will disappoint me if you do not at least try to accept the facts dispassionately, for I shall have done my duty to the utmost of my ability. No man can do more, and no one calling himself a man could do less.

I have always admired your amazing courage in the face of continual setbacks; in the way you have given me as good an education and background as anyone in the country; and always kept up appearances without ever losing faith in the future. My death would not mean that your struggle has been in vain. Far from it. It means that your sacrifice is as great as mine. Those who serve England must expect nothing from her; we debase ourselves if we regard our country as merely a place in which to eat and sleep.

History resounds with illustrious names who have given all, yet their sacrifice has resulted in the British Empire, where there is a measure of peace, justice, and freedom for all, and where a higher standard of civilization has evolved, and is still evolving, than anywhere else. But this is not only concerning our own land.

[1] Published in *The Times*, 18th June 1940.

To-day we are faced with the greatest organized challenge to Christianity and civilization that the world has ever seen, and I count myself lucky and honoured to be the right age and fully trained to throw my full weight into the scale. For this I have to thank you. Yet there is more work for you to do. The home front will still have to stand united for years after the war is won. For all that can be said against it, I still maintain that this war is a very good thing; every individual is having the chance to give and dare all for his principle like the martyrs of old. However long the time may be, one thing can never be altered—I shall have lived and died an Englishman. Nothing else matters one jot nor can anything ever change it.

You must not grieve for me, for if you really believe in religion and all that it entails that would be hypocrisy. I have no fear of death; only a queer elation. . . . I would have it no other way. The universe is so vast and so ageless that the life of one man can only be justified by the measure of his sacrifice. We are sent to this world to acquire a personality and a character to take with us that can never be taken from us. Those who just eat and sleep, prosper and procreate, are no better than animals if all their lives they are at peace.

I firmly and absolutely believe that evil things are sent into the world to try us; they are sent deliberately by our Creator to test our metal because He knows what is good for us. The Bible is full of cases where the easy way out has been discarded for moral principles.

I count myself fortunate in that I have seen the whole country and known men of every calling. But with the final test of war I consider my character fully developed. Thus at my early age my earthly mission is already fulfilled and I am prepared to die with just one regret, and one only—that I could not devote myself to making your declining years more happy by being with you; but you will live in peace and freedom and I shall have directly contributed to that, so here again my life will not have been in vain.

Your loving Son

These words of an unknown airman deserve to remain on record so long as the English tongue survives. Can anyone who reads them doubt that in him we lost one who would have been a spiritual leader in his generation? Those whose business it is to deal with young men know how terrible is the toll that air-war takes of our best. Can anyone doubt that the loss of such men in the last war goes far to explain the moral decline which followed it in Germany, France, and also this country? Wars, mechanized and totalitarian, must impoverish the material of human society to an ever increasing degree, and as never before in previous ages.

It is not the quality only of human society but its very existence which is now threatened by discovery in physical science.

The development in our own lifetime of internal-combustion engines has shown how physical discoveries, until they are controlled by an organized human conscience, can work far greater ill than good for mankind. Unless they are followed in time by adequate national and international control, they will threaten the very existence of man on this earth. This recalls to my mind an occasion when an able and representative group of Australians were deriding the idea that their country would ever abate one jot of national sovereignty. At length a professor of physics quietly remarked, 'If you gentlemen worked in a physical laboratory, I think you would quickly revise your views.'

In a word, the time is at hand when not merely our welfare but our very existence will depend upon how far we can make control of human beings keep pace with control of natural forces. That in a word is the problem with which the Atlantic Charter confronts us in terms. Our very existence as well as our future happiness now depends, not only on creating some international control of a really effective kind, but also on discovering how to give existing national governments a more efficient control of social conditions than they now have.

I believe that war can be stopped if the eyes of men are opened to see the true end of life on this earth. I believe that that object is to develop and perfect in each of us the sense of duty which moves us to see the interests of others as our own. It is that, and that only, which makes it possible for men to combine in a state to establish the rule of law. To develop by exercise this sense of duty in men is the object

for which the state exists, the final aim of all public policy.[1]
The prevention of war is not the *final* object of policy. When
governments treat the avoidance of war as their ultimate aim
their policy fails and ends in war. Having said this, I must
add that prevention of war is the next and most necessary
means to the final end. That, as proposed in the Atlantic
Charter, is the first and next practical step that has to be taken.

To approve this charter has become a convention, but how
many of those who render it lip-service believe in their hearts
that its promise of peace on this earth will be realized? In the
course of the last year I have noticed signs of a growing
doubt on the subject. Let me give one of many examples. In
a letter to *The Times* dated the 23rd May 1944, Mr. Robert
Boothby, M.P., writes: 'The president and secretary of the
Economic Reform Club are quite right when they say that
trade will only flow freely in the absence of fear. A durable
peace is another essential condition of any international
currency agreement which is going to work. And who can
say that we are in sight of that?' That similar doubts prevail
in America is shown by a report dated December 1943 by
the National Opinion Research Centre of the University of
Denver. To the question 'Are wars inevitable?' the report
shows that 62 per cent. replied that 'There will always be
wars'. Captain Grey, speaking in the House of Commons on
the 24th May 1944, remarked: 'A large number of the ideas
produced to-day seem to be based on the thesis that another
war, if not inevitable, is likely. I believe that if we approach
the problems of peace in that atmosphere, not only will
another war be likely, but it will become inevitable.'[2]

If so, then I think that civilization is doomed. By civilization I do not mean letters, art, music, culture. The tree on
which such flowers and fruits grow is a system of society

[1] Readers are advised to get and study Rohan Butler's *The Roots of
National Socialism*, published by Faber, a masterly study of the philosophy
which has led the German people to treat power as the final object of
policy.
[2] These words are a voice from the grave. Before they had been printed
here Capt. Grey was killed in action with his regiment in Normandy.
So does war continue to rob the world of men it most needs for its peace.

based upon moral values. The sap which enables that tree to live and to grow is conscience, the still, small voice that is always telling us that the interests of others are our own, and that final reality is of the nature of our own personalities, which exist and will always exist beyond time and space. If our consciences are liars, the concept of 'right' has no meaning. The only thing which counts is the will of the stronger, and anything worth calling civilization is an idle dream.

That civilization, a system of society based upon moral and spiritual values, is in danger of destruction, is no mere phrase. I will go so far as to say that civilization has now been destroyed in its cradle, Europe, except in Switzerland, Sweden, and Portugal. If you think I exaggerate, read a letter[1] which came by underground channels from Europe and was printed in the *Christian News-Letter* of the 29th December 1943. This letter depicts a condition more savage than existed even in the time of Augustine, when German barbarians were overwhelming the Roman Empire and opening the epoch we call the Dark Ages. When the Nazi gangsters have been scotched it will take generations for Europe to recover from the chaos they have wrought. This second world war has been more destructive of life, property, moral values, and human welfare than the first. That a third world war in the next generation may destroy civilized life in the other four continents as the second has now destroyed it in Europe, is no idle guess.

To return to the question, my answer is that I do believe that wars can and must be prevented. For I also believe

> Men at *some time* are masters of their fate.
> The fault, dear Brutus, is not in our stars,
> But in ourselves, that we are underlings.

[1] Reprinted by courtesy of Dr. J. H. Oldham from the *Christian News-Letter*, 29th Dec. 1943, as an appendix to this Chapter.

## Appendix to Chapter XXIII
### THE EUROPEAN SITUATION

We have received from a continental source the following grave account of the European situation. The writer of the letter, which was written in September, though it reached us only this month, is exceptionally well informed and has contacts with many different countries.

'There are few intelligent persons left in Europe who are not convinced that the end of totalitarianism is only a question of time. This applies just as much to Germany as it does to the occupied and neutral countries. National socialism is no longer considered as a force which shapes the future, it has ceased to count as an *ideological* factor or as a spiritual menace.

'But it remains a tremendous reality as a purely *physical* menace. The burning questions are: what the last stage of the war holds in store in the way of destruction and violence, and who and what will survive that most critical of all periods of the war. It seems already quite clear that just because national socialism knows that it is condemned, it will yet reveal its most demonic aspects. The coming months may well become months of even greater horrors in all territories controlled by the Nazis.

'So it is comprehensible that the general sense of relief that the end of tyranny is approaching, is tempered by the fear that those men and those groups which have shown most courage in resisting and who are most needed for future reconstruction will to a large extent be "liquidated" before the day of liberation. A poet in an occupied country has written a remarkable poem in which he describes the sentiments of a patriot who knows that the great moment of freedom is near, but that he himself will be shot before that hour arrives. This is typical of the mood of many in Europe to-day. There is no uncertainty about the outcome, but there is uncertainty as to who and what will survive the crucial moment.

'Nothing is more important for the understanding of the Europe of to-day and of to-morrow than the right appraisal of the effects of totalitarian rule upon the peoples. These effects are extremely difficult to ascertain, for the very nature of totalitarianism implies that the real life of the peoples becomes almost wholly invisible. Propaganda and terrorism produce a thick layer of official conformity which covers up the true currents of conviction and opinion. No one, not even the secret police, and

K

perhaps those least of all, can have more than a vague and inadequate impression of all that lives behind the façade. On the
other hand, the future depends on our conception of these underlying realities. We must have at least a working hypothesis on the
basis of the indications which are available.

'What are these indications? Totalitarianism appears first of all
as a great *destructive* force. It destroys not only the forces which
resist openly, but also those which, though not resisting openly,
continue to lead their own life. Thus it has not merely attempted
to break the resistance of political parties, of intellectual forces, of
the confessing Churches, but it has tried to do away with any
autonomous life outside its own orbit, e.g. universities and professional groups. Its purpose in doing so is to make any alternative
solution impossible and thus to make its own system indispensable
and final.

'In doing this totalitarianism (which pretended to fill a political,
social and spiritual vacuum) has in fact created a *vacuum* such as
has never been seen before. Individuals cease to think and to
react in a personal manner; self-governing responsible groups
cease to function; living traditions die; there is no other life except
the artificial life imposed from above. All the inner conditions
are fulfilled of mass-life, that is of irresponsible, impersonal, uprooted existence without creativeness and responsibility.

'There is then a vacuum of frightening proportions. It is in
the last resort a religious vacuum. The masses despair for lack
of a real substantial faith which holds on to the invisible realities.
*But there is one hopeful thing about a vacuum, namely, that it
demands to be filled.*[1]

'The full effects of totalitarianism have only now come to make
themselves felt, since total warfare creates a situation in which the
whole process of destruction and uprooting is accelerated in an
extraordinary degree. Total war means that the outward conditions of life become such that most of the last remaining strong-
holds of free, healthy life, which exist in their own right and not
merely as a product of the will of the state, are also destroyed.
Totalitarianism had already made an onslaught on the family,
but it is only through the process of mass-mobilization for the
army and the labour front, through evacuation and deportation
that the menace to family life becomes truly mortal. Similarly,
through the merciless liquidation for the sake of the total war-

---

[1] I have ventured to italicize this significant challenge.

effort of all professions, in which men retained a certain amount of autonomy, practically all classes become proletarian.

'It must be added that the wholesale bombardments which involve the complete blotting out of whole cities have the same effect. Men and women who had still a home and a job to defend, have suddenly become people who have nothing to lose and are thus thrown into the mass of uprooted creatures who are merely the passive playthings of forces which they do not comprehend. At the same time these bombardments create the impression that the whole world has gone totalitarian. It is believed that no country recognizes any longer the limits of consideration for human life and of moral standards. It seems that there is nothing left except the war of all against all.

'Thus total warfare achieves the work of destruction begun by totalitarianism. The result is a general deadening of the sense of responsibility and of purpose. Life becomes just a matter of survival. Everything else becomes indifferent. Any system of government will do as long as it gives bread and security. Moral standards belong to the past world of tranquillity and organic relationships. Human life is very cheap, and if one finds that the disappearance of this or that person is necessary for one's safety or prosperity, that person will have to disappear.'

## CHAPTER XXIV

# A CLINICAL THERMOMETER TO TEST SECURITY

As my readers will see, I am using this vague and over-worked word in its literal sense of *sine cura*, without care, such freedom from anxiety as free peoples enjoyed under the protection of the British sea power in the last century. It was just this freedom from anxiety in the minds of ordinary men that the League of Nations failed to create, except at the moment of victory. It soon began to decline, and fell with a rush when the economic collapse set in. So let us beware of illusions. The re-creation of this sense of security must be a slow and gradual process. That it should be growing and not decreasing as it did between 1919 and 1939 is the really important matter, and that growth or decrease will test the efficacy of any arrangements made for stabilizing peace after this war.

In one respect a marked change will be seen. Not many years ago the London County Council set its face against any form of military training in schools. The question of security did not come home to local authorities as of course it did to national governments. In future all this will be changed by the fact that local authorities now know better than anyone else what war from the air means.

The local authorities have to provide public services, water, drainage, gas, electricity, schools, and so on for new residential areas. They instruct their officers, engineers, and architects to prepare the necessary plans and estimates. In future those experts will have to advise a definite increase in their estimates, in order to provide greater security against the effect of air-raids. The mains will have to be buried deeper. Special storage tanks for water must be created and maintained. There will doubtless be provision for permanent air-raid shelters. The by-laws governing building will be drastically revised to ensure additional security against incendiary bombs. All this must result in a heavy increase in local expenditure. Nor will this increase in costs be limited to local authorities. It will also affect industrial and business undertakings. The banks and insurance companies, and indeed the business world generally will realize the necessity of duplicating all their records, and of depositing the duplicates in buildings farther removed from destruction than the cities in which they congregate. Directors will find it necessary to maintain alternative offices to which they can go on the outbreak of war. All this will involve an additional burden on the cost of production in countries exposed to air-raids, and will tend to weaken still further the financial capacity of Great Britain to bear the cost of providing defence for the Commonwealth as a whole.

This new factor in war which enables an enemy to destroy the lives of civilians and all their equipment, will in future provide governments with a clinical thermometer whereby to register the temperature of security. The percentage of additional costs which local authorities and directors of business and builders think it right to incur as insurance against the risk of air-raids will show for itself how far the arrangements which governments have made are providing security in the real sense of that word. When civilians have ceased on their own initiative to incur these additional costs, then, and then only, will the object announced in the recent Atlantic Charter have been attained. I will here make bold to record a prediction that this thermometer will never register normal, so long as provision against the outbreak of future wars rests on foundations no firmer than compacts, written or unwritten, between one sovereign state and another. The temperature of insecurity will only begin to fall when two or more states, including Great Britain, have co-ordinated their defence policy under a single control.

## CHAPTER XXV

# THE MILITARY FACTOR

*THE TIMES*, in reviewing *Decision* on the 23rd August 1941, raised the following query:

'The essence of his proposals is that the federal government shall control all issues relating to peace and war, that is to say, the entire field of foreign policy, including the maintenance of the armed forces of the federation, while the member-states have equally exclusive control of their own social structure.'

The reviewer goes on to describe with accuracy the means suggested to produce this result, and adds,

'It is questionable whether this device really draws the line of demarcation exactly where Mr. Curtis desires: what, for instance, if the federal government thinks it necessary to invade the social sphere by demanding compulsory military service?'

I must say, without hesitation, that the Union Government must have power to impose conscription in all the member States, whenever it deems such a step necessary for the adequate protection of the Commonwealth as a whole. Whether in actual practice it would be found necessary to impose conscription in peaceful times, on the continental pattern, I very much doubt. In time of peace military strength now depends less on numbers of men with rifles than on tanks, armoured cars, and planes manned by crews who know how to operate them. At times in this war Government has had to consider whether a number of men in the forces should not be transferred to factories and mines. If all the tanks and guns required to ensure victory in the event of war are in being, there should be no difficulty in finding the crews required to man them without resorting to conscription in times of peace.

There will always be some role for Infantry, that is to say, men serving in ranks and carrying arms in their hands will always be essential to victory, as they now are on the western front. Clearly the government, responsible for the safety of the Commonwealth as a whole, must have power to command as well as to invite the service of any number of men it requires, as the British Government did in Great Britain when this war was impending. And this power must extend not only to men of an age to fight, but to those older and also to women whose services are needed, whether as adjuncts to the forces or in the factories. The basic principle of this proposal is that in order to prevent the recurrence of war the government responsible for that task must be able to make it a first charge on *all* the resources, human as well as financial, of the countries it has to defend.

On the 26th September 1941 I listened to a broadcast from Colonel George Drew, a Canadian officer with a distinguished record in the last war. From conversation with young officers in mechanized corps, I had begun to suspect that there is in these islands no area in which mechanized divisions can be properly trained. This doubt was confirmed as I listened to Colonel Drew, from whose broadcast I now give the following extracts.

'The events of the past two years have imposed the needs of a special type of hitting force. It must be divided into fast, compact, hard-hitting units which can be transported easily by ships.

'. . . Such a force should be made up of extremely powerful and fast land units working in the closest co-operation with aircraft, parachute troops, and airborne troops. This would not do away with the existing land forces. They are necessary for the defence of Britain, and for the second phase of any offensive. But a clear distinction should be drawn between the existing mass formations and the shock troops or primary hitting force. It must be remembered that less than 140,000 Germans were in the forces which broke the French Army of five millions. Their large forces only entered the scene in the second phase as mopping-up and holding troops. Our task is to create a hitting force so much more powerful than anything Germany has yet produced that it will be able to overrun a superior number of Panzer Divisions and leave the way open for the larger holding forces. It can and must be done.

'But the very factors which make it necessary to maintain large forces in Great Britain for defence also make it extremely difficult to give combined training to the highly specialized hitting forces which will be needed for the type of offensive we must undertake on the Continent of Europe. The dense population of Great Britain; the numbers of men already in training; the weapons and vehicles massed for defence; the topography of the country itself; the necessity of avoiding the destruction of food crops which are so urgently needed; all make it impossible to train fast heavy-hitting land forces in close co-operation with aircraft and airborne troops over areas sufficiently large to give the necessary experience in the problems of manœuvre and supply at high speed.

'Canada, on the other hand, offers the space and freedom from air attack which would make it possible to give the right type of training to such an offensive force. The largest training area in Britain is Salisbury Plains. They can be crossed by some fast vehicles in about twenty minutes. In Canada, however, training areas are available which would make it possible to train troops under conditions similar to those to be found anywhere from the Arctic to North Africa. Areas of one thousand square miles or more could be set aside where dummy towns and strong points could be erected. Attacks could be launched by parachute troops, airborne troops, and the fast land forces under very much the same conditions as would be met on active service and straight across country without regard to highways or fences. Embarkations and landings could also be practised at many points along the thousands of miles of shore line which border our large rivers and lakes.

'Another reason why Canada seems to be the only logical place to carry out this training is that it has been chosen for the Empire Air Training programme which I assure you is coming along splendidly and will soon be meeting all requirements for air personnel from some eighty training centres scattered over the three thousand miles that lie between the Atlantic and the Pacific. If the Attack Force is to be properly trained it must be in close co-operation with aircraft and airborne troops. As nearly all air fields in Great Britain will soon be needed for actual operations it is hard to see how this combined training can be given in the British Isles.

'This force should be an Empire Force under the direction of experienced men from the whole Empire. It is not suggested that tanks and other vehicles be moved from Britain. They will be available very soon from the factories of the United States and Canada. The man-power for this force could be drawn very largely from Canada at the outset where there are a large number at present training in other formations. One great advantage of training in Canada is the fact that almost unlimited quantities of motor fuel and lubricants are available. It would also result in a great saving of shipping space, which would otherwise be required to ship fuel and supplies to the same men and machines if they were in Britain. When the force was ready for active service it could then be transferred to Britain as the assembly base.

'I believe that such a force should be free from the shackles of existing text-books and army conventions and that we should draw upon the inventive genius and scientific knowledge of the great industrial producers of the United States to provide such destructive hitting power as has not yet been imagined. I am sure that within the British Empire we have the brains and the initiative to create the most powerful land army the world has ever known. When we have done that, then we will be able to reap the fruits of the magnificent accomplishments and sacrifices of our navy and air force. Then, and then only, will blockade and bombing bring victory.

'We Canadians are your partners in war and in victory. We should make full use of all the advantages which that partnership offers. We have the space to train the force which is so urgently needed. I am sure that Canadians would welcome a decision that such a force should be trained in Canada. Apart from its military consequences it would be one more practical expression of the ever-strengthening bonds of affection within the British Empire.'

Next day I wired an invitation to Colonel Drew to meet and discuss his thesis with General Swinton, whose knowledge of tanks from their first inception is a matter of history. The meeting took place on the 1st October, and during the interval both officers had been following the manœuvres in cars. At the end of their technical discussions, to which I was privileged to listen for several hours, I found myself feeling that whilst we might turn out the finest tanks and armoured cars in the world, it is, and always would be, impossible properly to train divisions to use them in the space available for practice in these islands. The mechanized divisions which in 1940 swept the Allied forces from the Netherlands and France in a few weeks were trained in the ample spaces of Central Europe, largely in Poland. Their efficiency was due to the close co-operation of tanks and aircraft, made possible only by long and intensive practice in spaces where tanks could be turned at any moment *in any direction*, to attack

enemy formations visible only from the air. Such training is
out of the question in a country where armoured vehicles are
tied to the roads. It is as though some town which possessed
no football ground tried to win matches by training its team
in its own streets.

Colonel Drew was concerned with the question of winning
this war, a question outside the scope of these pages. We are
here solely concerned with the question how, when this
second war has been won, to prevent a third. But this we
shall only do, if Winston Churchill is right, as I think he is,
by remaining 'suitably protected ourselves'. In plain words
we must in peace possess mechanized forces strong enough
to defy challenge by aggressors who have ample spaces in
Central Europe in which to train such forces. The Government responsible for the safety of Great Britain and the
British Commonwealth must have an effective army. If
Colonel Drew's reasoning is sound, the situation has now
to be faced, that no British army competent to cope with
mechanized divisions trained in Central Europe can in future
be trained at Aldershot, Salisbury Plain, or indeed anywhere
in Great Britain. They can only be trained in Canada.

A consideration not mentioned by Colonel Drew may
here be added. Troops trained to operate on ski are now an
important factor on snow-bound fronts. Such British troops
could only be trained in Canada or New Zealand.

In 1943 wide spaces of rural England had to be cleared to
make room for the training of mechanized divisions from the
U.S.A. How those divisions swept from Normandy to the
Loire and west to Paris we know. General Eisenhower has
told us that we owe General Patton's brilliant achievement
to the patience of English peasants who had left their farms
to be laid waste by American tanks. Some of these peasants
who had listened to Colonel Drew may have thought wistfully
how their homes and fields might have been spared had some
of the higher authorities happened to hear what he was saying
two years before.

The problem is not an entirely new one. It must be remembered that before the war the British Government found

that it could not properly organize the Royal Air Force without the use of Canadian air fields. The proposal at once raised acute constitutional questions, the discussion of which seriously delayed the progress of the scheme. If it is true that, even in peace, the British Government will need to send its mechanized divisions to be trained in Canada, it is well to realize that technical aspects of military problems inexorably raise constitutional problems. With these we must deal in a later chapter. I may seem to have strayed away into purely military considerations; but my point is that it is these considerations which bring us straight to the issue of Empire defence *as a whole*, and therefore to the necessity for accepting the principle of co-operation in advance on a field which transcends the limitations of national boundaries.

## CHAPTER XXVI

# THE UNION CAPITAL

YOU ask me where best should an international government charged with the task of maintaining the peace of the world be seated? That is the one question to which is given no answer in the pamphlets I have published so far. I had better confess that, though I have thought of that question, I approach it with fear and trembling. One reason is that the Union of South Africa was almost wrecked in its final stage by the question where the capital should be. In the end it was only saved by a compromise like the judgement of Solomon. They even went farther than Solomon proposed; for instead of dividing the child between two mothers they cut it up to satisfy three. The union was only saved by deciding that Cape Town should be the legislative capital, Pretoria the executive capital, and Bloemfontein the judicial capital. Another reason for my hesitation has been the effect on public opinion in this country of the answer that I must honestly give. Australian airmen say to me here: 'You will have less difficulty in carrying your proposal in Australia than you will have in England.' For more than one reason I believe they are right. So far I have shrunk from giving my answer, because I believe that London is the worst possible place in which to centre an international union designed to secure the nations who enter it from war. Strategic and political objections combine to exclude any place in the British Isles.

In approaching this all-important question, let me hold in mind that the ultimate object I am keeping in view is a government responsible to men and women throughout the world for maintaining its peace. That, in ages to come, is the final object to be sought and found if civilization is to be saved and also lifted to higher planes. I also believe that such a government can only be realized step by step. Of all these steps the hardest and most important to take is the first; but if once the world can be shown that some international government of nations divided by oceans can function in practice, provide their common security, and also increase the power of national governments to control their domestic affairs, democracies outside it will be readier to join it than they now are. Difficult as it is to get any national states to merge their sovereignty into one union, the difficulty will be least in the case of the British democracies, with their common language and institutions. But I do not pretend that such a union can of itself preserve the peace of the world. A further step would be taken towards increasing the general security, if and when it were joined by the Netherland and Scandinavian democracies of western Europe and by France. It would then become an international union in a fuller sense than it ever can be so long as it includes only the democracies embraced by the British Commonwealth. My faith is that, if and when such an international union had demonstrated the greater security and national freedom of those who had entered it, in course of time the most powerful democracy, the people of the American commonwealth, would throw in their lot with it. I believe that whenever that happens the fear of world wars will be finally ended—security in the real sense of the word will be achieved. In those conditions I believe that nations outside it in Europe, Asia, and Africa will acquire the habits and practice of responsible government, and so qualify for inclusion in a union the central government of which must draw its authority from and be answerable to the citizens of the world and not to their national governments.

You now face me with the question what capital would be best if the British democracies attempt the first and most difficult step, by creating a government responsible to their people for their common security.

The seat of the government now responsible for this task is where it has always been, in Britain. The fleet, army, and air force it controls through the Admiralty, War Office, and Air Ministry are centred there. The events of history decided this fact and, so long as war was confined to sea and to land, this was also the best strategic point from which to direct the defence of an empire scattered all over the globe. But this strategic position is now changed by the fact that at any moment an enemy in Europe can strike from the air and strike without warning. In 1940 the future of freedom was in greater peril than it ever was since the ships of Athens and Persia were facing each other in the straits of Salamis. The chamber in which the Mother of Parliaments sat is lying in ruins. . . .[1]

But this was not all. Experience has also proved that neither on land nor yet in the air can mechanized forces be trained on an adequate scale in the British Isles. Provision had to be made for training a considerable part of the air force in Canada. Had similar provision been made for training mechanized troops in Canada, the devastation of the English country by tanks would have been saved. The space now used to train the millions of Allied troops in this country may gravely reduce its capacity to grow the food which is needed to win the war almost as much as are guns and shells. That space is wholly inadequate for the purpose of training. There is in this small island no space in which the land and air forces needed to ensure our freedom against attack can be trained. That is one inexorable fact that cannot be ignored in time of peace if we are really facing the problem how to make the free system under which we live too strong for any aggressor to attack.

Our object is to create for the British Commonwealth a system which will so far as is possible ensure it against attack. The brain and heart of that system should not in the future centre in an island so vulnerable to attack from the air.

The political objection to London is also important. For the present the United Kingdom contains more people than all the Dominions added together. With the Government of a union located in England the Dominions would feel, as they do now, overshadowed by its numbers, its power, prestige, and traditions. That 'complex' known as 'Downing Street' has not been allayed by 'equality of status' as enunciated in

---

[1] The rest of this paragraph has been omitted from the proofs, as originally printed, in deference to the censorship. When the war is over and censorship restrictions no longer apply, I shall hope to print what I wrote in a future edition.

the pages of the Balfour Report and the Statute of Westminster. One has only to spend an evening with politicians and public officials in Ottawa or Canberra to realize that.

For political as well as for strategic reasons I am forced to exclude these islands as the future centre of the Commonwealth. I have long felt that the first critical step might be taken by Australia and New Zealand. Yet no one from those regions has ever suggested to me that the capital of a world commonwealth could ever be fixed in the southern hemisphere. The reason can be seen by one glance at the map of the world; and the same applies to South Africa.

This first step in creating an international union would lose most of its value unless its structure could be widened to include more than the British Commonwealth. I am always thinking of how it can include the democracies of western Europe. Even so, the peace of the world will not be secured till the great American people have entered a union for the common defence of democracy. Whatever step is taken should keep that goal in view, however remote it may seem. For strategic reasons a world commonwealth for defence might well be centred in the U.S.A. which is and will be the most powerful national state in the world. But less powerful nations would feel that the international authority would be overshadowed and dominated by a nation so powerful as the U.S.A. The difficulty we are now facing in the fear of 'Downing Street' would be met in a different and wider form.

This method of exclusion has led me to think that the place on the map best fitted by nature as the capital of an international Commonwealth is Quebec, both at the outset and in the later stages of its growth. There, beyond the Atlantic, its naval, military, and air establishments, its executive, ministries, and legislature would lie outside the range of sudden and imminent attack by air from Europe or Asia. There, and in neighbouring harbours like Halifax and others along the Atlantic coast, its ships and their bases on shore could lie in security. In those harbours ships could be fuelled at the lowest possible cost with oil piped from Canadian and

American oilfields. The need to carry this fuel in tankers across the Atlantic would be greatly reduced.

Experience has shown that behind Quebec is that ample space, utterly wanting in the British Isles and also in the western democracies of Europe, for the training of mechanized forces whether on land or in the air. The world has come to realize that the power of aggressors to make war, and also of the democracies to prevent their making it, must in future rest with those countries equipped with factories in which such weapons as tanks and planes can be made. The world has yet to realize that space in which to train the crews to operate tanks and planes is just as important as factories in which to build them. In Britain no such space is available, nor is it in countries like Belgium, Holland, Denmark, or Norway. Mechanized forces and air fleets cannot be trained and made ready for battle in these small and thickly populated countries as they can in the wider spaces of central Europe. It is time that this vital fact should be faced by those who say so glibly that these lesser democracies are to supply their quotas of military force to the collective security of a League of Nations. It is only as states of an international union that their mechanized forces can be trained in some state of that union provided with ample space for the purpose. In a country like Canada, which extends into Arctic regions, such space will always exist. There will always be space for training mechanized forces in Australia and South Africa. In so far as an international union maintains mechanized forces, trained and ready for instant battle in defence of any of its states threatened with attack, those forces are less likely to be called into use. And as, in course of time, the danger of attack was reduced, so also would the scale of those forces be reduced, subject to the condition that they were always kept on a scale sufficient to ensure the safety of the union and the peace of the world if any attack were made on them.

In these days, when statesmen travel by air, Quebec is as easy to reach as London from New Zealand, Australia, and

South Africa. As a second step in the policy proposed, we are hoping that the French, Scandinavian, and Netherland democracies would join the union. It would then cease to be British and become international in the fullest sense of that word. London is nearer to them than Quebec; but for them political considerations would more than outweigh this physical fact. An international union, British perhaps at the outset, will only secure the peace of the world in so far as it ceases to be British and becomes international in the fullest sense of the word. That vital transition would be greatly impeded if its capital were still located in Britain. At Quebec two races, languages, religions, and civilizations meet. The Belgians and French would find themselves more at home in Quebec than in London. The government of the union would be working in a country which has long shown how to conduct government by discussion in more than one language. Norwegians would meet there a large number of Canadian citizens born in Norway and still speaking its language.

The third and decisive stage in this policy would be rendered more easy and probably quickened if the capital of the union were centred from the outset on the North American continent. That such a union would give the various nations united not less but much more control of their own national affairs will never be proved or disproved by arguments on paper. The question whether national sovereignty must really remain the last word in the growth of democracy can never be answered until an international union has been tried, and has failed or succeeded in actual practice. The American people will be able to answer these questions for themselves more easily if the first experiment is conducted at their doors and under their eyes. Until they join such a union the peace of the world can only be maintained in so far as its government is able to co-operate with the United States. The co-operation of Washington would clearly be easier with an international government located at Quebec than if that government centred in England.

A proposal to move the government which controls their defence and their foreign policy from the British Isles will

L

come as a shock to most Englishmen. So did Durham's proposal to create governments in Canada responsible to Canadian parliaments and electorates, and not to the Imperial Government in London. Yet in course of time the practical minds of Englishmen came to recognize that this was a necessary change, if the bonds which united the younger communities with them were not to be broken, as they had been broken with the older American colonies. To recognize facts as they change is a matter which needs time and reflection. The inexorable lesson of this second war is that these islands cannot in the long run be defended by forces trained and centred in the islands themselves. The land and air forces must be trained in regions more spacious, and the naval forces as well must have bases in some country less exposed to attack from the air. Above all, the authority which controls these forces must be located in some place less exposed to sudden destruction than it ever can be in Westminster. But the real key to defending the British Isles can only be found by creating a system of defence so strong that no aggressor in Europe will ever try to attack it. That can only be done by creating a system which in course of time will bring into being an authority backed by the American as well as the British and French peoples and also by other democracies on the continent of Europe. If and when that is achieved, the peace of the world will at last be assured, and the ultimate creation of a world commonwealth will then be in sight. The essential defence of the British Isles will only be found in a system which ensures freedom from world wars. From 1815 till the end of the nineteenth century we had such a system, till the progress of mechanization rendered it obsolete. By 1914 the security that system created had vanished and cannot now be restored until we rebuild it on foundations far wider than those of the British Isles. To create such a system we must learn to look the changing facts in the face. In doing so Englishmen will come to see that no system of defence which is centred in these islands can in future hope to protect them from attack. No system of defence will protect the British Commonwealth from attack unless it is centred in some place less vulnerable than islands exposed to the sudden impact of blows from Europe.

As I say this, flying bombs are dealing death and destruction in London streets, and the Prime Minister has warned us to be ready for the even more devastating rocket bombs which the Germans hope to shower upon us. When one thinks what has followed the first invention of submarines, aeroplanes, and tanks, one can see to what lengths the future developments of this latest weapon will go. If another world war should break out, fire and brimstone will rain on every city in these islands. The public men who are telling us to trust our security from war to a League of Nations will then be seen to have led us down the primrose path to the ever-lasting bonfire.

To reach security these islands must also face some reduction in population and the industries which support them. Any system under which the forces defending the Commonwealth are trained in the continents of America, Africa, and Australia will lead to a transfer of population from the British Isles to the Dominions. Factories to produce the weapons these forces wield must be maintained in considerable strength in the countries where those forces are trained. Young people from the British Isles who join those forces will to a certain extent elect to make their homes in the countries where they are trained. When their time of service expires they will find employment in the factories and farms needed to supply the forces trained in these countries. Such a system will in fact be a more effective scheme of migration from the Mother Country to the Dominions than any which has yet been devised. The United Kingdom can only afford such a transfer under a system which gives these islands a greater measure of security than they can hope to enjoy under the existing system. The same would of course apply to youths enlisted in the union forces from western democracies in Europe. Many soldiers and airmen from Belgium, Holland, and Norway, after training in Canada, Australia, or South Africa, would ask to stay there.

To secure the peace of the world and discharge our commitments under the Atlantic Charter we must have a short-term programme which leads on to a long-term programme. In any such programme the centre from which the forces required to ensure the peace are to be controlled is a question of vital importance. My own conclusion is that Quebec is not only the best place from which to provide security for all the British democracies, but would also be best for a system developed to maintain the security of free nations throughout the world.

The writer himself is responsible for every proposal in these pages, and no one else. They have all been made after full and often protracted discussion with people selected for their judgement and experience and knowledge of public affairs. The post-war policy worked out in these chapters was obviously incomplete until some answer had been suggested to the question where an international government should be centred. National sovereignties are not the last word in the growth of freedom and, whatever publicists may say, human society will sooner or later achieve control of itself through an international government. Such a government must be located at some spot on the face of the globe, and to fix on that spot will be easier if men have thought long in advance where it should be. When I came to think that an international government of the British democracies could best be placed at Quebec, I submitted my reasons to the criticism of three men whose judgement, knowledge, and experience of public affairs I had learned to respect. After long discussion one of them remarked, 'Had we not better realize that the question we are discussing is the future capital of the world?' This remark convinced me that the answer to this critical question here suggested has this merit, that it meets the need of the long-term policy no less than the need of the short-term policy.

CHAPTER XXVII

# A FROWARD RETENTION OF CUSTOM

IN discussing the Atlantic Charter with a highly intelligent lady, I was trying to explain the view I have stated in Chapter XVIII. 'I do so agree with you', she said. 'What you mean is that after this war we must break Germany up into a number of smaller states.' 'Your answer', I said, 'exactly illustrates the very danger I am trying to explain. You say that we are to prevent a further war by breaking Germany up. Personally I don't agree with your policy; but that is neither here nor there. Suppose, for the moment, that you are right, and that the way to prevent a future war is to keep Germany broken up. Now the question I have to ask you is this: suppose that in twenty or thirty years the Germans begin to reunite, how are we *then* to be strong enough to stop them from reuniting?' She was silent for a little, and then said, 'Now I begin to see your point.'

On a previous page I have said:

**'The safety of free systems is always to look to their own strength and not to measures for weakening their enemies.'**

I offer that statement here as the cardinal principle which must govern the future prevention of world wars, a principle by the observance or neglect of which the Atlantic Charter will stand or fall. It is for that reason that I so welcome the five pregnant words which Churchill used when explaining that charter—'while **remaining** suitably protected ourselves' —especially the word **remaining**. On the morrow of victory in 1919 we were *suitably protected*, until we began to liquidate our navy and air force as well as our army. On the morrow of victory in this war we shall again be *suitably protected*. The vital question is how we are to remain *suitably protected* for generations to come. That is primarily a financial question. **Can we remain suitably protected, so long as the Government responsible for the safety of the Commonwealth as a whole can make its defence a first charge on resources no wider than those of Great Britain and Northern**

**Ireland ?** Can those who have failed to see, as Lothian saw, that that is the question on which the future peace of the world and its hopes of freedom depend, lay claim to a genuine realism ? Politicians, civil servants, international lawyers, and professors of political science are prone to think themselves realists, because they cannot conceive any radical change in the system they have always practised and studied. I think that realists will agree with the view I share with Lord Cecil and Sir Rowland Evans, that the only way to prevent another world war—to realize the aims of the Atlantic Charter—is 'to build up the forces of peace sufficiently to make aggression by Germany or any other Power a hopeless proposition'. But until they have faced this crude financial question they are in fact unconscious visionaries.

Realists always brand as visionary any suggestion for a radical change in the system to which they are used, and, in doing so, appeal to that deep-seated factor in human nature—inertia. They dwell on the dangers they see in the change proposed, ignoring the actual and more imminent danger which a radical change alone will remove. It was so with realists when Priestley in England, and again when Garrison in America, were urging that the time had come to abolish slavery. I have before me a letter from a leading banker in London who writes:

'I very much agree with the importance of the question you raise. Twenty-five years is a short time in the life of a nation, and unless we work out something immediately after this war, something which effectively deals with that problem, our descendants will certainly face another war before so very long.'

That is the real danger inherent in leaving things as they are. My critics suggest all sorts of dangers in the constitutional change I propose. The worst of the dangers they suggest is that one of the nations, having entered the Union, might afterwards feel that its contribution to the common defence was too heavy a burden, or for some other reason, might wish to secede. The Union would then be threatened with civil war as happened in the U.S.A. Are all these hypothetical dangers, including a civil war, when taken together, so great, or so fatal to human welfare if realized, as another world war, the danger of which must remain actual and imminent in the system of national sovereignty under which we are living?

As with dangers so with difficulties. All sorts of difficulties in the way of a change are suggested as insuperable.

The fact is ignored that things as they are present insoluble problems. From Australia has come a demand for the representation of Dominion Governments in the War Cabinet. Now if the doctrine of equal sovereign status which inspired the report of the Imperial Conference of 1926 and the Statute of Westminster corresponds to the facts, the Australian demand for a War Cabinet in which Dominion Prime Ministers sit, is unanswerable. But Prime Ministers like those of Canada and South Africa cannot and will not sit in the War Cabinet, because they know that they cannot afford to be absent from Ottawa, Cape Town, and Pretoria. The difficulty is, in fact, insuperable, though no one has yet ventured to say so, because by saying it they would admit that the issues of war, like the issues of peace, must rest in practice with the government answerable to British electors, and not with the governments answerable to Dominion electorates. The alliance of the whole British Commonwealth with Russia was decided by the British Cabinet, and rightly decided, within twenty-four hours of Hitler's attack on Russia. In the time available Dominion Governments could scarcely do otherwise than give their assent. Was there any consultation at all with Dominion Governments when Mr. Churchill offered to France an organic Union with Great Britain, or when he was meeting President Roosevelt to frame the Atlantic Charter? The answer is, there was none, because none was possible.[1]

Advice to leave things as they are can always parade as a counsel of safety, and realists brand as dangerous men and as revolutionaries those who call for an overdue change. The men of the *ancien régime*, who could learn nothing and forget

---

[1] On p. 335 of *International Affairs, Review Supplement*, Sept. 1941, Graham Spry, a Canadian, writes 'the Atlantic meeting of the two great Powers is the measure of the significance of relatively small Powers. There was no Canadian, no Dominions, representative.'

nothing, were the real authors of revolutions whether in France or in Russia. Alcibiades with all his treachery did less to compass the ruin of Athens than Nicias, so upright, so pious, so cautious, so safe that he cancelled the order he had given for the fleet to escape from the harbour of Syracuse—

'. . . because an eclipse of the moon . . . took place . . . . Nicias . . . refused from that moment even to take the question of departure into consideration, until they had waited the thrice nine days prescribed by the soothsayers.'[1]

The morning paper before me repeats the verdict of history.

'What seems not to have been realized by the British and French was that the tank of 1939 differed from the tank of 1918 almost as much as that from the armoured cars of 1914. . . . The Germans did realize that. They saw that it could be used, not merely for pounding at the enemy in conjunction with infantry, but independently to sever his vital reserves. . . . But the implication was forgotten, or, one might even say, ruthlessly thrust aside. Some day the whole story of the opposition of the higher ranks of the Army to mechanization may be told. It will be a depressing narrative of prejudice and folly.'[2]

These words recalled to my mind a conversation to which I had listened years before between Lawrence, who was at the time a private in the Tank Corps, and General Swinton, to whose genius and technical knowledge, as we now know, the invention of tanks was largely due. My heart sank as I realized how little the authorities were doing to develop the new weapon which had gone so far to secure the defeat of the German armies in 1918. I then understood the craving which Lawrence had to escape from the stagnant atmosphere which deadened the Tank Corps, back to the Air Force, in which the vital importance of technical improvement was realized.

It is fair to add that General Swinton has since told me that failure to develop the tanks was mainly due to refusal by the British Treasury to provide funds necessary for the purpose. That fact should be noted for the light it throws on the in-

---

[1] Thucydides, chapter xxiii.
[2] Edward Shanks, *Sunday Times*, 28th September 1941, reviewing *War on Wheels* by C. R. Kutz.

ability of a government to discharge the task of defending the whole British Commonwealth from attack so long as it commands resources no wider than those of Great Britain and Northern Ireland.

We must, however, return to the point of this chapter, that world wars and great revolutions are less due to our wrongdoings than to our failure to get things done. The order in which these two kinds of sin are ranked in the General Confession is profoundly significant.

'We have left undone those things which we ought to have done; And we have done those things which we ought not to have done.'

Sins of commission have brought less evil on men than sins of omission. As Bacon wrote in his pregnant phrase:

'A froward retention of custom is as turbulent a thing as an innovation; and they that reverence too much old times are but a scorn to the new.'[1]

[1] *Essays*, XXIV: 'Of Innovations.'

## CHAPTER XXVIII

# THE PATH TO BRITISH-AMERICAN UNION

SOME notices in the press construed my proposals as a plea for organic union between the British and American Commonwealths. Letters have reached me from readers who are clearly under the same impression. Such proof of my failure to convey what I mean to others impels me to make a further attempt.

The danger of world wars will not, in my view, be *completely* removed, except by an international government, which includes the United States of America. Whenever the U.S.A. combines with other free states to make their common defence a first charge on all their resources, the era of world wars will be, I believe, at an end. I thought I had shown plainly enough that I did not expect that the U.S.A. would be ready to join such a union within one generation after this war. In *Decision* I was trying to argue that the only way to prevent a recurrence of war within one generation was for the sovereign States of the British Commonwealth and of Western Europe to merge their sovereignties into one international union for the purpose of common defence. I believe that this of itself would suffice to avert war for one generation. But I also believe that such an example is necessary to prepare public opinion in America for eventually joining the union.

Let us first deal with the question how to prevent the renewal of war within one generation. Think for one moment what would have happened if in 1919, or soon after, the British Dominions had formed such a union as I had suggested and again suggest in these pages. There would then have come to exist a legislative body to which Canada, Australia, New Zealand, and South Africa would have sent their members. A large proportion of these members would have had to travel across the world. Inevitably these distant members would have called on the Union Government to provide them with facilities for travelling by air. The early creation of a frequent commonwealth air service, to save the time of members and union officers in travelling, would have been certain. On the morrow of the war we had plenty of pilots already trained to man such a service.

It is worth considering why no such Imperial service was brought into being till years later and then on the most inadequate scale. In Central Europe Germany lost no time in developing civil aviation. In the U.S.A., Canada, Australia, and South Africa such services went ahead by leaps and bounds, because they had all to deal with distance on the continental scale. In Great Britain it languished, and a number of pilots trained in the war went unemployed, for the simple reason that the island was not large enough to make travel by air a practical necessity. If you wanted to travel from London to Glasgow or Edinburgh it was more convenient to go by the Scotch express. The railway was still an effective competitor with aircraft. It was only after years of agitation by private individuals that the Government was driven to establish Imperial Airways, and then on a most inadequate scale. There was too little in the constitutional situation to convince the Imperial authorities of the need for effective air service, not on the insular or even continental scale, but to serve a commonwealth spread over the world. The force which had conquered the air in the war, and was now needed to guard and maintain freedom of the air, was reduced for reasons of economy to the narrowest limits. Within two decades command of the air had passed to Germany.

If from 1919 onwards members from distant parts of the world had had to travel to one centre to attend the meetings of a Union Parliament we may be sure that they would have insisted on the establishment of an Imperial Airways regardless of cost. But that is not all. Accustomed to travel by air they would have insisted that the British Commonwealth must always maintain the safety of its airways, that it must of necessity maintain the mastery of the air as it always maintained the mastery of the sea. Why, for centuries, had we maintained our mastery of the sea? Because for centuries we had created a vast mercantile marine, and Parliament was full of members who knew that our very existence as a free people depended on its adequate protection. So the members of a real commonwealth legislature, accustomed to travel by air, would never have allowed our Air Force to be reduced, as it was, after the last war. They would have insisted that it must be maintained on a scale strong enough to defeat the air power of Germany or of any aggressive nation. The cost could have been met if Dominion resources, as well as those of Great Britain and Northern Ireland, had been available for the general defence. As it was, the British Treasury felt that it could not be met by the British taxpayer alone. Within two decades German air-power had become a dominating factor, as it proved at the time of Munich.

Behind all this is a point of profound importance. The most valuable aspect of the democratic principle is its tendency to bring the largest possible number of people face to face with the facts of life. As noted above, the British Parliament was so constituted that a large number of members could see that our freedom depended on control of the sea. After the last war the House of Commons was not so constituted that enough of its members could see that our freedom and the peace of the world must now depend on our power to control the air, as well as the sea.

This diversion on the subject of air-power is merely another approach to the question why organic union of the British Commonwealth is a necessary step to organic union between the British and American Commonwealths. In my own judgement the time is scarcely in sight when my friend Streit and his followers will succeed in persuading a majority of Americans to accept such a Union. I doubt their power to convince their electorate, merely by the spoken and written word, that this is the only way to obtain a new birth of freedom. My pessimism may be falsified (I hope that it will be) if Americans should be found to possess a leader of the courage and calibre of Washington or Lincoln. God alone, in His wisdom, can see to that; but otherwise I fear that in spite of all reason a number of Americans will continue to regard an organic union of the British and American Commonwealths as a loss of the freedom they now have—enough at any rate to prevent a change so difficult under their constitution. I think that this adverse condition will only be remedied when Americans have seen an international union in actual being, and at their doors.

My own unquenchable faith is that a Union, as outlined in these pages, would in time yield certain good results, and make their benefit obvious. The visible demonstration of those good results would go farther to convince an American electorate, than any mere spoken or written persuasion can do.

The first of these good results would be greater security. It is surely clear that a government responsible for the safety of the British Commonwealth as a whole, and able for that purpose to command all its resources and not, as at present, only those of Great Britain and Northern Ireland, would greatly increase the general security. Americans, as they compared the British Commonwealth before and after the change, would begin to see that war is rendered less likely only in so far as sovereign nations merge their sovereignty for the purpose of defence into one international sovereignty.

The trouble in the U.S.A., as elsewhere, is the widespread fear that an international union would diminish the power of national governments to control their own domestic affairs. I am one who thinks that control of domestic affairs can be divided from control of defence and placed under separate governments; but whether this is so or not can only be proved by an actual experiment. If once that experiment were tried in the British Commonwealth, and proved successful, then I am sure that each nation would find that its power to control its own domestic affairs had in fact increased—and this for several reasons. As the Union Government diminished the menace of war and increased the general sense of security, the national governments would obviously find it easier to tackle questions of social reform. Whenever security reached a point which made it safe to reduce armaments, then larger funds would become available for social reform.

The question of time is of no less importance. The executive and legislature of a modern government really tasked with control of defence will never have time to meet the demands of social reform. An extreme case in point is, of course, the Government of the United Kingdom.[1] There are not enough days in the year for the Cabinet and Parliament to digest the reforms which are needed. The failure of democracies to keep pace with the changes required by mechanization is mainly responsible for the swing which Europe has taken back to the methods of despotism. A Cabinet and Parliament which has to devote so much of its time and nervous energy to defence and external affairs will never be able to overtake the arrears of social reform. The first essential step to the social reforms we are promised is to relieve the Cabinet in Whitehall and Parliament of the time they now have to devote to external affairs. And this applies in varying degrees to the other responsible Governments of the British Commonwealth. At the opposite end of the scale is New Zealand, which has frankly left the control of external affairs, except as to minor details, to the British Government. I was in New Zealand at the time of a general election, on the morrow of Munich, when the clouds of war were visibly gathering. Yet scarcely a reference was made in electoral speeches to the international situation. The issues turned on domestic questions of butter and cheese. One could not fail to observe how much higher the general condition of social welfare was than in England. No people have ever been able to devote so much of their time and attention to their own social affairs as those of New Zealand. If all the Governments of the Commonwealth were relieved from the burden of defence and external affairs, they would soon find their capacity for controlling domestic affairs greatly increased. The fact would in time be plain to social reformers in the U.S.A. In spite of the federal system the state of congestion in Washington is fast approaching the state of congestion in Westminster. With actual examples before their eyes a time may come when Americans will see that Washington cannot really grapple

[1] In an article published in *The Sunday Times* on the 2nd Oct. 1941 Lord Vansittart seems to confirm this view. He has lifelong experience of over-congestion in Whitehall.

with domestic reforms until it is relieved from the pressure of attending to defence and external affairs.

I had just written this last paragraph, when I opened *The Times* of the 11th October 1941, and on page 4, column 6, read a statement by President Roosevelt that

'roughly 1,000,000 young men—about half of those examined—have been rejected as unfit for service in the U.S. Army on account of physical, mental, or educational defects.

'For years the American Government have been facing the fact that the distribution of services in the health field has lagged behind the production of services in the laboratories of the world and that, as the late William Welch said: "We know how to do a lot of things which we do not do or do on a wretchedly small scale." '

The case which would doubtless affect American opinion most strongly would be Canada. The trouble of Canada has been throughout that she has never quite known what she is or where she is. I gathered this from listening to the conversation of politicians and officials at Ottawa in 1909, and on many subsequent visits. The last of these visits was after the Statute of Westminster had been passed, which on paper gave Canada a status exactly the same as that of Great Britain. The conversations to which I listened were, none the less, exactly the same as in 1909. In spite of all that was written in the Statute of Westminster, experienced and thoughtful Canadians still felt that they did not know what their nation was or where she was. Personally I felt that when war came the Canadian Parliament would go through the motions prescribed by the Statute of Westminster, and Canada would find herself at war; but whether the war broke out or not would be really determined by things which were done, or left undone, at Westminster and not at Ottawa. As Mr. Menzies afterwards said:

'The fact will remain that the great issues of peace and war will be much more determined by the gentleman who sits in a room looking across the Horse Guards Parade than it will be by my colleagues in Canberra or one of our colleagues in Ottawa or Pretoria.'

And so it fell out in September 1939. The gentleman in

the Horse Guards Parade held office by virtue of votes cast in Great Britain, including my own, but not by virtue of votes cast by Canadians. Canada was a satellite state, under a British hegemony committed to war by a Government of the U.K. too weak to have taken the measures required to obviate the outbreak of war. If the change suggested in these pages were made, the Government which held in its hands the issues of peace or war would be just as responsible to a Canadian as to an Englishman. It would also command resources strong enough to prevent a recurrence of war. The status of Canada would then in fact, as well as on paper, be that of Great Britain. At last she would really know what her status was, and that knowledge, that certainty, would react on her own internal position. Her Government would be able to cope with the stresses which gravely menace her unity, her racial stresses, and those which threaten to divide the East from the West. Relieved from concern for external affairs her Government could grapple with her own domestic reform. Its control of national affairs would not be diminished but greatly increased.

I am asking the reader to consider the effect of this, if it happened in Canada, on public opinion in the U.S.A. Increasing complexity of civilization is imposing ever increasing tasks on Washington in foreign as well as in social affairs. Social reform in America will fall into ever graver arrears. Her people will find themselves losing control of their own domestic affairs by reason of over-congestion at the centre. The object lesson of a Government in Canada gaining control of national affairs, when relieved of international problems, would help to convince Americans that that is the necessary path to a new birth of freedom.

The federal union of Canada led to the growth of the British Commonwealth as it now is. This far-reaching constructive act achieved by Canadian statesmen in 1867 was only made possible by the example of the U.S.A., before their eyes and at their doors.[1] There is thus ground in ex-

[1] See *The Commonwealth of God*, by the present writer, pages 526–7. For the sake of brevity the historical details are not restated in this chapter

perience for thinking that if Canada were to open a new path to a higher freedom, the example set before American eyes and at their doors would in time have decisive effects on American opinion.

Whenever the citizens of the British and American Commonwealths unite to preserve the peace of the world, the era of world wars will be closed once and for all. With such a Union, the cost of the armaments, before needed to prevent the recurrence of war, will rapidly fall, releasing vast material resources to aid the progress of social reform. I think that the British Commonwealth, united as I suggest, can prevent the recurrence of war for a generation at least, by maintaining armaments strong enough for the purpose. If other nations joined the Union, the risk of war and the burden of armaments would be rapidly decreased.

Any union which included the citizens of the British and American Commonwealths, of French, Netherland, and Scandinavian democracies would be strong in the qualities and experience required for self-government. Then, and not till then, would the time have arrived to consider the inclusion of nations which have purged their souls from gangster rule and have shown themselves able to establish and work governments responsible to themselves. That will happen when Germans have seen with their own eyes that despotism fails and that popular government succeeds. I regard as chimerical any proposal to include the Germans in an international commonwealth which has not already included the American as well as the British Commonwealth; and that will not be within one generation after this war.

At the close of the last war public opinion was possessed by the one idea, the League of Nations, by the belief that the peace of the world could be based on compacts between most or all of its sovereign states. In this second war public opinion is again possessed by one idea, that in future the peace of the world can be based on unwritten compacts between the sovereign states of the British and American Commonwealths. The principle is the same, and its second application will, I believe, lead on to calamities great as the

M

first, and perhaps in one generation. American and British democracies can, I believe, put an end to war, but only in so far as they merge their sovereignties into one international sovereignty. Whenever the citizens of the British and American democracies have merged their sovereignties, the peace of the world will be finally secured—then and then only. But I do not believe this can happen till the British democracies, now fighting for life, have first shown for themselves how separate national sovereignties can be merged. I am urging the Union of the British democracies as a necessary step to an Anglo-American Union, which men of my age will not live to see. Holding such views, I feel bound to place them on record, though but a voice crying in the wilderness.

CHAPTER XXIX

# THE PATH TO SECURITY

THE question now before us is how to realize the prospect offered by President Roosevelt and Winston Churchill of a world freed from the fear of war and of unemployment, a world in which the nations can hope to secure a more decent standard of living. In these pages I have noted certain conditions which will, I suggest, have to be recognized and dealt with before we can set our feet on a path which will really lead to this land of promise.

I. There are two closely connected factors which together frustrate progress in social reform. One is fear of impending war; the other is the incapacity of governments, which have to attend to foreign as well as domestic affairs, to keep pace with both.

II. The fear of impending war can never be removed from the British Commonwealth by a government which commands resources no wider than those of Great Britain and Northern Ireland.

III. The mechanized forces required to remove this fear must be trained not in Great Britain but in the Dominions, and especially in Canada. They must have behind them in those countries the industries necessary to supply their equipment. The exigencies of air strategy are empire wide and cannot adequately be provided for on a local scale.

The system outlined in these pages would satisfy these conditions. It would make the defence of the Commonwealth as a whole a first charge on all its resources. It would bring into being a government of men able to devote their whole time and attention to the problems of defence. It would leave the existing governments of Great Britain and of the Dominions free to devote their whole time and attention to problems of social reform.

In an earlier chapter it was argued that the ultimate problem of free systems is not to secure adequate discussion of public questions, essential as that is, but to enable decisions to be reached, and reached in time. It is this failure to reach decisions which has always led systems based on compacts between sovereign states to disaster. The doctrine of unanimity reduces progress to the pace of the slowest, or more often to a standstill, because the slowest member so often prefers to stay where he is. The doctrine that any one nation of the British Commonwealth may loosen its relations with, or indeed go out of, the Commonwealth is now almost unquestioned. On the other hand, it is widely assumed that no two members of the British Commonwealth should agree to enter on closer organic relations until all its members are ready to do the same. My own view is that if two or three of the British democracies were to unite for their common defence on the morrow of war, the rest would follow their example in time to prevent that competition of armaments which must lead on to a third catastrophe.

The thesis advanced in these pages is that no government which commands resources limited to those of Great Britain and Northern Ireland can now undertake to preserve the British Commonwealth from attack, and prevent the recurrence of world wars. If a British Government voicing the views of all parties, as it might on the morrow of war, were to state this clearly, and invite the Dominions to share the burden and control, I believe that their electorates, some of them at any rate, would respond, when the question was put to them by their own governments. The benefits of the new system to those who had joined it would I think ere long become clear to those who remained outside it. They would come to see that the nations inside the union had acquired a firmer grip of their own domestic affairs. They would also see that the need for training mechanized forces in the Dominions was fostering the growth of their national industries and populations.

If Colonel Drew is right that effective mechanized forces cannot be trained in Great Britain, the same difficulty, I imagine, applies to the small democracies of Western Europe. They may build tanks and armoured cars, but they cannot in their restricted areas hope to train men to operate them as Germany can in Central Europe. If they entered the Union their nationals would have to train with the Union forces in the Dominions. Many of them, like the British, would elect to remain there. Again, the migration problem would be solved on lines welcome to all parties concerned.

I think South Africa would be slow to enter the Union, and fear that she may not do so without some internal convulsion. Still, I believe she will enter it at last, and for this compelling reason. The war is teaching her people, as nothing else could, that their national future is inseparable from Africa to the north of them. If the Union we are picturing is established, the control of the British Colonies must pass from the British Government to the Union Government. Such a Government will come to include Canadians, Australians, and New Zealanders, and also Belgians, Dutchmen, Scandinavians, and Frenchmen. South Africa will then find the control of the continent to which she belongs in the hands of a Government in which she alone has no representation. I cannot believe that the people of South Africa would be willing to accept that position indefinitely, more especially if they saw, as I think they would, that the peoples who had entered the Union had increased instead of losing their control of their own domestic affairs. Whenever she joined, she with her wide spaces would take her share in the training of mechanized forces. She would share in the social and economic results.

To tell people the things they like to hear is fatally easy. True leadership begins when a statesman like Winston Churchill has the nerve to dwell on distasteful facts. The future of freedom depends upon how far recognized leaders continue this practice when hostilities with all their horrors have ceased. I believe it is true that the freedom of the British Isles, of the Commonwealth as a whole, and the future peace of the world, can now be preserved only by realizing to the full the policy stated in Canning's resounding phrase: 'I called in the new world to redress the balance of the old.' This master-truth, with its practical implications, will convince the people of these islands when it is uttered by a statesman whose guidance the people have learned to trust. But if and when such a truth is uttered by a leader the people of these islands should also be told with equal frankness of the sacrifices needed to apply it. They ought to be warned in clear unmistakable terms that the days are gone when the peace and safety of this Commonwealth can be preserved by a weak British hegemony. Nay more; these changes are likely to mean a certain transfer of population from the British Isles to the British Dominions. Ere many generations have lived and died, the United Kingdom will have come to stand on a footing of real equality with the Dominions, not only in status but even in population. Canada at any rate is, I predict, destined to contain a number of people larger than the British Isles can properly support.

Such, I believe, are the probable effects on the future of England which the changes required to translate the Atlantic Charter from promise into fact will produce. There are in this country large numbers of men and women in whose marrow and blood the long-standing traditions of British hegemony are deeply inbred. They are often the people who in any great national crisis are the first to devote their strength, their substance, their lives in the public interest. There are many such who, I know, will view with distress and alarm the change in our future status described in these pages. I ask them to believe that proposals which seem to them revolutionary, are the fruit of long years devoted to the study of what measures are needed to save the mother of freedom and her children from the dangers which threaten them with destruction in a mechanized age. It is my profound conviction that nothing short of the change outlined in these pages can avail to secure these beloved islands, and all that they stand for throughout the world, from the fate which has overtaken Norway, Denmark, Holland, Belgium, and France, before the close of the present century, that is to say in the lives of children already born. I ask them to believe that my love of this dear, dear land and her greatness is no other than theirs. And I think she may keep the place she has won in the eyes of the world for all future time; but only if she can show, as I pray to God that she may, that it was not England that spread upon the world, but it was the world that spread upon England; and that was the sure way of greatness.

## CHAPTER XXX

# THE LINE OF DIVISION BETWEEN NATIONAL AND INTERNATIONAL FUNCTIONS

THE Atlantic Charter implies the need of strengthening national governments for the tasks of social reform which they alone can discharge, no less than the need for an international government strong enough to remove the fear of impending war. The creation of an international government means that a line has to be drawn between the powers that are given it and those reserved to existing national governments. That line, however drawn, will raise some difficulties and create some dangers. But it has to be drawn. The best that constructive statesmen can hope to do is to draw it where it will cause the least difficulties and dangers. My own suggestion is that the powers of the international government should be limited to defence, foreign policy, colonies, civil aviation, and effective means of making the cost of these services a first charge on the nations united, leaving all internal and social affairs, including the incidence of taxation between one tax-payer and another, to the national governments where they now rest.

No change like this is worth making unless the international government is given powers sufficient for its paramount task of preventing the recurrence of wars. But powers are inseparable from duties. Every fresh power you give to a government adds to its burden, a fact ignored in the common assumption that to strengthen a government you must add to its legal powers. I learned this truth from the lips of one who had been the most brilliant head of the Treasury in Whitehall, aptly described in *Punch* as 'The mute but not inglorious Lord Welby'. Let me here record what he said on this matter, if only because I have never seen it mentioned in any book on political science.

'A fundamental difficulty is to secure for a central Government the time and knowledge necessary for the men who administer it to do the work that a central government alone can do. It is a great mistake to assume that the strength of a government is increased by adding to its powers, because additional powers always impose additional duties. There are tasks which only a central government can perform. To enable it to discharge those tasks it is wise to devolve on local authorities all the functions you can, not only those that local authorities can perform as well, but even those that they cannot perform quite so well, but somehow or other. The *onus probandi* should always rest with the centralizer.'

Throughout his long career Lord Welby was an ardent social reformer. Through the second half of the nineteenth century he had watched an ever-increasing failure of government in Whitehall to cope with the need of social reform. In the twentieth century an overtaxed cabinet and parliament have, despite the most strenuous efforts, failed to keep pace with the growing need. In *The Times* of the 13th January 1943 Mr. R. D. Denman writes from the House of Commons:

'There is enough valuable matter in the Barlow, Uthwatt, Scott, and Beveridge Reports to keep us busy for years, and the sooner the Government let us get to work on them the better. . . . In especial the Education Bill should be presented with all possible speed. It would not have the ghost of a chance of breathing in the after-war Parliamentary scrum.'

This failure to use accumulating knowledge to rectify wrong social conditions is not peculiar to our British democracy. In Chapter XXVIII I quoted the alarming statement which President Roosevelt made in Oct. 1941 of the numbers rejected for active service on account of physical, mental, or educational defects.

General Lewis Hershey, Director of Selective Service in the U.S.A., has since 'disclosed that about one-third of the men called up were being rejected'.[1]

Social reform is at least as important as the stoppage of war. One cannot imagine unbroken peace in a world that continues to suffer from ignorance, want, ill-health, unemployment, and all the manifold ills to which it has long been heir. A friend to whom I was saying this remarked: 'We must look to the churches and schools rather than to Govern-

[1] *The Times*, 15th Sept. 1942.

ment to give us social reform.' To this I replied that churches and schools must do their part, but no one can produce proper conditions of human welfare in this or in any other country without enacting more drastic legislative measures more rapidly than any democratic system has yet been able to do. In answer to this I am told: 'We have too many laws and too many of them wrong.' But how are we to simplify the existing tangles of statutes and get them straight without drafting and passing amending and consolidating acts? Take the Beveridge report or any plan of social reform you like, and then examine how far you can give effect to it without legislative action. To reduce these evils and to bring their people a better life, governments must reform obsolete laws and the means whereby they administer them. Promise of social reform is a sheer illusion until governments have at their disposal the time necessary to draft and enact the necessary measures. It cannot be done by making speeches or wishful thinking. Orators and the listeners who punctuate their eloquent phrases with applause too often drift into thinking that when a thing has been said it has also been done. The reason why social reform has fallen into such grave arrears is that national governments have to attend to too many things to keep pace with their work. They cannot adapt their laws and systems in time to meet the changes imposed by mechanization at an ever-increasing rate. This explains the astounding ease with which dictators have convinced whole peoples that the principle of a government responsible to themselves must now be renounced, and to accept the only alternative, governments based on closely organized force. World wars are the certain result of governments based on this principle in large and powerful national states. The dogma that such wars have their roots in economic conditions is less than half-way to the truth. Their final cause is failure to develop a system of government responsible to ordinary men which is also competent to effect in time the changes they need.

This analysis brings us straight back to the fundamental truth which this Atlantic Charter grasps and proclaims. We cannot achieve social reform and attain to a better life until we begin to feel that peace amongst nations is firmly established; and we cannot establish peace unless national governments are really equipped to cope with the need of social reform. In a word, peace and social reform are two inseparable ends.

The real obstacle to social reform is that national governments have so much to do that they cannot keep pace with the changes that a mechanized age demands. They, and they only, can effect those changes, and the only way to give them the time they need for their work is to relieve them of the task of maintaining peace, and to give that task to an international government which alone can do it. Both must have powers sufficient for their respective tasks. The international government which derives its authority from an international electorate must have power to make security a first charge on all the resources of all the people to whom it is responsible. The national governments must have all the powers they need to see that the balance of national resources secures so far as is possible a better life for the people to whom they are responsible. The national government must have full power to control the composition and social structure of its own people. We thus reach the conclusion that the two inseparable aims of the Atlantic Charter, security and social reform, can only be attained when security is allocated to a new international government, and social reform reserved to existing national governments.

Here we come back to the point with which this chapter started, that a line has to be drawn between the powers given to an international government and those reserved to existing national governments.

We are thus confronted with the difficulty which always besets the government of men, that law and administration have to draw hard and definite lines across finely shaded facts. I can only think of three cases in which nature has given us definite lines between facts, the difference between the living and the dead, between male and female, and, strangest of all, the difference between human beings and

animals. If 'missing links' had survived, the tasks of legislators would be even more difficult than they are. But foreign
and social affairs are by no means an exception to the rule.
International and national problems are always reacting on
each other. Yet, none the less, we shall not begin to realize
the two inseparable objects proposed by the Atlantic Charter
until we commit one to an international government and reserve the other to national governments. We have to draw
a line and say that on one side the common government has
the last word, whilst on the other side of that line the national
governments have the last word.

My reasons for leaving to national governments the last
word on the incidence of taxation between one citizen and
another, on tariffs, industry, and commerce, are twofold.
Governments can only provide the better life foreshadowed
in the Charter so long as they control the composition and
social structure of the nations they rule. The government
charged with the task of securing the common safety of the
nations united would break down if charged in time of peace
with the task of deciding the composition and structure of
the several nations it protects from attack. Government
resides in the brains and characters of men, and no one group
of human beings could cope with tasks of such infinite diver-
sity. A power given them to do this would be cancelled by
the burden it imposed.

In brief, my proposal is that the international government
should be given power to make security of all the nations it
has to protect a first charge on all their resources, material
and human. All other powers, including the incidence of
taxation between one citizen and another, should in time of
peace be reserved to the national governments. I suggest
that this can be done if the burden of the revenue which the
international government needs for the common defence
were distributed between the nations defended in proportion
to their taxable capacity, as ascertained by a judicial committee of experts. These proportions would constitute a first
charge on the consolidated revenue of each national government, payable to the international treasury without a vote

from the national legislature. Each national government, in framing its budget, would then be free to decide what kind of national taxes were needed to provide a consolidated revenue large enough to meet its quota due to the international government as well as the funds required for its own national administration. The power to decide the distribution of wealth between one citizen and another and thus to control its own social structure would then remain, where it now rests, with each national government. That government would continue to control its own industrial system.

A friendly reviewer in *The Times* argued that this mechanized war has proved that no government could organize an effective defence of the countries it protects unless it controlled the industrial systems of those countries, as the British Government now controls the industries of Great Britain. Under my proposal the international government would lose this control of industry even in Great Britain and acquire no such control in the other nations united for defence.

The force of this criticism must be recognized and the proposal amended to meet it. The government responsible for defence must have power in war, and even when war seriously threatens, to control industry and indeed anything which is needed for effective defence. In times of piping peace the financial power of that government to place contracts will, I believe, enable it to bring into existence, and maintain, potential war factories wherever they may be needed, should war break out. This, in fact, is the situation now in the U.S.A. The powers of the central government to control industry, labour, prices, and food, which exist only in the most limited way in time of peace, become absolute when war threatens.

## CHAPTER XXXI
## 'INFLUENCE' AND 'GOVERNMENT'

THE last chapter had just been written when a letter reached me from an international lawyer who, after spending years at Geneva, is now in the service of one of the Allied Governments. The writer expressed his personal agreement with the general position outlined in *Decision* and *Action*, but added the following comment:

'I prefer the formula for defining the jurisdiction of international government set out on p. 49 of *Decision* (restricted to security and what is inseparable from it)[1] to that set out on p. 7 of *Action*.[2] A joint foreign policy goes, in my opinion, rather too far at the outset, for a great deal of it would not be directly a matter of defence or security, but would rather depend on commercial or social policy. The point is delicate because *no logical division will hold water and yet some division will be necessary*.'

In the last sentence the writer has put in his own words the point I have made in the last chapter, that governments have constantly to treat interests that fade into each other as if they were in separate compartments, with a definite line between them. The proposal to entrust matters affecting the issues of peace and war to an international government, whilst reserving to national governments the control of social, commercial, and industrial affairs is a typical example of this difficulty. Migration and tariffs are amongst the causes that contribute to wars. By the word 'control' I mean that the

[1] The control of social affairs in their widest aspect must be left to national governments, yet cannot be so left unless they continue to control the distribution of taxation and therefore tariffs within their several jurisdictions. The international government must be restricted to security and matters which are quite inseparable therefrom, for which purpose it must have effective power to make security a first charge on all the resources of the nations included.

[2] A joint foreign policy. A joint defence policy. A common budget for defence purposes. One joint legislative body for defence questions only which would discuss the foreign situation, the danger of war, the necessary measures of defence; and would determine not individual taxes but the proportion of individual State revenues to be devoted to joint defence. One joint executive body for defence questions only, responsible for framing the estimates necessary to secure the Union as a whole from attack, and to lay them before the legislative body.

authority in which it is vested has the last word, the final decision. A political system in which questions cannot be brought to final decision by some authority or other leads to deadlock, chaos, and therefore anarchy. It cannot live without the power to decide; but it cannot live by that alone. Nearly all the things which a government does are done by persuasion without resort to its power to compel; though, without that power, it comes to a standstill.

American history throws some light on the necessary parts which persuasion and the power to compel must play in the government of men. In 1783 Great Britain agreed to recognize the independence of the thirteen American States. The Congress of these States, as united by the Articles of Confederation, had then to face the task of carrying out the terms of the Treaty, and also of meeting the debt-charges on loans it had raised in the war. This it could only do by requesting the governments of the thirteen States to take certain action, and their thirteen legislatures to vote the money it needed to meet the debt-charges. Some of these States neglected to take the steps required to discharge the terms of peace, or to remit to Congress their quota of the funds needed to defray the charges on debt. By 1786 the Government of the United States had failed to discharge the terms of peace and was in default to its creditors. Then the mischief began to spread to the States themselves, in which private debtors, refusing to pay their debts and taxes, began to resist the enforcement of law by their own State governments. A rebellion against the Government of Massachusetts was headed by Colonel Shay.

Things had come to this pass when Colonel Lee wrote to Washington:

'My dear General,
We are all in dire apprehension that a beginning of Anarchy, with all its calamities is made, and we have no means to stop the dreadful work. Knowing your unbounded influence, and believing that your appearance among the seditious might bring them back to peace and reconciliation, individuals suggest the propriety of an invitation to you from Congress to pay us a visit.'

To this Washington replied:

'You talk, my good Sir, of employing influence to appease the present tumults in Massachusetts. I know not where that influence is to be found, nor, if attainable, that it would be a proper remedy for these disorders. *Influence is not government.* Let us have a government, by which our lives, liberties, and properties, will be secured, or let us know the worst at once.'[1]

Washington, however, did exert his influence to induce the States to send delegates to a convention at Philadelphia. There the question how the United States could be given the faculty of genuine government was faced and answered. Under the Articles of Confederation Congress consisted of delegates from the State assemblies. It could only obtain the funds it needed by asking the assemblies to vote their quotas. The request was widely ignored, and Congress had no power to enforce it. In a word, the influence of Congress on the States had failed to produce the funds without which Congress could not discharge the duties laid on it. So the delegates gathered at Philadelphia framed a new constitution under which Congress was empowered to impose the taxes it needed direct on the individual taxpayer. If he failed to pay, Congress could bring him before courts of its own, and enforce their judgements by sending police of its own to seize his goods. Congress was also made to represent, not the State assemblies, but the people themselves. A Congress elected by the taxpayers was empowered to enforce the payment of taxes on individual taxpayers. In practice it is seldom necessary to use this power because it is there and can be employed in the last resort. It was this change that established peace, order, and the rule of law on the continental scale in America.

I have often used these memorable words 'Influence is not government' in answering those blind leaders of the blind who have taught the world that international problems can be solved by co-operation only, and have helped thereby to lay it in ruins. I am frequently charged with teaching that such problems are soluble only by force. On the contrary, I know

[1] Marshall, *The Life of Washington*, vol. v, pp. 137–8.

by experience that a government must do most of the things which it has to do by influence, that is to say, by persuasion, without resorting to force. I remember a gifted man who was fond of saying that all problems are soluble in alcohol. He died of delirium tremens. It does not follow that alcohol is without its proper and indeed necessary uses.

In actual fact the government in Washington covers a vast field of activities in which it has no power to compel. When its constitution was drafted in 1787 no one had then thought that it might be its duty to provide people with any kind of security against illness or unemployment. More than a century later measures to provide such security in England were enacted at the instance of Mr. Lloyd George. This example started a movement for similar measures in America. Congress was powerless to legislate on the matter. But it had power to vote subsidies to State governments willing to enact the necessary measures, which went far to meet the cost. With its wide command of financial resources, the federal authority was thus able to meet the public need by virtue of influence. A government provided with funds can accomplish all sorts of things which it has no power to enforce by law. For this reason I think that a government of United Nations with a first charge on all their resources could exercise an influence sufficient to prevent fatal conflicts between the wide powers of the National governments over their own domestic affairs and its own narrowly restricted powers.

The results of American experience may be summarized as follows. The restricted modicum of compulsion or 'government' which the Congress of Philadelphia introduced into the central authority of the United States has made it possible for the system to work under presidents like Fillmore, Hayes, or Harding, men of very ordinary abilities whose names are now almost forgotten. The Articles of Confederation, in which that element was wanting, could not be made to work, even by the influence of Washington, an influence which was greater than any which any leader has ever exercised in a democratic community.

For these reasons I think that a government of United

Nations with a first charge on all their resources for the common defence widely interpreted, a government, therefore, in the real sense of that word, would have the influence necessary to prevent a fatal conflict between the wide powers of the National governments over their own domestic affairs and its own circumscribed powers. An international government responsible for the common security of the several nations it represents, cannot be otherwise than concerned with their policies in respect of trade migration and shipping.[1] It must therefore collect, and digest, and publish information on these matters on a scale more wide and impartial and thorough than could be attained by the national governments. On the basis of this information, it must develop views of its own as to what policies in respect of these matters are required to promote the well-being of the Union and also of the world at large. Such views to become operative must be discussed and accepted from time to time by the Union legislature. The Union government and legislature should formulate rules to which national governments and legislatures would be asked and expected to conform. Examples of such rules may be found on page 6 of a paper issued in June 1941 by the International Chamber of Commerce, entitled *War of Ideas*.

The fact that the electorates of all these nations would be represented in the Union legislature must be held in mind. As things now are in the British Commonwealth, the Government of the United Kingdom, and that government only, is responsible for the security of the Commonwealth as a whole. It in fact determines the issues of peace and war whatever the Statute of Westminster may say. But its influence over the Dominion Governments is fatally weakened by the fact that the Imperial Government is responsible to a legislature in which the Dominion peoples have no representatives. Obviously a government and a legislature composed of spokesmen from a number of nations could influence their national governments to a far greater extent than a government which represents one of those nations only. But the constitution

[1] See next chapter.

of any such Union must specify clearly where the ultimate decision in such matters rests. For the reasons given in these pages the ultimate power to decide in matters of trade migration and probably shipping must rest with the national governments. The influence of the Union government would, in my view, suffice to prevent any conflict with a national government which might lead to a rupture of the Union.

## CHAPTER XXXII

# FUNCTIONS INSEPARABLE FROM DEFENCE

THE conclusion reached in the last chapter may now be applied to the questions of tariffs, migration, and shipping. Some critics have started by rejecting these proposals as a whole, on the ground that no self-governing Dominion will ever consent to merge its sovereignty in an international government charged with control of the issues of peace and war. The same critics have then gone on to criticize the proposal in detail, on the ground that no government could control the issues of peace and war for a number of separate nations unless it also controlled tariffs and migration. They did not, however, mention the fact that the government of Great Britain and Northern Ireland had been left to control the issues of peace and war for the whole British Commonwealth, without any kind of control over tariffs and migration in the self-governing Dominions. I now go so far as to say that this situation has led straight to a war with Japan, which at one time threatened the very existence of Australia and New Zealand and indeed South Africa, not only as free, but as European communities. Can anyone doubt that one reason why Japan has attacked the British and American Commonwealths is because the Anglo-Saxon communities are as fixed in their purpose to maintain their character as European communities as Japan herself is to maintain her own character as an Asiatic community?

The question of migration is a greater menace to peace than tariffs. The policy of a white Australia and New Zealand was resented more by the Japanese than their policies of protection. Nor must we forget that this policy has also been used to exclude the peoples of India and China, immensely greater in number than that of Japan. The U.S.A., Canada, and South Africa are equally resolute to exclude Asiatics. We are thus brought face to face with the chief issue I raised on page 78 of Chap. XVII:

'Man, as science has now convinced us, has aeons before him

on this planet. We can surely foresee a world government and stabilized peace in course of time, without assuming a human society in which all the racial elements have been mixed in one conglomerate, following one standardized way of life. Such a human society would have acquired the uniformity of a jelly-fish, a one-celled organism, the lowest form of physical life. The highest form of physical life is the human body. Its component organs—heart, lungs, liver, brain, &c.—are all of different chemical composition, and highly different structure, all harmonized in one supreme unit. The highest form of organism is made up of highly differentiated organs, fitly joined together in one. And so the supreme unity which human society should attain is one in which its component nations are highly differentiated in composition as well as in structure. It has been the function of national states to accomplish this. To preserve and develop this differentiation will still be their function. But the chief impediment to the discharge of this function is now the insecurity caused by the state of anarchy between them.'

I do not recede from this position. A world in which nations are free each to develop their own individual character is to me the hope of civilization. They must each control their own composition and social structure. But free nations cannot do this except in so far as they unite their resources in peace, as in war, to make themselves jointly too strong to attack. The practical way to prevent war on the British Commonwealth is not to create an Imperial government to control the migration and fiscal policies of its component nations, but a government competent to marshal all its resources in a system of common defence too strong for any aggressor to challenge. Japan herself never attacked the British Commonwealth until it was locked in a struggle for life or death with two major powers which controlled the whole of Europe west of Russia.

This leads me to deal with a further point which I have not touched in the previous chapters. Before Japan attacked the British and American Commonwealths she was able to establish a basis for her forces in Indo-China with the aid of the Vichy Government. From this basis her armies have conquered Malaya, Burma, and the Dutch East Indies. Australia,

New Zealand, India, and Ceylon were threatened with invasion. Her achievement in sinking American ships at Pearl Harbour and British battleships off the coast of Malaya had given her naval command of the sea-routes to the countries she had conquered and to those she threatened with invasion.

We must hold in mind the length of these routes across which these armies must be supplied from Japan. Her route to Indo-China is about 3,000 miles, to Rangoon 5,000 miles, to Australia about 4,000 miles. Troops and supplies across those miles must be carried in merchant vessels. If she has not enough vessels her victorious armies will presently languish and ultimately perish.

The same is true, on an even larger scale, of the United Nations. Their production of munitions exceeds that of the Axis. But these superior supplies of munitions are of no more value than scrap-iron until they are transported across the seas to the battlefields. On the 1st June 1942 *The Times* correspondent in New York wrote as follows:

'Great quantities of American goods and munitions are being shipped constantly to Europe and to the Near East and the Far East, but not so great as could be shipped if there were more vessels to carry them. It is no secret that at this time United Nations ships are being sunk faster than United Nations ships are being built.'

In time of peace merchant ships are normally built, owned, and operated by private owners, while warships are built, owned, and operated by governments. But in world wars merchant ships are as essential to victory as warships. The merchant marine and the navy are each useless unless both exist or can be created in adequate strength.

The 38th report of the British Imperial Shipping Committee published in 1938 shows how much more clearly this vital strategic factor had been grasped in Japan than in any of the countries now at war with her. This report shows how after the last war the Japanese Government set itself to ousting ships under the British flag from the carrying trade of the Far East. This she was able to do with far-reaching success by playing off against each other the conflicting interests of

Great Britain, India, Australia, New Zealand, and of their respective producers and mercantile interests. The results of her operations were briefly given in the House of Lords on the 4th June 1942 by Lord Craigmyle. In the years between the two wars British tonnage went down by over 1,500,000 tons, and when this war broke out we had over 2,000 fewer vessels than in the last one. In the same period Japanese tonnage had increased from 1,500,000 tons to well over 5,000,000 tons. To begin with, the whole trade between India and Japan was carried in British ships. When this war broke out 73 per cent. of that trade was carried in Japanese ships.

These results were attained by Japan partly by government subsidies and loans enabling shipowners to scrap obsolete vessels and build new ones, but even more through the agency of her vast commercial organizations. To take one instance, the wool-growers of Australia and New Zealand were offered lower rates on Japanese ships. They accepted the offer, closing their eyes to the fact that the disappearance of British shipping, including Australian and New Zealand ships, would not only weaken their defence as partners in a maritime commonwealth, but would presently leave them at the mercy of a foreign monopoly. The relative cheapness of Japanese labour, of course, made it easy for their ships to offer the lower rates.

We now see the results. The ships which enabled Japan to conquer our Eastern Empire and threaten Australia, New Zealand, India, and even South Africa, were largely paid for by producers and merchants under the British flag. The 38th report of the Imperial Shipping Commission shows what happens in practice when sovereign nations have accepted co-operation as a panacea for ensuring their safety. It is time that the dreams of the realists should be brought to the test of experience and facts.

The immediate point with which we are here concerned is this. The experience we are now facing has shown that any international government charged with the task of averting war must have the power to secure that it has under its own flag a merchant marine large enough to secure its transport needs in war, should war break out. The power such a government will need is, I think, the power of money, which under these proposals it would have. I do not think that it would be necessary to take from any of the legislatures of the United Nations the powers they now have to control their own mercantile marines. Should experience prove, however, that the international government cannot in fact ensure the maintenance under its flag of the merchant shipping it would need in time of war by its power to grant subsidies for the maintenance, and loans for the building, of merchant ships, it must be given whatever additional powers are needed for the purpose of rendering itself too strong to attack. The problems involved in control of shipping are so intricate that experience alone can decide the point.

We are now in a position to answer the simpler question where the control of transport, whether of persons, mails, or goods, by air between the nations united should lie. The experience of this war may possibly show that no power however strong can really control communications by sea against the submarines which a highly industrialized enemy can construct. It may show that development of transport by air on a scale undreamt of before is needed to win the war. In order to render the free nations immune from attack by aggressors, the maintenance of an adequate equipment of carrier planes may be just as essential as the maintenance of a large enough mercantile marine. Such a service lies in the future and has not behind it the long and complicated history of shipping with all the vested interests concerned. The argument in favour of giving the international government complete control of all aviation between the nations united, and with it the duty of creating an adequate service would seem to be conclusive. The national governments would continue to control and to exercise power to develop civil aviation in their own territories; but the power of the international government to promote and control civil aviation between those territories should be absolute.

## CHAPTER XXXIII

## COLONIES

IN previous chapters I have tried to explain what I mean by faith. The necessary prelude to any action that can lead to useful results is a clear vision of the object we are seeking to obtain. Too much that passes for faith has begun and ended in mere vision, swallowed like a cocktail to produce a feeling of exaltation. Faith and works are not really opposed, but are so much parts of one whole that each will perish apart from the other. As action will go utterly awry without clear vision of its aim, so faith will decay and perish unless those who hold it think out the positive tasks it imposes upon them, and nerve themselves to the effort of discharging those tasks. The sound course for men with a faith is to look squarely at the world as it is, see where it falls short of the vision before their minds, think what steps must be taken by them to move the world towards their vision, and then take them with all their might.

As I write, the world is involved in a struggle, in all its history the most widely destructive of life and property. The number of peoples not actively engaged as belligerents are a minority, and even their lives are profoundly affected. For the moment our efforts are bent on winning the war; but even so, we cannot evade the questions—What is our object in fighting it? What is our aim when we have won it?

For myself I find these questions answered in outline by the Atlantic Charter. We are fighting this war to secure a better life for all who inhabit this planet. That is the final object of all public policy rightly conceived. The greatest mistake which public opinion and governments can make is to treat the maintenance of peace as the final end of policy. That mistake has always led, and will always lead, to war. War and the constant threat of war are the immediate obstacles to the better life, which must always be kept in view as the final end. The prevention of further war is the first thing to be done when hostilities cease; but by no means the last. I therefore suggest that the first thing we have to consider is our own actual power as things now are to prevent the recurrence of future wars.

This task was, on the whole, discharged by one government for the century after the world war which ended in 1815. In the words of Professor Carr, 'the British fleet not only guaranteed immunity from major wars, but policed the high seas and offered equal security to all'.[1]

The security thus established enabled the U.S.A. in the course of the nineteenth century to include thirty-five other states, in addition to the thirteen which had founded the Union in 1787. By this inclusion the U.S.A. became the greatest power in the world founded on free institutions. This security also enabled free institutions to take root in Canada, Australia, New Zealand, and South Africa. The predominant power of the British Government at sea also enabled it to establish the rule of law for the whole sub-continent of India, and thus to lay the foundation on which alone its people, one-sixth of the human race, can hope to establish self-government for themselves. Predominance at sea also meant that the British Government was unwillingly led to assume that ever-growing responsibility for the government and protection of backward races in the Atlantic, Pacific, and throughout the African continent. How unwilling it was is shown by a resolution which a House of Commons committee recorded in 1865:

'that all further extensions of territory or assumption of government or new treaty offering any protection to native tribes would be inexpedient.'[2]

Even in those days there were Englishmen anxious to spread British dominion; but that policy was not favoured by the British Government till the closing years of the century. With governments in Europe it was otherwise. The craving of German, French, and Italian chauvinists to bring wide areas in distant continents and oceans under their own flag was reflected in their national policies, and made the

[1] *The Twenty Years' Crisis*, p. 297.
[2] The Royal Institute of International Affairs, Information Dept. Papers, No. 18, p. 6.

pace. The British Government was forced to abandon the policy formally enunciated in 1865 for reasons which were partly strategic, partly economic, but also humanitarian. When in 1884 Bismarck initiated the policy of German annexations, the British Admiralty, responsible for safeguarding the route to India, could not afford to see the harbours of Walfisch Bay or of Santa Lucia go under the German flag.

The governments of Europe by no means adopted the British policy of the open door. Some annexations meant the exclusion of British trade from the areas annexed, though British colonial possessions were open on equal terms to foreign traders.

Humanitarian reasons were also urgent. So long as the territory of a primitive people was not controlled by a civilized government, European traders were free to exploit it in search of gain and without restraint. Let us glance at four separate examples in widely distant parts of the world. In New Zealand German traders developed a lucrative trade in tattooed Maori heads, for specimens of which museums were ready to pay as much as £500. The Maori tribes were slaughtering each other to obtain such heads to trade for arms. When the British and French Governments had established a court to decide the claims of European adventurers to hold land in New Hebrides, the claims were found to amount to 14 times the total area of the island. The Sandwich Islands became an emporium of the traffic in opium, till the Government of the U.S.A., more opposed to a policy of expansion than even the British Government, was forced to annex the islands to suppress the traffic. In Swaziland the paramount chief, whom the British Government had recognized as a sovereign, sold to foreign concessionaires for liquor the whole of the land, and every right that his people possessed. For humanitarian reasons alone, civilized governments would have been forced to annex primitive countries, to protect them from spoliation by their own nationals.

Such motives combined with reasons of strategy and trade to force the British Government, against the policy formulated in 1865, to join in the scramble for annexations. In

Africa considerable areas were taken by Germany, France, Spain, Portugal, Belgium, and Italy. But as always when sovereign nations compete, the result was largely decided by relative power. The major share fell to Great Britain, whose fleet controlled the routes to these territories.

In result a continent much larger than India, with a population smaller in size and more uniform in race, was parcelled out amongst a number of sovereign powers in Europe. There was for tropical Africa no one government, as in India, to view the interests of its people as a whole, and plan their future.

By the end of the nineteenth century the people of the British Isles had become responsible for the peace of nearly a quarter of mankind, scattered all over the globe, and for maintaining internal order, except in the self-governing Dominions. Through the Parliament of the United Kingdom, which they, and they only, elected, they were answerable for peace, order, and good government in India, Ceylon, Burma, Malaya, for numerous islands in the Caribbean and Pacific, and for great parts of tropical Africa.

That these special responsibilities rested on the people of the British Isles and nowhere else came to be regarded as the order of nature, not only by the British themselves, but also throughout those communities whose freedom and institutions had sprung from these islands, in America, Canada, Australia, New Zealand, and South Africa. In ages to come historians will marvel that men could ever have thought that a system on which the peace of the whole world depended could rest securely on foundations so narrow.

These pages are based on the postulate that the duty of each man to his fellow men is the basis of human society. That postulate implies a duty owed by civilized peoples to backward peoples who lie at their mercy. The nature and scope of this obligation can be seen if we concentrate on the case of the African people. The opening of the seas to America by Columbus and to Asia by Vasco da Gama brought into general use in Europe three new products, sugar, cotton, and tobacco. The tropical and subtropical regions of the newly discovered Americas were suitable for raising all three—given the labour for planting. The problem of labour was met by the importation of slaves from the African coast. To supply the demand the interior of Africa was left at the mercy of Arab slave-hunters. Bloodshed and anarchy closed it for centuries to any other kind of trade than that in human flesh. In the nineteenth century the trade in slaves was stopped in time to save the remnants of these backward peoples from extinction.

The stoppage of the slave-trade opened the continent to traders who came in quest of products other than human beings, such as ivory, copra, fibre, rubber, and cocoa. To obtain these products the traders naturally offered things which savage tribes are most anxious to get, which always include guns and liquor, the abuse of which they learned from civilized men. The immediate results on African society were only less tragic than those of the slave-trade itself.

If the postulate on which these pages are based be true, it follows that all civilized people who use for their own comfort tropical products like cotton, tobacco, cocoa, or rubber, and produce articles like guns and liquor to give in exchange for them, have a moral responsibility for effects which such trade has on tropical peoples. The only effective means whereby this responsibility can be discharged is through their governments. To control their traders, governments had to administer the countries in which they traded. We have seen the course of events whereby, in the English-speaking world, this responsibility was concentrated on a government responsible only to the British Isles. Except in a few minor cases no responsibility for governing backward races was assumed by the peoples who lived in America and the self-governing Dominions. If the British Government and people had shirked the overwhelming responsibility which the course of events laid upon them, the disasters now visiting the world might have been even greater than they are. But these disasters are now showing how inadequate the resources of these islands were to the task assumed.

No one would now suggest that in England the poorer

districts, the depressed areas, should be left to subsist on the revenues which they themselves can produce. Every thoughtful man would agree that the richer districts must always contribute to the well-being of poorer districts. This also applies in a field wide as the world itself. In his *African Survey* Lord Hailey has pointed out that backward communities in tropical regions cannot hope to attain to a decent standard of life until they receive substantial help from civilized countries. He thinks that the British Government should spend at least £10,000,000 a year on its African colonies. In the same spirit Miss Perham pleads that the British Government should find another £3,000,000 a year for a long period, to help Abyssinia on to its feet. In a letter to *The Times* of the 31st August 1942 Mr. Patrick Donner, M.P., writes:

'Cheeseparing will not do. A new deal is required for all the colonies—let us face it—in which hundreds of millions will have to be spent. The Government cannot sit back and rely upon the démodé ideas of the nineteenth century. . . .

'What is required is a Lend-Lease Act. We must recognize that the Government will have to lend great sums carrying at first no interest, and for many years afterwards a very low rate.

'. . . The colonial problems which the war raises are a challenge and an opportunity. It is my faith that we shall not be found lacking in vision and in statesmanship.'

Such proposals, sound as they are, involve a break with the recognized policy of the British Treasury. That policy has been that each separate colony must be made to live on its own resources. There have been exceptions to the rule; but if Lord Hailey and the Royal Commission on the West Indies are right, the general observance of this Treasury policy has meant, and if still followed will continue to mean, a deplorably low standard of life in the Crown Colonies.

In the same column as Mr. Donner's letter another M.P., Mr. John Dugdale, wrote as follows:

'With the exception of question-time—and I admit that it is a big exception—there are scarcely more than a couple of days in the year devoted to a discussion of colonial affairs. And when they do take place, debates are as likely as not concentrated on one particular aspect of the affairs of a single colony. I have not got a Hansard beside me as I write, but I would hazard a guess that the affairs of such colonies as Fiji, Mauritius, British Guiana, and Gambia—to pick out a few at random—have not been discussed by the House during the past five years. . . .

'Whatever method is adopted, however, I hope that something is done at an early date to enable colonial affairs to receive the consideration that is their due—a consideration that in some cases has been withheld until disaster has overtaken them.'

The Treasury was right in its judgement that the British Isles, rich as they are, could not hope in the long run to afford the charges required to create a decent life for the vast communities brought under their government—charges such as are now proposed. Will anyone in touch with political realities assume that Members of Parliament, acutely conscious of the needs of their own constituents after this war, will continue to vote £13,000,000 a year for the next generation for African territories, in addition to sums they would have to vote on the same principle for the West Indies, Pacific regions, and countries like Malaya? There a vast expenditure, as Mr. Donner points out, will be needed to repair the immeasurable destruction of war.

The United Kingdom electorate is responsible for the peace, order, and good government of somewhere about 440,000,000 people who do not as yet govern themselves. As the complications of modern life have multiplied the tasks laid on the British Government, and therefore the issues upon which the electors are asked to decide the question 'Who is to govern?', these issues are now so many that in practice some of them are never before the electors' minds. Colonial issues are rarely mentioned at general elections. Electors naturally think first of issues which touch them at home. Fear of storms from the field of the Home Office is usually foremost with Government Whips. When I was serving in Whitehall it seemed to me vigorous, efficient, and alert, a stream kept clear by the strong current of public opinion and interest that flowed down its bed; for millions at its doors were concerned

with its work. The Colonial Office seemed like a backwater;
for members of the public interested in its work were limited
to earnest specialists and the few thousands who read what
they wrote. When colonial estimates come before Parliament,
the House is empty because members know that the issues
they raise will not be in the minds of the voters when next
they come up for election. When Mr. Harold Macmillan
was introducing the colonial estimates, the *Spectator* remarked that eight Members of Parliament were present.

In Lord Hailey's view[1] the end and object of British colonial
policy is to fit the backward peoples under our rule to govern
themselves. Such an object is not too easy for officers who
administer backward peoples to keep uppermost in their
minds. Their immediate task of maintaining order and efficiency must tend to push into the background the idealist aim
of the distant government they serve. When a new official
or magistrate is needed, it is much easier and more effective
to import a countryman of their own from England than to
appoint a native to the post. Yet no real progress will be made
towards self-government unless more and more of the natives
are trained and exercised in administrative and judicial work.
Public opinion in Great Britain is not so active or well informed as to bring this about, for such issues are never before
the voters at general elections.

The British colonial system will, I believe, bear comparison
with any other: but no one can examine its working at close
quarters, as Lord Moyne's Commission has done in the
West Indies, or Sir Alan Pim and Lord Hailey in Africa,
without becoming aware of some grave short-comings. On
these public opinion fastens in the English-speaking communities which have assumed little or no responsibility for
the government of backward peoples. It is now more than
thirty years since I first visited the Dominions to study the
Imperial problem. The impression I got was that in intellectual and labour circles the government of subject peoples
by civilized states was regarded as something so inherently
wrong that they wished to have nothing to do with it. It was

[1] *Romanes Lecture*, May 1941. Oxford University Press.

pitch, sure to defile them if touched. The results of leaving capitalists free to exploit the vast resources of regions like tropical Africa or Malaya had not been before their minds. It was not till Australia and New Zealand had accepted mandates in the neighbouring islands that these peoples began to grasp this side of the problem.

Thus British sea-power, while preventing world wars for a century, made the fraction of civilized society resident in the British Isles responsible for the peace, order, good government, and future welfare of at least 440,000,000 people as yet unable to govern themselves. The world wars of this century have been widely regarded as a struggle between 'the haves' and 'the have-nots', between satisfied and unsatisfied powers, between countries like the British and American Commonwealths, France, Belgium, Holland, and Russia on the one hand, and Germany, Italy, and Japan on the other. The phrase shows that the future of backward peoples in Asia, Africa, and the Pacific is one of the great issues at stake. But that issue has been obscured by the equivocal meaning of the word 'have'. To commonwealths this word has meant political control of subject territories, to be exercised primarily for the benefit of the people who live in them. In the British and American Commonwealths it has meant that this control was to be used to help these people in time to govern themselves. As stated above, our administrators have tended to lose sight of that ultimate goal, through lack of adequate knowledge and supervision on the part of the government and people of the British Isles. But whatever our local failures in detail, no truthful historian will say that exploitation has been our dominant motive. Nor will he deny that sincere, if inadequate, steps have been taken towards helping backward peoples to acquire self-government. With governments like those of Germany, Italy, or Japan, the word 'have', as applied to colonies, means exactly what an estate with serfs tied to the soil meant to a Russian Boyar in the last century. They have never disguised their view that colonies and their peoples were to be held for the benefit of Germans, Italians, and Japanese. Their régimes as established in

Damaraland, Abyssinia, and Korea were expressions of this idea. Nor would they become 'satisfied' nations till the regions under the British flag were divided amongst them. Such principles work to their practical issue with inexorable logic. As the 'Herrenvolk' conquers Europe the same principle is applied not merely to Poles, but to kindred peoples of Nordic race in Norway and Holland. In the 'new order' every people in Europe is to work for the Herrenvolk, supplying food and raw materials for Germans whose monopoly of industry would empower them to hold the subject nations about them under their iron control.

The responsibility of all civilized peoples to backward races is thus inseparably connected with world peace and world war. That the people of the British Isles were alone responsible for the peace, order, and good government of 440,000,000 politically backward people was, throughout the English-speaking world, assumed as part of the order of nature. They and they only were responsible for defending this vast Empire as a whole, for the measures required to prevent attack on it and attempts to dismember it.

In circles beyond the English-speaking communities an idea took root that the main responsibility of keeping the peace of the whole world lay on the shoulders of the British people. On the 14th March 1925 Sir Austen Chamberlain, as Secretary of State for Foreign Affairs, addressed the House of Commons in the following words:

'The British Empire, detached from Europe by its Dominions, linked to Europe by these Islands, can do what no other nation on the face of the earth can do, and from East to West alike there comes to me the cry that after all, it is in the hands of the British Empire, and if they will that there shall be no war, there will be no war.'[1]

Ten years later the Abyssinian crisis revealed how completely the world had learned to look to the British Government alone for the forces needed to prevent aggression. On the 19th December 1935 Sir Samuel Hoare, speaking in the House of Commons, said:

[1] *Commons Debates*, 5th series, vol. clxxxii, col. 332.

O

'We alone have taken these military precautions. There is the British fleet in the Mediterranean, there are the British reinforcements in Egypt, in Malta, and Aden. Not a ship, not a machine, not a man has been moved by any other member state.'

When in 1925 Sir Austen Chamberlain told the House of Commons that the whole world was looking to the British Empire to prevent an outbreak of war, he himself in 1921 had signed the treaty which gave Dominion status to the Irish Free State. Even he had not paused to consider, or to ask the world to consider, whether a government whose resources were limited thereby to those of Great Britain and six counties in Northern Ireland had still the power it wielded in the previous century to prevent the recurrence of world wars. The will of the British people to prevent such wars was never in doubt. The real question was whether it still wielded the necessary power. Events had answered that question in 1914 and were destined to give it the same answer in 1939. At the moment of writing Japan controls the Pacific. Hong Kong, Penang, Singapore, Rangoon, Mandalay, the Dutch East Indies, and the Philippines have fallen to her arms. Till 1944 Australia, New Zealand, Ceylon, and India were threatened with invasion.

The key to this situation was Singapore. It was fortified at a cost of £18,234,000. To this cost New Zealand contributed £1,000,000, Hong Kong £250,000, Johore £500,000, the Federated Malay States £2,000,000. The balance of £14,484,000 was paid by the taxpayers of the United Kingdom.[1] It has taken this war to reveal to Australia, what New Zealand had seen, that Singapore was at least as important to her as to the British Isles.

As Admiral Richmond has pointed out (see appendix to this chapter), these £18,000,000 spent on the military equipment of Singapore were a present to Japan, unless at the same time we were able to make sufficient provision for controlling the sea routes in the Pacific as well as in the Atlantic and the Mediterranean.

[1] Answer given in the House of Commons, 24th June 1942, to a question put by Sir John Power, M.P.

As always the cry goes up for scapegoats; but historians will ask how anything else could have happened under a system which placed the security of this Far Eastern Empire on less than two small islands, the most remote from that Empire on the face of the globe. The position will, we hope, be retrieved by the aid of American forces. But when retrieved it must then be maintained,

> 'And duller shouldst thou be than the fat weed,
> That rots itself in ease on Lethe wharf'

who believes that it can be maintained, as in the nineteenth century, by the government of Great Britain and Northern Ireland on the opposite side of the world.

## Appendix to Chapter XXXIII

### Extracts from Admiral Sir Herbert Richmond's article in the Fortnightly Review, *March 1942*

Singapore has fallen. It is the greatest disaster that we have suffered since the collapse of France, the most serious blow that has been struck not only at the British Empire but also at our allies, China and Russia. It paves the way to invasions of the British possessions in India and the Indian Seas. Australia and the Dutch Indies, the trade of India and the communications of the armies of the Empire, of Russia and of China, the supplies which pass through the Indian Ocean are threatened. The Burma Road can be cut as effectively at sea in the Bay of Bengal as in Burma or China. Japanese ambitions, now whetted with success, embrace the capture of every port in the Indian Ocean as far as Aden; and they will not stop there.

The immediate impulse in many minds is to find scapegoats for this grave disaster. The blame is variously thrown on the recent Commander-in-Chief; on the Administrations which, it is said, in the years before the war neglected to provide for an attack by land, their eyes being confined to the sea front; on those who rejected the advice of Lord Trenchard to confide the defence to the Air Force. Blame is thrown too on the present Ministers for failing to send reinforcements of land and air forces in adequate numbers, or to accompany the two battleships with aircraft. Australian critics complain that the Government in

London, focussing its attention entirely on the security of Britain, has neglected the interests of the Empire in the South Pacific.

The Prime Minister has given his explanation of the reason why it was not considered possible to provide at the same time for the armies in Egypt, give Russia the aircraft and tanks and other munitions, of which she was in urgent need, and send reinforcements to Singapore. Whatever may be the right and the wrong in this matter, the real reason for the loss of Singapore lies further: and the persons and policy that are responsible for it are not far to seek. The persons are those Ministers who have directed the policy of our armaments for the last score of years; the Parliaments which have silently acquiesced in that policy; the Press which, with a few notable exceptions, has either supported the policy of reduction of British sea power or failed to point out the danger into which the folly and vanity of Ministers was leading the country; the successive Boards of Admiralty whose members, knowing (it must be presumed) the inadequacy of the provision that was being made, and the erroneous strategical conceptions of the Ministers, kept silence and left the public to assume that their silence implied their concurrence. The public itself is not free from blame. Indifferent to the matter, and concerned with its own comforts and pleasures, it allowed the questions of national defence to be settled without enquiry. Nor are the Dominions without their share of censure. Ever since the first Colonial Conference in 1887, when the need for sharing the burden of the cost of Imperial defence was pointed out by Jan Hofmeyr, attention had been drawn to the need for the Dominions to take a proportionate share—proportionate either in terms of population, value of sea-borne trade or some other criterion—in the cost of the common defence, the maintenance of sea power which is the only possible form of security for our scattered Commonwealth of islands. The expenditure per head of population on the navy by the several Dominions and the United Kingdom was given by the late Lord Lothian (*Round Table*, November, 1910) for the financial year 1909–10 as follows:—United Kingdom 15s. 6d., Canada nil, Australia 1s. 6d., South Africa 1s. 6d., New Zealand 2s. 2½d., Newfoundland 3d. An increase in the Dominion contributions was agreed to in the Conference of 1909 but the disproportion still remained and has never been adjusted.

The fundamental reason for the loss of Singapore and the further losses that will follow is not the lack of local defence either in the present war or in the past preparations. Errors there may have been. It may well be—on this I can offer no opinion—that the defence could have been prolonged if the land and air defences had been differently arranged and in greater strength. But no fortress in the whole history of warfare that is isolated has ever survived. Unless there were sea power to bring relief, drive off the attacker at sea, and cut the communications of the forces he had landed for the siege, the place was bound to fall. The British and Dominion Governments which had failed to maintain a navy adequate to its responsibilities, which set aside the teachings of history and the eternal lesson that the security of such an Empire as ours depends on sea power, are the real authors of the disaster.

Though the disablement of the American fleet is the immediate cause of the lack of allied command which has resulted in the loss of Singapore, the Philippines and the Dutch islands, it is idle to lay the blame on that event. This country, as Lord Stanhope had said, should rely upon itself alone for its security. It never could be foretold with that certainty that a question of this importance demands that the United States would either be attacked by Japan or would, if she was not attacked, come to the help of the Commonwealth to preserve its possessions and guard the Dominions in Australasia. To depend upon either of these events would be the height of folly, equalled only by the folly of not providing adequately for the command of the sea in a two-ocean war. For a two-ocean war was a possibility after Japan had set her feet upon a course of aggression and the twin dictators were beginning their careers of crime. No one could reasonably expect that if war should break out with Japan, it would be possible to send the whole fleet of Britain to the Far East: and less than the whole would not be enough. The temptation to our late enemies and the land-grabber of Rome to seize the opportunity to attack us in Europe if we had sent the whole fleet away was one to which no one could be blind: and, as the danger in Europe grew continually nearer with the rearmament of Germany, and the several acts of aggression by her and by Italy, Australia became anxious. England's difficulty would be Japan's opportunity, and Australian writers drew attention to the gravity of the situation that would then confront her.[1] The remedy that was suggested in Australia was local defence by submarines, destroyers, mines and aircraft. The utter inadequacy of local defence, the impossibility that it

[1] *Japan and the defences of Australia* by 'Albatross'; *Australia and War to-day* by the Right Hon. W. M. Hughes, 1936.

could replace a defence arising from the command of the sea, was not realized by these writers any more than the need for a two-ocean navy was realized by the successions of British Governments which tampered (to use Burke's expression) with the Navy.

Lord Jellicoe had seen clearly the need. When he made his world cruise with the object of discussing the problem of Imperial defence with the ministers of the several Dominions, he had recommended the creation of an Eastern Fleet of 16 capital ships with the proper proportion of cruisers and flotilla craft, and the building of a base at Singapore, the cost to be borne by the United Kingdom, Australia and New Zealand in the proportion of 75, 20 and 5 per cent. respectively. The proposal expressed recognition of the true fundamental principles that the defence of the Empire depends on sea power and is the joint concern and responsibility of all its members. But it did not find support either in this country or in the Dominions except in so far as the building of the base was concerned, and that was undertaken at the cost of the United Kingdom. A base was a very necessary thing, but a base without a fleet is no more use than a sentry box without a sentry.

## CHAPTER XXXIV

# FILED FOR REFERENCE

To remove the fear of impending war is the first task proposed by the Atlantic Charter. However the present conflict may end, I do not myself believe that a third world war will break out in the next twenty years. For two decades at least a peace of sheer exhaustion will follow. To judge by experience, our only guide, the imminent risk of a further struggle will not begin to mature till the third decade after this war is over.[1] That will not, of course, mean that we have security in the real sense of that word—freedom from fear. Such fear will distract public opinion, preoccupy national governments, and paralyse social reform. Thereby it will foster the forces which will presently lead to renewal of physical conflict, as in the last twenty-five years.

In the years that followed the last war the victors believed that another could be prevented by virtue of a covenant between national governments. We have tragic reason to know that they failed. In previous chapters I have given the reason for that failure as I see it. I can see no reason to doubt that the same cause must always in future operate to produce the same result.

In view of the facts it is hard indeed for anyone to argue that the League of Nations can be trusted to prevent the recurrence of further wars. But the real question is whether its failure was due to the shortcomings of those who ad-

[1] Some of those to whom I have submitted this passage in proof challenge this view, which is, I feel, open to question. I have thought it best to leave the sentence as printed and to quote the comment of one of these critics who has served in Parliament and as a minister. He writes to me as follows: 'I do not trouble you with my views except that I must say that I think your proposals are the most satisfactorily conceived of all the plans for preventing war. I feel that it is rather optimistic to believe that mere exhaustion will ensure some 30 years of peace. We ought to face the position that an ambitious and unscrupulous power, if it could gain a momentary ascendancy in the air, might choose its moment to destroy simultaneously American and British powers of resistance. Germany won't commit for a third time the blunder of waiting till she has disposed of others before she attacks us or America. There is a great risk in any opinion that nothing much will happen to permit that.'

ministered the League, or to the principle upon which it was based. Can the peace of the nations ever be based on a system which so concentrates the minds of voters at elections on their own national interests, that they fail to consider the interests of the other nations, and so blinds them to the fact that the common interest of all those nations is really their own? We have yet to hear anyone who speaks with authority on behalf of any of the United Nations suggest any departure from this principle. In all their utterances on the Atlantic Charter they assume that future outbreaks of war can be prevented by compacts between existing national governments. As one of them said in my hearing, 'we must have the League; but in a new presentation'. This phrase recalled a remark made by a cynic when the Government of India had ordained that in future Eurasians should be called 'Anglo-Indians', that governments think that problems can be solved by a change of names.

To estimate public opinion, or to say whether or no two or more sovereign commonwealths will ever consent to merge their electorates and establish an international government strong enough to maintain their common freedom from war is not in my province. Near the close of a lifetime given to the study of the question, with some practical experience of public affairs, it is in my province to record my opinion that until two or more nations do so, the world will inevitably drift towards the vortex of war. A growing sense in the minds of ordinary people that another war is sooner or later inevitable will preoccupy national governments, and everywhere paralyse social reform. Until definite steps are in train to establish a government responsible to an international electorate the promise of a better life will remain a dead letter, and the Atlantic Charter a scrap of paper as futile as the Covenant of the League. For, in my view, there can be no genuine transfer of sovereignty from national governments to an international government until that government derives its authority direct from an international electorate. I print that opinion now and so file it for reference, to be verified or falsified by events which I shall not see but will sooner or later show whether it ranks with 'truths for want of which whole nations fare the worse'.

Let me formulate, therefore, as briefly and as clearly as possible, the considered opinion I have reached in the light of comments received.

I believe that the following conditions must be realized before any real effect can be given to the two closely connected objects proposed in the Atlantic Charter, the prevention of war and social reform.

I believe that the practical execution of the charter will not begin until the task of preventing war, together with functions quite inseparable therefrom, is entrusted to an international government formed by two or more self-governing nations while powers to control their own composition and social structure are reserved to the national governments.

The international authority will not be a government in the real sense of that word, nor be able to protect the nations who compose it from attack, unless it draws its authority direct from the citizens composing those nations. It must be entitled to make security a first charge on all the human and material resources of the countries it protects: but national governments must control the incidence of taxation between individual taxpayers.

These two objects can be reconciled if the estimates of the international government are distributed between the countries it protects in proportion to their taxable capacities, and the quota due from each national government is made payable to the international government, as a first charge on the consolidated revenue of each national government, without being voted by the national legislature.

The international government must have general power to spend its revenues on any purpose which it deems necessary to render the countries it protects immune from attack, e.g. to secure that the merchant shipping and aircraft of those countries will be adequate in the event of war.

It must also have power to control dependencies not ripe for responsible government.

All other powers, including control of migration and tariffs, should be reserved to existing national governments, save and except that, when war is seriously threatened or has broken out, the international government must be entitled to exercise any power which it deems necessary for the common security.

There must be a supreme court by which powers claimed by the international government can be tested.

CHAPTER XXXV

# WHAT THEN MUST WE DO?

THE United Nations, in adopting the Atlantic Charter, are committed by Article VI to the dual task of establishing 'a peace which will afford to all nations the means of dwelling in safety within their own boundaries and which will afford assurance that all men in all lands may live out their lives in freedom from fear and want'.

Article VIII is designed to show that this goal is not to be reached by wishful thinking. Aggressor nations must be disarmed 'pending the establishment of a wider and permanent system of general security'. What is that system to be? What must we do to make it exist? These are questions which stand to be answered, if ever the Atlantic Charter is to be brought from Utopian cloudland to the solid ground of practical politics. In the last chapter I have summarized the conditions which, in my view, will have to be satisfied before the hopes set forth in the charter can begin to be realized in fact.

Let those who think that a world system such as Roosevelt and Churchill have figured can be brought into being at one step waste no time in reading these pages. They have meaning only for those who believe that a system to secure the peace of the world, and to all men freedom from fear and want, can only be realized little by little, step by step. They are written for those who have learned not to despise the day of small things.

Yet, even so, I do not presume to address the world at large. In appealing for action, I must deal with the question what *we* are to do to realize the faith expressed in this charter. I must, therefore, say whom I mean by this word *we*. The world is still in the epoch of national commonwealths which each demand an unlimited devotion from the citizens that compose them, from whom their governments draw the authority to make that claim. The government which makes that claim on me is the British Government. It draws that authority from the 47,000,000 who inhabit Great Britain and

Northern Ireland, of whom I am one. Our votes control the British Government only. So where in this chapter I ask what *we* are to do to give effect to this charter, I mean by the word *we* the people of Great Britain and Northern Ireland. For us 47,000,000 the question is what steps the British Government should take, when hostilities cease, to implement the charter.

Consider the relation in which the Dominions now stand to us, the 47,000,000 who constitute the United Kingdom of Great Britain and Northern Ireland. It is surely unnecessary to argue here that the peoples of Canada, Australia, New Zealand, and South Africa had to become nations distinct from our own in the full sense of that word. By a nation I mean a people in one territory with full control of its own composition and social structure. I have argued elsewhere that the organization of the human race in such national units was not only a necessary step in the progress of civilization but must always remain so. The development of Canada, Australia, New Zealand, and South Africa as nations distinct from our own was recognized long before the Balfour Report or the Statute of Westminster; though the statute was needed to reconcile law with the fact.

What I question is not the Statute of Westminster, but its general presentment as the final settlement of future relations between the Dominions and us. Of their own willing choice the Dominions recognized the sovereignty of the British Crown, and by doing so were recognized as remaining integral parts of the British Commonwealth. The United Kingdom, as a matter of course, had always recognized her responsibility for defending all territories under the British Crown. From 1815 to the close of the century she was able to do so with such effect that no foreign power essayed the destruction of the Commonwealth. The United Kingdom gave to this quarter of mankind security in the real sense of the word. By the end of that century a change had set in. The outbreak of war in 1914 was of itself a conclusive proof that the United Kingdom had ceased to be strong enough to render the Commonwealth immune from attack. It also proved that she had ceased to be strong enough to defend even herself, when standing alone. Yet, when the Statute of Westminster was passed, the Dominions were allowed, and indeed encouraged, by us to believe that the United Kingdom remained as before responsible for the safety of the Commonwealth as a whole. That she was so responsible was constantly emphasized by all her spokesmen. That no Dominion was committed to war by a declaration of war by or against the British Government was widely argued. When the United Kingdom declared war in 1939 Dominion Parliaments went through the motions of declaring war on their own account.

It remains, however, a significant fact that neither the British nor the Dominion governments had notified foreign powers that no Dominion was committed to war by a declaration of war by or against the Government of the United Kingdom. Responsible statesmen silently shrank from a step which would have raised the question whether the people of a Dominion were still British subjects in any possible sense of that word.

As the British Government continued to assume responsibility for defending all parts of the Commonwealth, so was left in its hands a final responsibility for all decisions affecting the issues of peace and war. Dominion governments were told everything and consulted on everything. The pledge to do this more often than not delayed and embarrassed decisions. The final decisions were, none the less, made by ministers in Whitehall. Dominion governments were fully informed of all that happened at Munich. The government of New Zealand disapproved the decisions then made. They were none the less involved in all the results that followed.

By 1926 the British Government had ceased to command the resources of most of Ireland. Before the outbreak of war it relinquished control of the naval stations in Southern Ireland, retained under the Irish Treaty, for want of which hundreds of allied vessels and thousands of lives have been lost. Yet the question whether a government which commanded resources no greater than those of Great Britain and Northern Ireland was still physically able to ensure the defence of the whole British Commonwealth scattered all over the face of the globe and containing a quarter of mankind was never faced nor even raised. The British Government had indeed realized that an effective air force could not be trained in the space available in this small island. But negotiations for facilities to train crews for the British Air Force in Canada were gravely delayed by long discussions on constitutional issues. While allowing and encouraging Dominions to think that we still undertook to defend every country under the Crown, we never recognized ourselves, and, therefore, we never told the Dominions that we now utterly lacked the power to give effect to that undertaking. When we guaranteed the frontiers of Belgium were we really able to defend them in fact?

The results are before us. It is futile now to apportion blame, for God Himself cannot change the past. Our business is to read the lessons which this past has taught, and then to apply them. When hostilities cease our government will be face to face with the question what they must do to give effect to the Atlantic Charter. In the light of all that has happened in these two wars, can the so-called Imperial Government, as now constituted, hope to render the British Commonwealth as a whole immune from attack?

In Parliament, on platforms, in the Press, and by political experts, public attention is constantly fixed on points where the British Commonwealth has met with success, on facts which are pleasant and easy to state. How the British Commonwealth has twice in this century failed of its major purpose, that of averting wars and of keeping the world at peace, goes without mention. On this great outstanding unpalatable fact the voices that millions can hear are silent as graves—as the graves that their silence may open for millions unborn.

The first essential step is that we, the people of Great Britain and Northern Ireland, should be brought to confess this distasteful truth, a thing which will only begin to happen when recognized leaders speak it aloud. Such speech will, of course, be overheard in the Dominions. When hostilities cease our leaders must meet those of the self-governing

Dominions to discuss what steps are to be taken in pursuance of the Atlantic Charter to prevent the recurrence of war. That the British Government has always felt itself responsible for defending the whole British Commonwealth, and has been so felt by all parts of it, is beyond question. Can the British Government honestly tell the Dominions that it is still in a position to discharge that responsibility so long as it commands resources no greater than those which it now commands? It is time for our ministers to tell the truth to the Dominions, whose future's safety is in question no less than our own. They can say with conviction that the people of these islands can be trusted to do their best to defend every part of the Commonwealth. They should also have the candour and courage to add that with such resources as they now command they cannot in future hope to render the British Commonwealth immune from attack. Great Britain and Northern Ireland can no longer provide the security which the United Kingdom was able to provide in the nineteenth century. The outbreak of two major wars in this century has proved no less. Dominion governments must, therefore, consider what policy can now provide them with such security as Great Britain and Northern Ireland with their present resources can no longer provide. Since the Statute of Westminster every Dominion is as free in law as in fact to follow whatever course its people find best. They may think it wise to discover, for instance, what degree of security the U.S.A. might be able and also willing to guarantee them under its constitution.

It could, however, be pointed out to the Dominions that a government which commanded the whole resources of the British Commonwealth would be strong enough to lay the spectre of war for the next generation. They could say that they themselves were prepared to advise the British people they represent to authorize them to consider how such a government might be established with representatives of any Dominion authorized to explore that alternative.

I am not suggesting that the British Government should formulate proposals for solving the problem at this stage;

but I think that it should be prepared to work out proposals in consultation with any Dominion government which expressed willingness to discuss the matter. My belief is that the formulation of a practical proposal which any one Dominion government was prepared to recommend to its own electorate would lift the question to a new plane.

To make defence of the British Commonwealth a first charge on the resources of one Dominion, even of Canada, as well as those of Great Britain and Northern Ireland, would not, of course, suffice to solve the problem of security. It is my fixed belief that the problem of security for the United Nations will only be solved when the peoples of the American and British Commonwealths have merged their resources under one organic government charged with their common defence. Nothing short of that will complete the task of the Atlantic Charter to which the United Nations are pledged. That is the objective which, when achieved, will in time lead on to the ultimate objective—a world government in the final sense of that word.

The moment hostilities cease our present Allies in western Europe, the French, Belgian, Dutch, Danish, and Norwegian democracies, will want to know what guarantees we can give them that their territories will not again be invaded and their people enslaved. *We*, at any rate, the people of Great Britain and Northern Ireland, and our government will have to face that inevitable question.

Here again I submit that our answer should be based on facts as revealed by the present war and the last. Experience has proved that no such guarantee as we gave to Belgium can avail to save them from these disasters. In pointing this out, our position will have been strengthened, if our ministers have told the Dominions that Great Britain and Northern Ireland can no longer pretend to be strong enough to ensure the security of the Commonwealth as a whole, nor even that of the British Isles, and are discussing how the burden of a common defence could be shared. An invitation to join these discussions is the answer we could make to our present Allies in western Europe.

My purpose in these pages is to suggest a policy whereby, step by step, we might realize the objects to which we are now committed by the Atlantic Charter. Let us recall some memorable words which Milner once used in the House of Lords:

'There is nothing which braces the mind so much as facing the naked truth.'

Our greatest obstacle in facing the truth has been our pride in our own past. It was well said that humility is merely a question of knowing the truth about ourselves. The time has come to brace our minds by facing the naked truth, and with all humility to confess that our own strength is no longer equal to the tasks we have undertaken, a fact which two wars have now revealed.

The best way to assess the merits of a policy is to suppose that effect has been given to its earlier stages, and then see how far the results would tend to its ultimate completion. Let us, therefore, suppose that some of the nations now fighting for freedom had combined to create a government for their common defence with a first charge on all their resources for that purpose, and responsible, therefore, directly to the taxpayers themselves of all the nations united. Suppose that the first union included Great Britain and Northern Ireland, one or more of the self-governing Dominions, and one or more of the western democracies of Europe, France, Belgium, Holland, Denmark, or Norway. We must hold in mind that every attempt to conquer the world from Europe has always meant an invasion of the Low Countries, and will now mean the invasion of Denmark and Norway. The change would mean that in future an aggressor would no longer be dealing with countries too small and weak to resist pressure, diplomatic or military. Any threat to the Low Countries or Scandinavian frontiers would mean, without question or parley, war with a new United States, including the British Commonwealth with all its resources. The Government of those United States would have to maintain in the western democracies of Europe land and air forces strong enough to resist the first impact of any attack. The

P

German technique of dealing with disunited nations and enslaving them one by one, applied with resounding success in the present war, would no longer operate. What German government would violate the frontiers of Holland or Norway if it knew that an international state of which they were members would and could rain bombs on Berlin the following night?

The national governments, relieved of concern for external affairs, would then be free to concentrate their minds and their time on social reform. They would find themselves able as never before to handle their problems of unemployment, education, housing, and health. Experience itself would expose the widespread fallacy that national sovereignty is a condition of genuine freedom. If this were proved beyond doubt by example, other democracies would be readier to merge their sovereignties, and to strengthen the Union by joining it.

Our own conception of the younger British democracies as sovereign nations, equal in status with the United Kingdom, has never been grasped by the world at large, and certainly not in the United States. There Canada, Australia, New Zealand, and South Africa are still regarded as something less in their international status than countries like France, Belgium, Holland, and Norway. An international state which included the democracies of western Europe would to the American mind assume a different complexion from one which included only the British Dominions. It would, I think, be strong enough to prevent the recurrence of war for one generation. If, for that period, it had proved its stability, the vast American electorate might come to feel that they could join their forces with it to preserve the peace of the world once for all, without the danger of losing their own national identity.

When once there has come to exist a government to protect free institutions directly responsible to the people it protects, and those people include the inhabitants of the U.S.A., the first aim proposed in the Atlantic Charter will have been achieved; then and then only. Mankind will then have come to believe that the era of world wars has been ended once and for all. It will come to enjoy security in the real sense of that word. When free institutions are safe where they now exist, they will start once more to spread to communities which have not learned what those institutions mean, and how to conduct them. In a world where peace is established they will spread little by little to countries like Germany, Italy, and Japan, and more rapidly, perhaps, to countries like Russia, China, or India.

In Chapter XXXIII I have argued that the civilized peoples cannot disown responsibility to communities less advanced than themselves whose products they use. The creation of an international government which included the democracies of Holland and Belgium with those of the British Commonwealth would have brought the great majority of the tropical peoples under one authority. The inclusion of America and France in that government would practically meet the responsibility which civilized men have in common to the backward peoples whose lives are profoundly affected by the need which civilized men have for their products.

In my view, the prevention of war to which we are committed in the Atlantic Charter can only be effected by an international government, responsible, not to national governments, but to the people they represent. The League of Nations has failed in that paramount object, and in these pages I have given my reasons why I believe that a League so constituted must always in future fail. On the other hand, the League and the International Labour Office have met with conspicuous success in the field of finance, of health, the traffic in drugs and white slaves, in the co-ordination of measures to solve the problems of labour, and in collecting information on world affairs.

There is every reason why such an international government as is here proposed should join such a league with nations outside it. Experience has shown that the nations composing the international government could also be members of such a league, as the self-governing Dominions now are, side by side with the whole British Commonwealth.

But the Covenant must be free from commitments which none of the members of the League have observed or are likely to observe. So long as political leaders present a League of Sovereign States as a panacea for preserving peace they are dooming this planet to an endless succession of world wars.

I am here looking forward into a future which can, I believe, be realized within measurable time only if we ourselves take the initiative when hostilities cease. My case is that to take that initiative our ministers must first bring home to the people of this country the truth that history has laid on them a burden far too heavy for this one small unit of society to discharge. The fact will of itself lead the rest of the world as well as ourselves, step by step, to the only effective solution, if we have but the courage and humility to avow it.

In order to reach that solution and to realize the promise to which we are pledged by the Atlantic Charter two other questions have to be faced. Should a system which has failed to prevent the outbreak of two major wars be commended, as it has been commended, to our Allies as one which can be trusted to prevent future wars? Can national governments, especially our own British Government, succeed in coping with the problems of social reform so long as they are preoccupied with the task of maintaining peace?

## CHAPTER XXXVI

# THE SILENCE OF PUBLICISTS

THE questions raised at the end of the last chapter have never as yet been faced by the people of Great Britain and Northern Ireland; nor will they be faced until they have been put to them with authority by their recognized leaders and spokesmen. And because these questions have never been so put, public opinion in these islands is unprepared to accept the practical changes which must be made if once they are really faced. Public opinion in these islands has not been prepared to share the control of defence, of foreign affairs, of the issues of peace and war for themselves with the people of the self-governing Dominions.

How comes it that questions so vital are treated, with rare exceptions, as taboo by Parliament, the Press, and also by those teachers of international law and politics whom the public have learned to regard as men who can speak with authority on matters like this? For brevity I propose in this chapter to refer to the politicians, journalists, and political experts, who have the ear of the masses, as publicists.

We are often told by the politicians that their function is to ascertain public opinion and give effect to it. The growing attention paid to Gallup polls shows how prevalent this doctrine is. Too little account is made of the obvious truth that the main factor in shaping public opinion is what recognized leaders say to the public, and what journalists write in the Press. No popular government can give real effect to a policy until a sufficient number of the voters who keep them in office approve that policy. At any moment a recognized leader can make himself heard by a far greater number of people than the writer of a book, especially since the invention of broadcasting. In time of war the superior power of reaching the public ear which politicians and journalists have is greatly accentuated by the shortage of paper. This special power they hold of creating and guiding public opinion and their special responsibility were never so great as now.

When discussing the questions set forth at the end of the

last chapter with various audiences and especially with men in the Forces, I have found an eager readiness to face them. On the other hand, I find an almost complete silence with regard to them in discussions on post-war settlement in Parliament, on the platform, and in the editorial columns of the Press.

In June 1942 Lord Selborne uttered his personal opinion that the British Commonwealth could not be rendered immune from attack unless, in peace as well as in war, the Dominions shared with the British Isles the burden and control of defence. His remarks, I gather, were received with disfavour in political circles and were not repeated.[1]

In editorial columns, whether of daily or weekly papers, I have so far been unable to trace any reference to such questions except in *The Western Mail* and *The Glasgow Herald*. As I cannot read many papers myself, I asked the press-cutting department of Chatham House to keep a close watch for any reference to such questions in editorial columns. Up to the moment of writing these words (27th Sept. 1942) that department reports that, with the two exceptions mentioned above, they have been unable to trace any such reference in the papers they read.

The question that lies behind all others is that which Lothian raised. In a pamphlet entitled *The Ending of Armageddon* shortly before the outbreak of war he wrote as follows:

'That cause (the cause of war) does not lie primarily in defects in policy by any nation but in the system of international relationships in which we have tried to live both before and after the world war. The real cause of our troubles is that the nations were living in anarchy—by far the most fatal of all political diseases— the consequences of which have been intensified a hundredfold in recent times by the conquest of time and space and the breakdown of the old Pax Britannica of the nineteenth century. The Covenant of the League of Nations disguises but does not end anarchy, because while it is a contract to co-operate, it leaves intact the root of anarchy, national sovereignty.... **Leagues of**

[1] An M.P. has told me that he went to a debate in the Commons on post-war aims with a speech prepared to raise these questions, but failed to catch the Speaker's eye.

**Governments are necessarily concerned with making the world safe for national sovereignty and not either for democracy or the people. . . .**

'Finally national sovereignty has been the hidden hand which has wrecked the League ideal. For national sovereignty implies that every nation sets its own interests first, and requires every individual to obey his own state and not the decisions of the League.'

Was Lothian right when he pointed to the maintenance of national sovereignties as the essential cause of war? If so, the human race can never hope to be delivered from this scourge until we find some way of merging national sovereignties in one international state. My own experience is that the practical difficulty lies not with ordinary men, when once the issue is before their minds. The moment they come to think that we have to choose between peace on earth or the maintenance of national sovereignty, the vast majority are ready to let national sovereignty go. With publicists it is otherwise. To them national sovereignty, Leviathan, is the god of their idolatry, and any proposal to supersede it is anathema. They regard as fantastic any proposal to establish an international government which draws its authority from the same source as the national governments, that is to say, from the people themselves. In the face of all human experience they insist that peace must and can be maintained on the basis of compacts between sovereign governments.

The fact that politicians and journalists are more tenacious of national sovereignty than the masses they represent or address is not confined to this country. It is true, I believe, of every democracy. On a later page we note the startling result of the poll taken by *Fortune* in the U.S.A. The conclusion based on this poll was that over 35 per cent. of the population, and over 50 per cent. of those with opinions on the matter, approved of some federal world government. I would hazard a guess that had the poll been confined to politicians and journalists not 1 per cent. would have been found to approve any step which meant a surrender of national sovereignty. The result would, I suspect, have revealed the same difference in readiness to face this issue between ordinary citizens and the publicists that I notice here.

Frankly I admit that the view taken in these pages is rejected (with few exceptions) by those who have given their lives to the study and practice of politics, who may therefore claim to be experts and to know best what is right. I, indeed, believe that the vast majority of ordinary men would decide to discard national sovereignty if the question at issue could be brought before their minds. But how can I dare to suggest that the vast majority, mere amateurs in politics, would be right when most of the experts think they are wrong?

My reply is that in all fields of human activity experts drift into treating the instruments and methods they use as ends in themselves, and lose sight of the ends for which those instruments and methods were devised. Let us take a few examples from widely different fields.

In a polytheistic world a series of Hebrew prophets beginning with Abraham felt their way to the truth that God is one. The vehicle which carried and preserved this truth for centuries was the people of Israel and the worship of one invisible God which centred in the Temple at Jerusalem. This worship developed an elaborate ritual in the hands of the priests. 'Scribes' and 'Pharisees' grew up as professions, as teachers and interpreters of the Scriptures, books written, or supposed to be written, by Moses and the prophets. A nationalist conception crept in, favoured by prophets like Ezekiel, though combated by others like Jeremiah, that the tribes of Israel were a chosen people standing apart from all other peoples described as Gentiles. Then Jesus of Nazareth appeared, reasserting and emphasizing the doctrine of Jeremiah, that all men are brethren, children of God, and equal in His sight. He discounted the value of the Temple ritual and of ordinances elaborated by scribes and Pharisees. It was in the nature of things that the priests who had spent their lives practising their ritual and the scribes and Pharisees whose profession it was to teach their ordinances should find it hard to accept this religious teaching.

To them these things, developed as tactical means to the worship of one true God, had become ends in themselves, which obscured the essential truth revealed by the prophets and now reasserted by Christ Himself. But the 'people'—peasants from Galilee and pilgrims from every part of the Roman Empire—heard Him gladly. Ordinary folk were more receptive of a fundamental religious truth than the experts in religion.

'Red tape' is another instance of how forms come to be treated as ends in themselves by officials, and obscure and defeat the purpose for which those forms were devised.

Another familiar case is that of the war services. In the last war it needed civilian pressure to force the convoy system on the Admiralty. Tanks were a British invention, but the German conquest of France and Europe was partly due to a failure of the experts who controlled the French and British War Offices to recognize the change which mechanization should impose on military organization. Politicians and journalists have rightly commented on this failure.

Mr. Walter Nash, the New Zealand Minister at Washington, on his recent visit to England, observed and warned us against a similar tendency in business circles.

'With all the credit due for the splendid spirit of the people of Britain and the thoroughness of its executives and administrators, they are handicapped, and the value of their efforts reduced by the policy of minimum interference with the existing channel of production, trade, custom, and tradition. What has struck me most is the apparent determination of some influential sections not to interfere unduly with ordinary business. We are probably paying a very heavy price for this policy, and *later will have to pay a higher and more dangerous price unless it is altered*.

'There is as much initiative, enterprise, and courage in the British character as in that of any other nation and race, but it is restricted by the determination to stick to "existing channels".'

This tendency of the human mind to move in channels cut by the wheels of its own routine is not confined to religious, official, military, or business circles. It exists in all professions, and in none with more subtle, and therefore dangerous, effects than in those of politics, journalism, and teaching.

The creation of national commonwealths was a necessary step in the progress of man towards freedom, a means to that end, the highest expression of freedom as yet attained. Lord Simon's speech of the 5th August[1] shows how for the practical politician national sovereignty becomes an end in itself. It is the highest expression of freedom Lord Simon knows. Just because he has had so much to do with it, and has made so very many speeches about it, he, with his rare intelligence, is less able than ordinary and simpler folk to conceive that there may be a higher expression of freedom, the approach to which is dangerously blocked by the maintenance of national sovereignties. The same is true in the field of journalism. A man who for years has written such leaders as appear on the morning of Empire Day or when an Imperial conference meets, finds it harder than ordinary people to revise the idea that the British Commonwealth as established by the Balfour Report and the Statute of Westminster is the last word in political achievement. And so in the teaching profession. For one who has lectured for years on international law it is difficult indeed to imagine a human society which is not fragmented into national sovereignties. As Tolstoy said:

'I know that most men—not only those considered clever, but even those who are very clever and capable of understanding most difficult scientific, mathematical, or philosophic problems— can very seldom discern even the simplest and most obvious truth if it be such as to oblige them to admit the falsity of conclusions of which they are proud, which they taught to others, and on which they have built their lives.'[2]

As Tolstoy saw, minds able to escape the habits of a lifetime and to question the assumptions which underlie them, which they themselves have affirmed for years, are rare. He had here discerned a deep psychological truth which explains why publicists avoid discussing the question which Lothian raised. In the whole range of human activity there

[1] See Chapter XVI Appendix.   [2] *The Life of Tolstoy*, Maude, vol. ii, p. 516.

is no 'channel' worn so deep as this obsession of national sovereignty in the minds of the publicists. The words which Mr. Nash used of the 'channels' in which business circles are moving apply with deadlier force to the 'channels' in which political minds are moving:

*'We are probably paying a very heavy price for this policy, and later will have to pay a higher and more dangerous price unless it is altered.'*

I have elsewhere quoted the famous words of Garrison when he started the movement which led to the abolition of slavery in America. 'I am in earnest—I will not equivocate—I will not excuse—I will not retreat a single inch—*and I will be heard.'* Now what was the point which Garrison had raised, which the politicians, the journalists, and political experts, the publicists of New England, were refusing to discuss? It was not the evil of slavery; for every thoughtful man in New England was agreed that slavery was morally wrong. The point which Garrison raised was this, that if slavery is a moral evil, then the Constitution of the United States, which legalized slavery, was morally wrong and ought to be changed. To the publicists of New England the American Constitution was the last word in political wisdom. That belief had always inspired their speeches and writings. They could not combat the thesis which Garrison raised, that if slavery is morally wrong, then the Constitution which legalized slavery was also wrong and ought to be changed. So each of them instinctively avoided the question and refrained from discussing it. There was no conspiracy of silence. Each publicist found that he could not discuss the question at all without beginning to throw doubt on the excellence of a constitution he had spent his whole life in proclaiming. So each and all, they left it alone and never referred to it.

And so in the British Commonwealth to-day. Since 1926 the publicists, with rare exceptions, have acclaimed its constitution, as now defined in the Balfour Report and the Statute of Westminster, as the last word in political wisdom. Our Allied democracies are invited to observe our success and to believe that by adopting our principle of partnership between equal and absolute sovereignties the outbreak of war can now be prevented, and effect be so given to the Atlantic Charter. So when the point is raised that the British Commonwealth as now constituted has in fact failed to prevent the two greatest wars in history, they cannot deal with this stubborn fact without beginning to question what they have said or written in hundreds of speeches and articles. Their minds recoil from the effort. They simply avoid the question. There is no conspiracy of silence. The instinct to bury one's head in the sand when one's fixed ideas are threatened is too strong to resist. The result is that the real questions raised by the Atlantic Charter are avoided in political circles, in the Press, and the lecture-room.

A commonplace factor like the shortage of paper makes this silence of publicists a more than ordinary danger. Such awkward questions can only be broached in pamphlets, which owing to the restriction of paper can at best reach a few thousand readers, too few by far to create an effective public opinion. The millions can only be reached through the Press or by speeches they hear on the radio. Those millions, accustomed to look to their publicists for guidance, never hear of these questions at all, and cannot begin to answer such questions until they are put to them by their recognized leaders and guides.

Our publicists realize better than most that millions of lives hang upon what they say. But do they realize that millions of lives may also depend on what they refrain from saying?

On one point let me be clear. I am not complaining that my own views are rejected by the great majority of those who have given their lives to the practice and study of politics. Had my own life been spent in operating or expounding a system of society based on national sovereignty, I should probably be convinced that any challenge to national sovereignty as the natural and necessary basis of human society was a form of lunacy. For the reasons explained in this chapter I have never expected that the publicists would accept views like these. But readers can judge for themselves whether such questions as those here raised should be brought up for consideration by the multitudes whose children may again have to pay the price which their parents are now paying for ignoring them. My point is that the publicists, with rare exceptions, avoid any reference to the questions raised.

Much time has been spent in Parliament and much paper in demanding freedom of public discussion and freedom of the Press. For the vast majority of people Parliament and the Press are the only arenas of public discussion; and what real freedom of discussion and opinion can exist, so long as questions of capital importance are excluded from the agenda? When the politicians and journalists demand freedom of discussion, I would ask them to reflect on Northcliffe's cynical boast, 'The greatest power of the Press is to suppress.'

CHAPTER XXXVII

# A TALK TO THE FORCES[1]

As a young man I was so impressed by Admiral Mahan's *The Influence of Sea Power*, that I afterwards read everything he published. The distinction he drew between strategy and tactics caught my attention. I once had the privilege of discussing it with him when I met him in New York. His doctrine may be stated as follows:

'A general whose strategy is sound can afford to commit tactical errors. No tactical skill will save from disaster a general whose strategy is unsound.'

You have only to compare Hitler's strategy with that of the Allies to see how profound this aphorism is. But to grasp its full meaning you must realize what the admiral meant by strategy. 'The strategist', he says, 'is a man who sees and always holds in mind the object for which the war is fought; and that object is always political.' In these last words he was saying what the Greek historian Thucydides had said long ago when he wrote that 'States only make war to attain a higher condition of peace.' Mahan was of course thinking in military terms; but I have come to believe that his distinction between strategy and tactics applies to every field of human activity, and most of all to the field of politics.

The end for which we are now fighting this war is not as so many people glibly say 'to win it'. Victory in war is only a means to the true end, which in my view is now sufficiently stated in the Atlantic Charter. I think of this Charter as an ellipse drawn from two foci

(1) to prevent further wars,
(2) to provide a better life for all on this planet.

I shall try to convince you that we cannot attain either of these objects except in so far as we attain them both. They are so inseparable that they are in fact as much one as if they were the centre of a circle.

Such then is the object with which we are fighting this war as stated in the Atlantic Charter. We are thus confronted

[1] See Preface.

with the practical question, 'How far are we able to carry this object out when the war is won?'

I must pause, for a moment, to tell you the sense in which I am using the word 'we'. These proposals are not addressed to the Dominions, still less to Americans, or to any of our Allies. They are only addressed to my fellow voters and tax-payers in the United Kingdom of Great Britain and Northern Ireland. Of course, I am glad if people in the Dominions or in Allied countries read them, provided they hold this in mind. It is not for me to suggest to people who are voters and taxpayers in other countries what they should do.[1]

.    .    .    .    .    .    .    .

With the single exception of Eire, the Dominions in both these wars sprang to arms when the British Government declared war. Neither then nor at any time have they ever been asked by the British Government to commit themselves to action of this kind in advance. Such proposals, when made by writers of books or in the Press, have found no support from Dominion Governments. No British Government would ever have thought of asking an Imperial Conference to adopt such commitments as those assumed by the governments that signed the Covenant of the League. The reason why Dominion Governments signed the Covenant so readily was because membership of the League would give them an international recognition of their status as sovereign and independent states. Their minds, with those of the other governments assembled in Paris, were preoccupied with the question of national sovereignty.

Dominion Governments can claim that in going to war they alone of the States Members of the League redeemed the pledges they signed in the Covenant.

The sovereign status of each Dominion was asserted in terms by the Imperial Conference of 1926. In 1931 its report was given a legislative sanction in the Statute of Westminster. The Conference of 1926, however, declared that equality of

[1] I here omit four paragraphs which were given in this talk to the forces, because in this book I have printed them as Chapter XII, where they can be read.

status between the United Kingdom and the Dominions did not imply equality of function. Whilst each Dominion was primarily responsible for its own local defence, the United Kingdom remained as before responsible for defending the Commonwealth as a whole and for keeping open the routes by sea and air which connect its widely scattered territories. The cost of the forces required for the purpose had still to be drawn from the taxpayers of Great Britain and Northern Ireland. The inevitable consequence was that, whatever the Statute of Westminster might say, the issues of peace or war were controlled as before by the British Government. I can recall only one case in which this obvious fact has ever been mentioned. In the summer of 1939 the Foreign Secretary, Lord Halifax, made an important speech on foreign policy at the annual dinner of the Royal Institute of International Affairs. He was followed by Mr. Menzies, a member of the Australian Cabinet, who made the following observation:

'In spite of the theorists—and there are many theorists in the world—the foreign policy of the British Commonwealth is to a large extent in the hands of the Foreign Secretary of this country. We may, as indeed some of our predecessors did, claim that we are equal in all things in point of foreign policy, but the fact will remain that the great issues of peace and war will be much more determined by the gentleman who sits in a room looking across the Horse Guards Parade than it will by my colleagues in Canberra or one of our colleagues in Ottawa or Pretoria. The nations of the world will not be prepared to sit down for a few weeks or months while the members of the Commonwealth have an intimate chat as to what they are to do.'

The fact which governs this whole situation is that political responsibility cannot be divorced from financial responsibility.

Our rulers combine to present this Commonwealth to our Allies as the model of a system whereby the United Nations can accomplish the aims they are pledged to accomplish under the Atlantic Charter. They always repeat with emphasis that twice in this century the Dominions have rallied their forces in defence of the Commonwealth when attacked. Thank God they did, and unless they had done so in time, we must all have gone down to destruction. But Lord Halifax alone has mentioned the obvious fact that the British Commonwealth failed to prevent these two attempts to destroy it—attempts which involved, as they must always involve, the world in war: and he was taken to task for doing so. The fact is ignored that the object for which we have fought these wars, to which all the Allies are pledged in terms by the Atlantic Charter, is to prevent such wars happening again. The system our Allies are asked to copy has twice failed to achieve that object.

Last year Walter Lippmann published a book called *U.S. Foreign Policy*. It is short, contains no unnecessary word, a masterpiece, which deserves to be read as long as *The Prince* of Machiavelli. In this book he endorses Lothian's view that the freedom from world wars which prevailed for a century after the battle of Waterloo was due to British sea-power. He argues that no single democracy, not even the U.S.A., is now strong enough to prevent such wars. That, he thinks, can only be done by an alliance between the American and British Commonwealths and Russia, to which I suggest he would now add France reborn. I agree that such an alliance is needed to keep the peace for the next generation. I hope that such an alliance will be made, but I do not believe that any alliance between sovereign governments can endure, or prevent the recurrence of world wars in the long run. Lippmann is, of course, a hundred per cent. American, and his mind cannot conceive that his country will ever agree to merge its sovereignty with other democracies. He may be right, but my own conviction is that the world will not begin to develop any real feeling of security from war till two or more democracies have shown how to merge their external powers in one common authority or union for defence. My deepest conclusion is that the danger of world war will be finally ended only when there has come into being an international authority for defence which includes the U.S.A. with other democracies.

Having said that, I must add that I do not myself expect to see such a union come into being in my own lifetime. In

Q

the meanwhile I believe that a government which commanded the resources of all the British democracies in alliance with America and Russia could prevent world wars for the next generation, but scarcely for longer than that.

Our worst danger is a widespread presumption that practical problems can be solved by phrases. Such slogans as 'international co-operation' and 'collective security' are cases in point. You may also remember the popular cry that the one thing wanted to end this war was 'a second front'. I need scarcely tell you people in uniform that something more was required to establish a second front than speeches, articles, or resolutions at public meetings. Any civilian can now see what laborious and intricate staff work had to be done to make our landing on the beaches of Normandy possible. This is equally true of political problems. I say with conviction that the root cause of world wars is the anarchy which exists between sovereign states, and the only way to stop them is to entrust defence to a common authority. But the problem will not be solved by repeating a phrase like that. In my three papers, *Decision*, *Action*, and *Faith and Works*, I have done my best to work out in detail successive steps which will have to be taken to replace the anarchy which must exist between sovereign states by a genuine rule of law, with authority to enforce it.

The question before us is how a number of sovereign democracies can unite to create an authority for their common defence. To prevent war such an authority must be able to create forces by sea, land, and air so strong that no enemy will dare to attack them. The next question to be faced is how the cost of these forces is to be borne by the nations united for their common defence. My suggestion is that this question should be answered by applying the basic principle of taxation propounded by Adam Smith and accepted by all economists. For obvious reasons you can pay for such services as gas, electricity, or water, which can be measured on meters, according to the benefit received. But no instrument can tell what is the exact benefit which each citizen derives from the safety which government gives to our lives and property.

And this is true of most of the services which a government has to provide at the public expense. It has therefore to distribute the cost of these services between one citizen and another in proportion to the ability of each to bear the burden, that is to say, his taxable capacity. A Minister of Finance in framing his budget and devising the taxes to pay for it is trying to distribute the burden on that principle. My suggestion is that in an international union created for the common defence of several democracies the cost should be borne in proportion to the taxable capacity of the several nations composing the union. The taxable capacity of every nation which enters the union should be ascertained by a standing commission of financial experts. This assessment of taxable capacity should be revised by the Commission say every five years.

There would then be a common authority charged with the task of creating and maintaining such forces by land, sea, and air as may be required to secure the nations included in the union from attack. It would frame estimates for defence, show the total sum required for the purpose, and submit them to a legislature elected by the citizens of all the component states. The representation accorded to each of these states might also be based on their taxable capacity, allowance being made for more generous representation to the smaller states. In an upper house the states might be equally represented as in the American Senate. The estimates when voted would then be apportioned amongst the states in the ratio of their taxable capacities, as declared by the standing commission. The contributions due to the union authority would constitute a first charge on the consolidated fund of each national government. Under the constitution of the union they would be payable on demand to the union authority on the warrant of its office of finance, without any vote by the national legislatures. National governments and legislatures would have to provide that each year their consolidated funds were sufficient to meet the quotas due to the union authority for defence as well as the cost of their own domestic services. It would thus be left to each national government to decide the incidence of taxation between one individual taxpayer and another, as they do at present.

My reason for this proposal is my conviction that the powers of the union authority must be confined to defence and to functions clearly inseparable therefrom, of which the control of foreign relations which determine the issues of peace and war is obviously one. The union authority must be empowered to make their common security from war a first charge on all the resources of all the nations it safeguards. But the second object of the Atlantic Charter, the provision of a better life for all on this planet, cannot possibly be undertaken by the union authority. Social reform must remain as it now is in the sole control of the national governments. Each nation must control for itself its own structure and composition. In any measures for social reform the most vital instrument which any government can wield is the power to control the incidence of taxation between one citizen and another, which must largely determine the distribution of wealth. Under this plan the power to control tariffs and also migration is left where it now stands, with each national government. The scheme is designed to give the union authority a first charge on all the resources of the nations it protects, whilst leaving their national governments in control of their national and social affairs. The system is designed not to diminish, but to increase that control.

To explain why I think it would have this effect I will tell you a story. Some weeks after *Decision* was published the telephone bell rang one night when I was in bed. In some irritation I went down to it to find myself summoned by a courteous voice from a house in Bedfordshire, the voice of Sir Malcolm Stewart. I had never met him, but of course knew of him as the cement manufacturer who had done a superb job of social reform in the depressed areas. Sir Malcolm explained that he had just read my pamphlet and had ventured to ring me up to inquire whether I could use any money which he would be glad to supply to promote its circulation. My temper began to improve; so I told him that strangely enough funds would not help me just then, and I feared that even he, a cement manufacturer, could not give me the one thing I needed at the moment, paper on which to print more copies. We then and there agreed that he should come over and stay with me in college for the next week-end. When he arrived and had shaken hands I asked him, 'Why does this pamphlet interest you so?' His answer was:

'All my life my real interest, like my father's before me, has been in social reform. However, I have found myself up against two insuperable obstacles. One cannot get people to interest themselves in social reform while their minds are preoccupied with fear of a world war which is threatening. Apart from this, it is quite impossible to pass the measures needed for social reform in the present congested condition of Whitehall and Westminster. Your plan, if realized, would kill both birds with one stone. A Union Government charged with the common defence would in time remove the fear of impending war. It would also relieve the national government of all concern with external affairs. It would then be able to devote its whole time and attention, as it cannot do now, to the tasks of social reform; and we should begin to get the measures we need.'

Now perhaps you will see why preventing war and advancing social reform are as closely connected as the foci of an ellipse. You will only achieve either in so far as you achieve both. We are always told that vested interests stand in the way of social reform. That is true; but the reason why cabinets and parliaments cannot cope with these vested interests is because there are not enough days in the year for cabinets to frame and parliaments to pass the measures required to control these vested interests. The mere factor of time limits the power of sovereign governments. Mechanization is now changing conditions of life faster than any one set of human beings in a cabinet or parliament can adjust the framework of policy or law to meet the changes. The only effective remedy is to divide the tasks of government, to entrust those of external affairs to a single new cabinet and parliament, leaving those of internal and social reform to existing cabinets and parliaments.

A few days ago I found myself on a bus by an airman in the uniform of New Zealand. He spoke with justifiable pride of the notable progress made by his government in social reform. 'We can do all this', he added, 'because we leave our external affairs to be handled by England.'

This transition from a national to an international control of defence is the most important transition that man has ever been brought by the march of events to face, and also the most difficult. The British democracies, with their common language and institutions, can render the greatest service in history to the world at large if they can show how that first and most difficult step can be taken. I do not pretend that I think that a union of the British democracies will ensure the peace of the world. Again let me say that the peace of the world will be finally secured only when the most potent of all free peoples, that of the U.S.A., decides to merge its external relations in an international union for the purpose. But I do not myself believe that that vast and conservative nation will ever consent to join a union which might be at the outset mainly British. Let me quote an extract from a letter written by an eminent American lawyer who is now on military service in Australia:

'A poll by the magazine *Fortune* last October showed that in the previous year and a half the number of those who approved of some federal government had increased from something like 6 per cent. to over 35 per cent. of the population, and to over 35 per cent. of those with opinions on the matter. *The large majority of the federal-minded wanted a government that would not be exclusively Anglo-American even at the start.*

'That was one of the big points on which Streit misjudged the public and also, I think, political realities.'

His view, which I share, is that the U.S.A. will never consent to link their own external relations with those of a British Commonwealth, but would be prepared in time to join what they felt was an international union in the fullest sense of that word.

My proposal is simply this, that when hostilities cease the British Government should have the candour and courage to tell the Dominion Governments that Great Britain and Northern Ireland can no longer provide the resources required to maintain forces by sea, land, and air strong enough to protect the Commonwealth from further attacks, in accordance with the resolution passed by the Imperial Conference of 1926. In their own interest it should ask them to review the position in the light of a fact which is plainly beyond dispute. But already the French, Netherland, and Scandinavian democracies are asking the British Government what guarantees will be given them that Germany will not in future be allowed to do to them as she has done in this war. Here again our answer should be based upon indisputable facts. Twice have we guaranteed the frontiers of Belgium; yet twice in this century has Germany raped and enslaved her. What is the use of our offering our democratic allies in Europe a guarantee which we have not the power to make good? Our answer should therefore be that we are telling our sister nations in the British Commonwealth that we, the United Kingdom of Great Britain and Northern Ireland, are no longer strong enough to prevent aggression, and are asking them to discuss with us what should be done to restore the security which the United Kingdom was able to provide in the nineteenth century. We therefore invite the French, Netherland, and Scandinavian Governments to join these discussions, which might lead to the creation of some common authority equipped to provide a common defence for these countries as well as for the British democracies from all their resources.

With such a union in being the position would then be as follows. If one German tank or plane were to cross the frontiers of France, Belgium, Holland, Denmark, or Norway as in this war, there would then be no parley nor any discussion how far to restrain the aggressor with sanctions. (While the League Assembly was debating that question Mussolini was raining mustard gas on the helpless people of Abyssinia.) If one German tank or plane crossed those frontiers, there would then be instant war with a new United States which included the democracies of western Europe and the British Commonwealth, having an air force which would at once accept the challenge in overwhelming force. Then and then only the western democracies would have such a guarantee of their frontiers as a German government might learn to respect.

The world has seen no higher act of political construction than that which led thirteen American states to merge their sovereignties in one commonwealth. The drafting of the plan and even its rapid acceptance by the people of those states were only the first steps in that great achievement. It might soon have ended in failure but for the work afterwards done by Washington as President and Hamilton as Minister of Finance to show how the principles they conceived and expressed in the Constitution could operate in practice. In the course of that first decade they convinced the American people that the system provided them with government in the real sense of the word and would work. How this practical demonstration led on to vastly greater results we can see by recalling that no less than thirty-five other states have since joined the thirteen which founded the union.

In the light of these facts let us think what results might follow if British democracies joined with those of western Europe in a union for their common security which allowed their national governments to concentrate all their time and attention on social reform. As in America, much would depend upon how far the novel machinery was found to be workable in the first decade. I hope and believe it would stand that test if it were started by democracies so experienced as those of the British, the French, the Netherland, and Scandinavian countries. I think that in ten years they would find themselves moving to a greater sense of security, and also that their own national governments would be able to cope with the tasks of social reform as never before. My faith is that if other democracies saw such a union in being, they might come to join it almost as readily as the thirty-five states came to join the thirteen which established the American Union. I believe that even the great conservative American people would come to see that here was a new birth of freedom, and would join themselves to it. And this I am sure would happen if Canada were in the union, and they had watched the results in their own continent. An international union of defence which included the United States would then be strong enough to include any nation which has learned how to make their national government responsible to the people themselves. Sooner or later all nations will learn that lesson, when once the free peoples have rendered their freedom inviolate by aggressors. Democratic states are those best fitted to form the spearhead of an international union. A successful practical start opens the door for effective co-operation with nations having other forms of government.

There is a long-term policy for the prevention of war and the provision for a better life for all on this planet. It can only be realized by a series of steps of which the first is by far the most difficult. In my view the hopes of the world may depend upon how far we of the British Commonwealth can so 'elevate our minds to the dignity of our great calling' as to take that first difficult step. We British should apply to ourselves what Bacon meant when he wrote: 'It was not Rome that spread upon the world, but the world which spread upon Rome—and that way greatness lay.'

CHAPTER XXXVIII

# THE LEAGUE OF NATIONS

WHAT about the League of Nations? The Allies are pledged to its reconstruction, in one form or another, so the question is apposite.

In *The Times* of the 18th August 1944 the following statement by Mr. Cordell Hull is reported:

'In the Moscow Declaration the four nations placed themselves on record as advocating a "general international organization" based on the principle of sovereign equality of all peace-loving States and open to membership of all such States, large and small, for the maintenance of international peace and security; this statement was embodied in the Connally resolution passed in the United States Senate by an overwhelming vote of 85 to five.'

In 1919 the League was created to prevent the recurrence of wars and to make the world safe for democracy. It was also entrusted with certain social functions which could only be handled by international action, for instance the spread of disease, the control of drugs, and the white-slave traffic. In the outline I gave you I merely referred to its utter failure to achieve its primary function, the prevention of war. I am glad of this chance of mentioning its success in promoting health and in dealing with traffic in drugs and women and with economics and finance.

What is called 'a functional approach to security from war' is now a fashionable doctrine. This means that after this war governments should concentrate their energies on international organizations for feeding the starving peoples of Europe and Asia, for restoring their economic equipment, for promoting health, and so on. The argument is that they will thus develop such a habit of acting together that without any conscious change they will find themselves able to act together to deal with aggressors who threaten the peace of the world.

'A page of history is worth a volume of logic', said Mr. Justice Holmes as quoted by Mr. Cordell Hull in his Easter broadcast. In reading the page of history which is headed 'The League of Nations' we find how much their governments achieved in twenty years in the functional field, which covered not only such matters as health, but also the achievements of the I.L.O. But in twenty years this functional approach had failed to create a habit of co-operation strong enough to induce the States Members of the League to restrain Japan when she violated China, Mussolini's invasion of Abyssinia, or Hitler's rape of Czechoslovakia and Poland. On the 7th September 1939 the British Government wrote as follows to the Secretary-General of the League:

'The position to-day shows clearly that the Covenant has, in the present instance, completely broken down in practice, that the whole machinery for the preservation of peace has collapsed.'

With this page of history before us the United Nations are now told by their governments that the preservation of peace is to be entrusted to another League of Sovereign States.

The whole page should be read, including the great achievement of the League in the field of its secondary functions. It proves how useful and effective a League can be in this field, and so long as the world is divided into sovereign states some organization through which their governments can meet to discuss their mutual relations is clearly needed. My thesis is that democracies will not begin to allay the fear of war until they have shown how it is possible for some of them to merge their powers in one international union entrusted with the task of their common defence. The experiment, to succeed, must be made by experienced democracies. All attempts to create a world government at one stroke are doomed from the outset. There must for a period be states unfitted and unable to join an international union. But the first international commonwealth must have relations with those states, and the closer their contact the sooner will states outside it become fitted to join the union, and anxious to do so. So long as society is divided into sovereign states, there must be some regular system of consultation between them, and for such common action as can be achieved in the functional field. The practical need for a League of Nations will only vanish when they all have joined the international union and have thus brought into being a genuine world government. Then and then only will international law be law in the true sense of the word. A League may help to prevent some local wars as it did in the past. But the statesmen who are telling the world it can trust its peace to a League of Sovereign States are using a logic which ignores the experience written in the page of history before them. To them their national sovereignties are the Ark of the Covenant. Any movement to change the sovereignties they cherish and wield awakes a jealousy which blinds them to history. When they say that peace can be founded on leagues of national sovereignties they are throwing the dust which has blinded themselves in the eyes of the nations they rule. Leviathan blinds his worshippers.

I think that there should be a League of Nations, in which such a union as I am proposing would take its place. As was seen in the case of the old League, the national governments which compose the union might also be represented there, as well as the union government.

The same applies to the other policy which Allied governments have already adopted and proclaimed—the policy of an alliance of the British and American Commonwealths and Russia to maintain the peace, the policy advocated by Walter Lippmann. For the British democracies and those of western Europe to form an international union is consistent with both the policies which the Allied governments have announced. Such a union could speak on terms of equality with partners so powerful as the U.S.A. and Soviet Russia. In such an alliance the British Commonwealth will weigh but little so long as it speaks with five or more separate voices.

History has shown how stable organic unions are when once they are made, and how prone a league or alliance is to fail and to break in a moment of crisis.

> ' Men do their broken weapons rather use
> Than their bare hands '

for what they are worth. At best a league and alliance may

help to postpone war. But my case is that no league or alliance can avail to preserve the peace upon earth which the Charter has promised. Democracies will not begin to assuage the fear of war that bedevils mankind until they begin to merge their external powers of defence into one international union. Nor will they begin to overtake their growing arrears in social reform until by creating a government charged with the task of their common defence they have set their national governments free to concentrate all their energies on their own domestic affairs.

## CHAPTER XXXIX

# DUMBARTON OAKS

PROPOSALS for a world organization discussed by British, American, Russian, and Chinese officials at Dumbarton Oaks have now been issued in the form of a White Paper. I must preface my comments on these proposals by repeating what I said in the last chapter. So long as human society remains divided into sovereign states, some world organization in which their governments can meet to discuss their mutual relations, will, I believe, be essential. My quarrel is not with Dumbarton Oaks, but only with those who are using their high positions and seats in the legislature, especially those whose seats are hereditary, to convince the world that an organization based upon compacts between sovereign states can be trusted to secure it against a renewal of war.

In *The Times* of the 22nd December 1944 the following letter was published:

## OPINION AND PEACE

*To the Editor of 'The Times'*

Sir,—The report of Mr. Bruce's speech in your issue of December 13 and your own leading article on the subject, both emphasize the necessity of 'an enlightened public opinion' behind the government of the United Nations, 'demanding that the efforts to obtain general agreement (in economic and financial as well as in political matters) should succeed'. To create such a public opinion has been the specific object of the League of Nations Union since its foundation 26 years ago. Such will continue to be its object in the future; and we are grateful to Mr. Bruce and to you for pointing out how important it is that such an enlightened public opinion should exist.

As soon as the proposals of the Dumbarton Oaks conference become embodied in an international agreement, and a new world organization takes the place of the League of Nations, we shall make the necessary changes in our title and constitution, and apply for permission to amend our Royal Charter, to conform with the new situation; so that we may perform for the new organism the same service that we previously performed for the League of Nations.

> I am yours, &c.,
> LYTTON, Chairman, Executive Committee, League of Nations Union.
18, Chester Street, S.W.1.

We are thus informed that the League of Nations Union propose to continue their long and effective campaign 'to enlighten public opinion' under cover of a Royally Chartered smoke screen. If these priests of Leviathan succeed, they will, I believe, secure to their idol his appropriate offering of millions of young lives and rivers of blood.

In Chapter XV I remarked that 'All political systems are of two kinds, organic and inorganic. The organic systems are sovereign states such as Great Britain, France, the U.S.A., Germany, Italy, Russia, and Japan. Examples of inorganic systems are the Holy Roman Empire, the American Confederation, the Grand Alliance, the German Confederation, the Austrian Empire, Scandinavia before the partition, the Alliances which lost and won the world war, and the League of Nations.' The tentative proposals from Dumbarton Oaks clearly belong to this second class.

Sovereign states are based on a sense of duty in the persons who compose them. The cement which binds them is what Lincoln called 'dedication', a unilateral motive not subject to change by changing conditions, and, therefore, relatively stable. Alliances and confederations are based on compacts between sovereign states, a bilateral or multilateral bond. It is therefore subject to change as conditions change. Such international systems have in fact proved highly unstable. Theory and practice both point to the view that Dumbarton Oaks is likely to prove no exception to the rule, a rule to which there have so far been no exceptions in history.

That is my general comment on Dumbarton Oaks. It is in a word the League of Nations patched to cure defects that its own parents have to admit. The principle on which it is based is none the less that of the old League, that and no other. The fact is not masked by changing the name of

'Covenant' to 'Charter' or the name of 'League' to 'World organization'. As a cynic remarked in India, governments seem to think that problems can be solved by changing their names.

Let us now turn to examine the patching. That the League was unable to act in time to prevent aggressions in China, Abyssinia, Austria, Czechoslovakia, and Poland, aggressions bound to involve the world in war, is beyond dispute. These delays were largely due to the fact that every State member of the League possessed a *liberum veto*. Neither Council nor Assembly could reach decisions, until each and all their members were agreed.

Mr. Justice Roberts of the Supreme Court in the U.S.A. has sent me an article by Mr. Grenville Clark, a New York lawyer of international reputation, which was published by the *New York Times* on the 15th October 1944. It puts my own point of view so much better than I can put it myself that I shall not scruple to quote from it. Mr. Clark opens with two questions.

Do the Dumbarton Oaks proposals offer reasonable assurance for the realization of the basic purpose—the maintenance of 'international peace and security'? Or are they so deficient in principle and detail that they offer no such assurance, and should, consequently, be radically modified?

With regret I am constrained to the latter view. It is my firm conviction that these proposals repeat the essential errors of the League of Nations, which so signally failed in its prime purpose; that the proposals are demonstrably ineffective to the end in view, and that drastic changes are imperative if we are to avoid failure and disillusionment.

The Dumbarton Oaks proposals call for three main organs:

1. A General Assembly, with one vote for each member country, irrespective of population or resources;
2. A Security Council of eleven members, five of whom would be permanent members representing the United States, the Soviet Union, the United Kingdom, China, and 'in due course' France, the other six to be chosen for rotating terms by the Assembly; and
3. An International Court of Justice with a jurisdiction evi-

dently intended to resemble closely that of the present World Court. Since space forbids a discussion of the judicial organ, I confine myself to the proposed Assembly and Council.

It needs no argument that with the rule of one vote for each country the proposed Assembly must necessarily be a subordinate organ. It would indeed be contrary to all reason and common sense to confer important powers in vital matters upon a body in which Panama and Luxemburg have an equal vote with the United States and the Soviet Union, and in which Costa Rica and Ethiopia have an equal voice with the United Kingdom, China, and France.

In recognition of this obvious fact, the Dumbarton Oaks proposals carefully exclude the Assembly from any direct participation in the concerting of definite measures to prevent or put down aggression, which is the basic purpose of the organization. It would be virtually confined to the election of the rotating members of the Council and the supervision of various auxiliary agencies.

It will be seen that this restricted scope of the proposed Assembly results from the unsound conception that the doctrine of the 'sovereign equality' of all States implies that each country shall have an equal vote. From this perversion of the idea of sovereign equality comes the ironical result that, while all the members of the Assembly are accorded a vote, the very fact that the votes are equal necessitates a narrow restriction of the subjects upon which these votes can be cast. The net result is an Assembly subordinate to the super-directorate of the Great Powers, to be exercised through the proposed Security Council.

Turning to this proposed Council, we find an almost equal ineffectiveness, but for a different reason. This is the requirement of unanimous consent by the representatives of the Big Five, at least with relation to the most important decisions.

Much discussion has occurred as to whether any one of the Big Five should be permitted to veto sanctions against itself. But it is necessary to bear in mind that if this problem were solved tomorrow, the requirement of unanimity for sanctions against any other possible aggressor would remain intact.

The proposition, incredible as it may seem, is that any one of the Big Five may, by its sole fiat, paralyze the whole world organization. . . . If we go through to our objectives—the unconditional surrender or complete defeat of Germany, and the stripping from Japan of all her conquests since 1895—it will be like having two rattlesnakes in one's bedroom that will need to be watched with an eagle eye and a heavy club for a long time to come. Nothing less, therefore, will suffice than international machinery that can operate with maximum certainty and promptness in bringing to bear irresistible power.

I submit, therefore, that this combination of a nearly impotent Assembly, on the one hand, and, on the other, a Council that is hamstrung, or at best hampered, by the right of any one of the Big Five to veto sanctions, must be a weak reed to support the peace of the world. . . .

To these searching comments by this highly qualified writer I may now add one of my own. We have often been told that the new world organization must give adequate weight to views of the smaller states. Supporters of the League have always been loud in insisting on this. Dumbarton Oaks will give the smaller states about the same part in reaching decisions that the guinea-pig jurymen enjoyed in *Alice in Wonderland*.

In October the proposals prepared at Dumbarton Oaks were discussed in the House of Lords on the motion of Lord Winster. On the following day the main page of *The Times* carried a special article and also a leader on the subject. The author of the article remarked 'the basis of the association is to be a conventionally assumed sovereign equality which, however, does not extend to function'—thus adopting a typical Balfourian phrase from the Report of the Imperial Conference of 1926. Finding no further reference either in this article or in the leader to the cardinal principle of the proposal I turned to the report of the debate itself. There Lord Winster in opening the debate is reported to have said that 'the real issues in such Conferences as that at Dumbarton Oaks were not machinery and organization but the question of whether nations were prepared to sacrifice to try to secure peace by, among other things, surrender of sovereignty, agreement not to be judges in their own cause, alterations of frontiers, and racialism. If the answer was "No", then the old causes which drenched Europe and the world in blood over and over again would continue to operate and once more to produce war.'

Lord Winster was followed by Viscount Samuel, Viscount Cecil, the Earl of Perth, Viscount Cranborne, and the Earl of Huntingdon who is briefly reported to have said that 'the only device to prevent war that had so far worked was that of federations'. The report of the four previous speeches contains no reference to the principle which the draft itself describes as the basis of the whole plan nor to the main point raised by the mover that surrender of sovereignty is the real issue. Are we then to infer from their silence that the basic principle of the whole plan ought in the view of these peers to be excluded from public discussion?

This silence on the part of Lord Samuel calls for special remark. In February 1940 Lord Lothian, speaking as British Ambassador to the House of Delegates and Senate of Virginia said: 'To-day an anarchy of sovereign States cannot escape chronic war or preserve individual liberty or create the conditions of prosperity and employment within their own boundaries unless in some way they can bring themselves collectively under the reign of a single constitutional law.'

Lord Lothian was here repeating what he had said in his memorable Burge Lecture of 1935 under the title *Pacifism is not enough, nor Patriotism either*.

I am under the impression that Lord Lothian was leading the Liberal Party in the House of Lords when the present Viscount Samuel was leading that party in the Commons. It is strange therefore that Lord Samuel should ignore a point raised by Lord Winster, upon which his former Liberal colleague in Parliament had expressed so clear a view in his Burge Lecture and again when speaking as British Ambassador in the U.S.A. Lord Lothian's words, though addressed to the oldest American legislature, were obviously meant to be heard by English-speaking peoples throughout the world.

Should the Marquis of Lothian, Lord Winster, and the Earl of Huntingdon prove to be right, the next generation will, in Lord Winster's phrase, 'be drenched in blood'. So long as Parliament withholds this issue from public discussion the main responsibility for a third holocaust will rest there;

and the fact will need no further proof than the columns of Hansard.

Sooner or later historians will say who was responsible for a failure which will cost millions their freedom and lives. Their posthumous verdict may be useful as a warning to future statesmen; but we, while this second war is in progress, should look round us and say now where the responsibility lies for preventing a third and more fearful disaster, however painful the answer may be. I may illustrate the point by a hypothetical case. Suppose that some resident at Pearl Harbour had observed a neglect of precautions to forestall a treacherous attack by the Japanese air force. In my view such a resident should then and there have said in public that he would regard the officers in command as responsible for any disaster to which such neglect of precautions might lead. Had he happened to have been on a footing of friendship with the officers in question, it would still, in my view, have been his public duty to take such distasteful action.

To me it seems that Ministers in office are not, so long as the war lasts, in the best position to say what changes are needed to prevent the recurrence of world wars. For the moment, their task is to win this war, and not to raise issues which raised by them might impair the unity of the Cabinet and of the Allies. But if Lothian and those who agree with him should prove to be right, it is of vital importance that the question whether they are right or wrong should be made the subject of public discussion *now*, so that public opinion may be informed before decisions have to be made. In my own view the free discussion of this vital issue is for members of Parliament who are not burdened with executive office. The task is not so easy for the House of Commons, busied with a mass of urgent legislation, the members of which are faced by electorates. From both impediments elder statesmen in the House of Lords are exempt. They have ample time and no electorates to embarrass them. So far these elder statesmen have met the questions raised by younger peers with silence or else with strings of the clichés that have

long done duty in speeches on Imperial and foreign affairs
and in leading articles on Empire Day. (The word *cliché*
is French for a worn-out coin which has lost its value by
over-use.) Should a third and more terrible disaster befall,
those chiefly responsible, in my view, will be these 'blind
mouths' sugared with clichés which lure nations down paths
that wind through the dim shades of Dumbarton Oaks to
the edge of a precipice, and to utter destruction on the rocks
beyond.

## CHAPTER XL

# DEMOCRATIC PATHOLOGY

YOU ask me whether this policy has met with any support in political circles. **My unqualified answer must be 'with none whatever'.** If mentioned at all by politicians, it is only as something to be dismissed as beyond the limits of practical discussion. Let me quote two examples. In April 1944 the House of Commons discussed the Imperial problem for two whole days. Mr. Hore-Belisha dismissed this policy as one that 'suffers from the supreme demerit of being rejected by all the parties concerned'.[1] That this was the general opinion was shown when Lord Winterton said:

'I speak with the greatest discretion, as all speakers in this debate have spoken, when I say that alliance is and never can be anything but a voluntary alliance of sovereign Parliaments and Governments under a common flag and Throne. It should not go out from this House, and, indeed, it has not gone out in the course of this two days' Debate, that the powers of the sovereign Parliaments of the Dominions should be abated by one jot or tittle.'[2]

That, I believe, represents the attitude taken in political circles, not only in this country, but in all the other countries concerned. Mr. Sumner Welles, for example, in his able and important book, *The Time for Decision*, has a chapter on World Organization, in which an organic union of states is not even mentioned as a possible form of world organization. It is not an idea which a practical statesman should ever discuss.

I am not surprised, for I always expected it. The reasons lie in the natural history of freedom, the ultimate object for which we are fighting. The practical expression of freedom is a system which makes governments responsible to and therefore changeable by the people they govern. It vests political power in the people themselves, and is therefore called democracy, a Greek word which means rule by the

[1] Hansard, vol. cccxcix, No. 64, col. 498.
[2] Ibid., col. 569.

people. In my own view democracy is to human society what physical health is to your body and mine. Because we know how important health is to our bodies, we study the diseases which attack it and so learn how to cure or prevent them. It is just as important to recognize that democracy is subject to diseases, to study their causes and learn how to cure or prevent them.

As diseases come from the nature of our bodies, so those of democracy come from its nature. Where government is responsible to a people, they must have power to change that government from time to time, and rulers must gain and hold their position as such by winning elections. The result is a tendency in those who are asking voters to elect and support them to think what their voters want and to say what they like to hear. Politicians are thus led to think that their first duty is to find what public opinion is and to follow it, and forget that their primary duty is to form and lead public opinion. Leadership is vital to democracy. The average man does not like taxation or military service. Before this war Winston Churchill was almost alone in telling electors that unless they could face costly rearmament and compulsory service they were heading straight for disaster. You may note the fact that he now commands an authority greater than any leader in English history. In a crisis people follow the leader who had told them *before the event* the truths they least wanted to hear, the rare statesman, who grasps that imperishable truth revealed to the poet who sang:

'Yet, Freedom! yet thy banner, torn, but flying,
Streams like the thunderstorm *against* the wind.'[1]

Now I come to another and a more subtle disease of democracy. All systems become sacred in the eyes of those who control their mechanism. They tend to lose sight of the end for which the system exists, and the system becomes an end in itself. It was so with the Church founded that men might learn how better to serve God and their fellow men. To most of the priests it became an end in itself. They were

[1] Byron, *Childe Harold*, xcviii.

blind to abuses which the laity felt, till the Reformation blew it in pieces. And so it is with any great system, an army, a navy, a civil service, and even business organizations such as railways. To any drastic changes in such systems the most resolute opposition usually comes from those who control them.

This is equally true of the politicians who control the system of democracy as it now is. That system sprang from the tiny cities of ancient Greece. The living principle which inspired their commonwealths has grown through the ages. The English devised representative government and created democracy on the national scale. It was based on the principle that the nation must tax itself through its own representatives. By the eighteenth century our politicians had come to regard the sovereignty of Parliament as sacred. They forgot the principle on which it was based, and taxed the American colonies which elected no members to Parliament. The result was a revolution. That will always happen when people come to regard their system of democracy as final and static. For the principle of the commonwealth like a living thing must always grow, and begins to languish if its growth is arrested.

The American revolution set the principle free for a further growth. By devising the federal system the Americans showed how to apply the principle to a national democracy on the scale of a continent. Since then we have seen a world cut up into upwards of sixty sovereign states, including national democracies as great as the United Kingdom and the U.S.A. To politicians in all these democracies their claim to sovereignty becomes such a habit of mind that they come to regard it as an order of nature which can never be changed. A proposal to deprive their national government, as they have always known it and worked it, of its power to decide all public questions is to them too fantastic for serious discussion in legislatures. Any measures proposed for carrying out the Atlantic Charter must always be subject to one condition, that no such measures must interfere with national sovereignties. The right of ultimate decision must always rest where it now resides, in the national governments. You will find that condition affirmed in every public pronouncement, in the Atlantic Charter itself, in the declarations of Moscow and Teheran.[1] You will find it in every speech which statesmen and politicians of all the United Nations have uttered on the subject. It stands in the forefront of the programme issued by both American parties.

The worship of Leviathan as an idol too sacred to touch leads on to suppression in public debate of facts which point to the perils involved. In the two days' debate of April last particular stress was laid on the sovereign equality of Dominions with the United Kingdom, and their absolute right to control their defence and foreign affairs as declared by the Imperial Conference of 1926. But no mention was made of the fact that, whilst each Dominion assumed responsibility for its own local defence, the task of maintaining by sea and air the routes that connect them was left as before to the United Kingdom.

In the course of the April debate Mr. Vernon Bartlett remarked that after this war 'the United Kingdom will not be in a position to carry that main burden'.[2] Mr. Shinwell hazarded a guess that this war might not have happened at all 'if the Empire countries, twenty years before this war began, had collaborated for the purpose of defence'.[3] Apart from these two gleams of reality little was said to dispel the clouds of rhetoric and make-believe which always envelop our public discussions of Imperial questions.

In democracies public opinion is the governing factor. Their success or failure will depend on a public opinion which is properly informed. The speeches of politicians as reported in the Press and telegraphed in cables are of all the means of informing public opinion the most important. Debate by their own members in parliaments is the most powerful agency for forming that public opinion, which is in the last instance the determining factor in politics.

Democracies are thus subject to three specific and closely

[1] See the page opposite the frontispiece Leviathan.
[2] Hansard, vol. cccxcix, No. 63, col. 419.     [3] Ibid., col. 400.

related diseases: the tendency of politicians to follow instead of leading public opinion, to regard the system they operate as one too sacred for structural change, and so to avoid mentioning facts in debate which point to the need for such change. This explains why reforms needed to save the cause of freedom are usually opposed at the outset by a great majority of public men. A few examples will show you how such reforms were carried.

After the War of Independence the Confederation of thirteen states went bankrupt and lapsed into anarchy. Though Washington believed that public opinion was against such change in the Constitution as would save the American people from disaster, he persevered till he got the states to send delegates to Philadelphia to consider amendments to the articles of Confederation. He opened the Congress with these words:

'It is too probable that no plan we propose will be adopted. *Perhaps another dreadful conflict is to be sustained.* If to please the people we offer what we ourselves disapprove, how can we afterwards defend our work? Let us raise a standard to which the wise and honest can repair; the event is in the hands of God.'

This lead was followed by the men he addressed. Exceeding their terms of reference they framed a proposal whereby the sovereignty of the thirteen states was in fact merged in the sovereignty of the United States. And this was so because they proposed the creation of a central government charged with the interests common to all the states, which derived its authority not from the governments of those states, but from their citizens, and could exercise its authority over those citizens. It made the adoption of this proposal depend, not on consent of the thirteen state legislatures, but on consent of the citizens who elected them.

The result surprised Washington himself. The proposed constitution was to come into force when accepted in nine states by conventions directly elected. The delegates dispersed from Philadelphia in September 1787. The ninth state confirmed the union in June 1788. The lead given by Washington and followed by the Congress of Philadelphia had worked this political miracle in less than twelve months, and this the American people did because their trusted leader had told them that the only practical alternative to anarchy was this novel contrivance. But even a leader of Washington's calibre could not have accomplished this unless a handful of young followers, of whom Alexander Hamilton was foremost, had grasped the cause of anarchy and had worked out in detail the minimum changes needed to remove this cause and establish a government for the American people.

The hope of freedom in America was saved thereby; but in course of time a further step was needed to save and extend it. A movement was started in the North to abolish slavery in the Southern States. The movement was discounted by politicians even in the North, on the ground that the necessary change in the Constitution could only be made by a civil war, which public opinion would never be ready to face. Even in the North abolitionists were treated as dangerous agitators, till a Member of Congress, Abraham Lincoln, called on the people to face the fact that America must be all free or all slave. They elected him President and faced the issue of civil war. The Union was saved and slavery abolished. And let me add that but for the work that Washington did in the eighteenth century to create the United States and that Lincoln did in the nineteenth century to save the Union, Americans would not have been able to marshal their vast resources to save their own freedom and that of the world, as twice they have saved it in the twentieth century.

Let us now take two cases from the British Commonwealth. By 1881 most thinking people in Australia had come to see that they could not hope to control the future and fate of a whole continent through six colonial governments. Time and again the colonial governments and legislatures sent delegates to conferences, and drafted plans for a Union which came to nothing. At last Sir Henry Parkes appealed to the people over the heads of the legislatures. He demanded and got a convention directly elected by the people themselves. The convention met in 1897 and framed a constitution which the voters of five colonies accepted in 1899. In 1900 the Commonwealth of Australia came into being.

In 1902 the South African War was closed by the Peace of Vereeniging. In 1905 the Transvaal and Orange Free State were promised responsible government. Some of us thought and said that if four democratic governments in Cape Colony, Natal, the Transvaal, and Orange Free State were left to control the tangled affairs of South Africa, we should all be shooting each other again in a few years. Politicians indulgently said that all young men talked like that. Union would come, no doubt, perhaps in the time of our grandchildren. The matter was not yet ripe. Our arguments would have had no effect, even though backed by the High Commissioner who published and endorsed them. But the whole situation was changed by four public men, Botha and Smuts in the north and Jameson and Francis Malan in the south, who told their followers, Boer and British, that a Union effected then and there was the only alternative to another civil war. By 1909 the Union was an accomplished fact.

In all these cases the world was ripe for what Abraham Lincoln so aptly called 'a new birth of freedom'. In all of them the operation required to deliver a world in travail was regarded by politicians as the visionary project of troublesome busybodies. The combined opposition of politicians in all the democracies to any proposal to merge their national sovereignties in an international union is a normal occurrence and perfectly natural. But note the means in all these cases from Washington onwards by which this opposition was overcome. At the critical moment some politician who stood head and shoulders above his fellows, some statesman, that is, whose voice could be heard by millions of people, rose up to tell them that some such change was the only way to escape disaster. When millions believed what he said, politicians began to think and to say so, too. As if by a miracle the change was made. I have said that fear of war will continue to paralyse the world until some democracies show how to merge their sovereignties in an international union. The pamphlets in which I say this can at best reach a few thousand readers. Some of them may be convinced by my reasons, but never so many as to create a public opinion strong and widespread enough to effect the change. Mere argument does not reach the millions and create an effective public opinion. In democracies the masses take their opinion from some recognized leader, whose judgement they trust, and when he utters such a truth they accept it in masses, and the change that he tells them is needed is faced and accomplished.

To all this let me add one closing remark. We are told that it rests with the British and American Commonwealths in close alliance with Russia to secure the peace of the world, and to exercise the necessary force for the purpose. Americans, surely, will see that if in practice the British Commonwealth consists of a confederation of five democracies, the strongest of which commands resources limited to Great Britain and Northern Ireland, the confederation will be a negligible factor in providing the forces necessary to support its allies in the task of ensuring peace.

## APPENDIX TO CHAPTER XL

A FRIEND, with whom I was discussing the question of answers to prayer, said to me, 'Remember that God sometimes answers prayers in ways we do not expect.' On the 11th November 1944 (a memorable date) *The Times* published the following leading article, which in all fairness I must append to this chapter. I had always felt that if the President of the United States or the Prime Minister of the United Kingdom were to follow the example of Washington by warning the world that, until democracies had merged their national sovereignties in one international union for their common defence '*another dreadful conflict is to be sustained*', the necessary step would be taken in a few years. I had not realized that a voice might come from the Press which could reach almost as far as the voice of the President or the Prime Minister.

### 'THE WESTERN POWERS [1]

'The impending visit of the Prime Minister and Mr. Eden to France, following on the visit of the Belgian Foreign Minister to this country, throws into relief a subject of first importance—the future relations of Great Britain with the newly liberated European countries of western Europe. The question has already engaged

[1] Reprinted from *The Times*, 11th November 1944, by permission.

the attention of the leaders of these nations themselves. As long ago as last March General de Gaulle discussed the prospects of a "western union" based chiefly, though not exclusively, on economic collaboration. Last week the Belgian Prime Minister, in the Chamber of Representatives in Brussels, spoke of the "essential common interests" of Great Britain and Belgium "especially concerning security", and looked forward to "closer relations and preparations for practical collaboration in several directions". That Norway and the Netherlands, once liberated and freed from the weight of their most pressing preoccupations, will share these sentiments and these hopes need not be doubted. The journey of Mr. Churchill and Mr. Eden to France will doubtless provide the occasion for some corresponding declaration from the British side on an issue which is at least as vital to the foreign policy of Great Britain as to that of her continental neighbours.

'The position of Great Britain differs in one respect from that of her two major partners in the world alliance for victory and peace —the United States and the Soviet Union. While they naturally seek the closest partnership with the geographically contiguous countries of Latin America and of eastern Europe respectively, the most intimate ties of sentiment, tradition, and interest bind Great Britain to the widely dispersed countries of the British Commonwealth of Nations. The United States and the Soviet Union are, it is commonly said, continental Powers; Great Britain is an oceanic Power. But it is possible to press this obvious distinction too far. It has been part of Great Britain's strength in the past that she has never been content to consider her position in the world as one irrevocably determined and incapable of evolution. Not only will relations between Great Britain and the nations of the British Commonwealth demand fuller and more fruitful development after the war, but there will also be room and need for an altogether new development of relations between them and the nations of western Europe; and since these relations will help to strengthen Britain and British security, they will also promote the strength and security of the whole Commonwealth.

'The demand for a new orientation of policy is most clearly recognized in the field of security. In the nineteenth century the traditional British policy of splendid isolation from Europe was never absolute; the contingent obligation of the Belgian Guarantee treaty of 1839 had constituted at least a formal exception to it. Forty years ago the Franco-British *entente* brought even the form of isolation to an end. Since that time the question has never really been whether Great Britain might be compelled by certain contingencies to take military action in Europe, but what were to be the scope and timing of that action. The present war has taught two clear lessons. The first is that the British commitment is necessarily more far-reaching and more automatic in its operation than the British people had hitherto been prepared to believe. The second lesson, valid for all the nations of western Europe, is that no commitment providing for common action in certain contingencies but not for common organization in advance to make such action prompt and effective will in future suffice. Even "staff talks", the most practical form of preparation ever seriously envisaged in the period between the two wars, are in themselves a totally inadequate expedient. Nothing short of common military organization and planning, with pooled and coordinated military resources and joint bases serving the needs of all the United Nations, has sufficed to make the strategy of the United Nations effective in war. Nothing short of this will suffice to meet the lasting requirements of security in every part of the world, Europe—and Germany—included. It is no longer a question of guarantees given by Great Britain to other nations, but of common policies and common preparations to execute those policies which are as vitally important to Great Britain herself as to any of the European Powers.

'Such policies would fall directly within the category of "regional arrangements or agencies" for the maintenance of peace and security foreseen in the Dumbarton Oaks plan. But the principle is also valid, and its application is indeed equally necessary, beyond the strictly military sphere. Whatever conclusions may be reached by the Chicago conference on civil aviation, some regional system of joint control and organization for civil flying in western Europe will be a paramount condition of security which cannot be taken into consideration too soon. Nor is it only the exigencies of security which are common to the nations of this western region. Most of them are faced with identical or similar problems of economic readjustment arising from a balance of payments in dislocation, a high degree of dependence on foreign trade, and a developed industry working on imported raw materials. Most of them have vast dependent colonial territories, the greater part of the African continent being divided between them. All these nations have accepted the challenge of social justice at home and of policies of development and welfare for colonial peoples; and they will be seeking together to meet this double challenge through the processes of reconstruction. Common economic planning will be required, as well as joint military organization, if western Europe, Britain included, is to face the future with united strength and confidence.

'Some moves have already been made towards the establishment of common monetary policies for Great Britain, France, Belgium, and Holland; and it is certain that whatever universal framework be evolved there will be a place within it, as within the Dumbarton Oaks plan, for "regional agreements or agencies" aiming at the promotion of full employment and the free exchange of goods within specific areas or groups. A correspondent who reviews on this page to-day the past and future of the so-called "sterling area" suggests that this flexible conception, whose wide potentialities had been demonstrated before the war, might hereafter become—no doubt under another name and other forms of organization—"a firm basis of mutual understanding and practical cooperation for countries which wish to participate in the experiment of stabilizing national income and providing full employment". The more immediate task is, however, to set going once more with the least possible delay the wheels of production and trade in the liberated countries. Great Britain can directly contribute to this process in two ways—by ascertaining what these countries require (other than immediate relief requirements to be met by Unrra) that she can supply, and what she in turn requires that they can produce, and by matching the one against the other. This cannot, however, be done—especially in the economically primitive conditions of the present state of emergency—through the unsupported enterprise of individual traders, each interested only in one range of commodities and in one-way trade. A broad view of the whole field is required. If these mutually fruitful processes of exchange are to be set in motion in time to restore the economic stability—and perhaps to save the political stability —of these countries, strong Government initiative will be needed; and the British Government must be the prime mover. The visit of Mr. Churchill and Mr. Eden may give the much needed impetus to action already too long delayed.

'The development of closer military and economic links between Great Britain and the countries of western Europe fits into a general picture of European and world security of which it is an essential part. On the one hand, western Europe, including Great Britain, is, as American opinion has come increasingly to recognize, an outer bastion of the defence of the western hemisphere; and the strengthening of this bastion is a decisive interest of the American nations as well as of the whole British Commonwealth. On the other hand, the security of this region, assured in the first instance by an integration of its own resources, is a necessary complement to the system of security which Soviet Russia herself is building up in eastern Europe. Both for Britain and for western Europe development on these lines represents a departure from tradition which may court and encounter prejudice, misrepresentation, and genuine misunderstanding. But for both it has become a necessity of the first order. The revolutionary changes wrought by the war allow of no return. The option of continuing to stand where they stood is no longer open either to Britain or to her closest neighbours in Europe. The choice which remains is to recede into a secondary role on the stage of world affairs, or to move forward through hitherto untried experiments in common policy and organization to fresh fields of achievement.'

The policy set forth in this article was further developed in *The Times* leader of the 20th November, entitled:

## 'MECHANISM OF PEACE'[1]

'The outlines of the structure of peace sketched at Dumbarton Oaks have still to be filled in, and given concrete solidity, in forthcoming talks between the principal leaders of the United Nations. But they suffice to show that full account has been taken of the main lesson taught by the disappointed hopes of 1919 and by the five years of struggle to retrieve the consequences of the disappointment. Peace has to be maintained by the same weapons and the same organization that have made victory possible. The lesson is not new. An organized preponderance of power has been the hall-mark of all the relatively peaceful periods of the world's history. In the nineteenth century the *pax Britannica* acted in restraint of war through the exercise of unchallengeable sea-power. This power depended upon the possession not only of fleets but of fortified harbours throughout the world on which their operations could be based. But it was effective only within the limits of this system. The veto of Canning could prevent a war by Spain for the recovery of her revolted dependencies in America; on the other hand, the *pax Britannica* could do nothing to stop Bismarck's continental campaigns against Denmark, Austria, and France.

'The political conditions are now entirely changed. Action in

[1] Reprinted from *The Times*, 20th November 1944, by permission.

S

defence of world peace has long ceased to be within the strength of a single nation, or indeed of the whole English-speaking world, and must be a responsibility shared by all the great peace-seeking Powers. But the strategic principle is the same as ever; whoever are the trustees of peace, they require, with the command of decisive force, the means to transfer it rapidly to any assigned part of their combined territories, and to place it athwart the communications of any possible aggressor. The scope of this principle is now enlarged, and indeed completed, by the entry into strategy of the element of air, which gives direct access to every point of both land and sea. A chain of bases for the operation of combined forces, on land, on sea, and in the air, is therefore the logical foundation for the strategy of world peace. The use of such bases, available as military need dictates to all members of the alliance, has been essential to the conduct of the war; it will be no less essential to the joint action of the United Nations as guarantors of the future peace. The technical developments of modern warfare, including the range, variety, and power of modern weapons, have made the old conception of alliances based on contingent obligations inoperative and obsolete. Standing military establishments are henceforth a condition of security.

'These general postulates have won a wide measure of acceptance. But the enunciation of broad principles of universal scope is no longer enough. The time has come to concert practical measures in terms of the specific conditions of particular areas; for though security is a world-wide theme, its detailed demands vary from ocean to ocean and from continent to continent, and call for the working out of the regional arrangements foreseen in the Dumbarton Oaks plan under the general superintendence of the supreme Security Council. Though security in the Pacific will before long present its particular problems, the progress of the war at this moment gives proper precedence to the consideration of European security; and whatever the precise forms of organization the key to that security lies in a system of permanent joint bases. The system will be one; and the link between its diverse elements will be provided not only by the over-all authority of the Security Council and its agencies but by the Anglo-Soviet treaty of May 1942, and by the agreement which may result from General de Gaulle's forthcoming visit to Moscow. But within this European system it is reasonable to suppose that Britain with the western Powers will play a principal role in the west and Russia with her European neighbours in the east. Strength and unity are overriding conditions of security both in the west and in the east.

'Great Britain has thus an urgent double task. On the one hand she must coordinate her action with her great partners in the world alliance and with her partners in the British Commonwealth; on the other hand she must with the cooperation of France and in the company of the Low Countries and the Scandinavian kingdoms build up a common organization of mutual defence, the lack of which bore such tragic fruit in 1940. These countries, taken together, form a single buttress of security in western Europe corresponding to the buttress in the east of which Russia will be the main support; and the emergency of war has forged a link between them which should henceforth be indissoluble. Nothing could do more to cement it than agreement among these countries for the common user of certain strategic bases, carrying with it agreement for common action by their armed forces; and never has the prevailing sentiment among their peoples been more favourable to the contracting of such engagements.

'Some of these common bases will be established, as they have been in time of war, on the territory of the United Nations themselves. Others will be established on the territory of the defeated enemy and will remain as a permanent guarantee of security. The military occupation properly so-called imposed on Germany after the war cannot, for obvious reasons, be indefinitely prolonged; and whether its duration be long or short, it will be imperative, at the moment of its withdrawal, to bring Germany within the scope of the general security system. The lasting instrument must be the maintenance on German territory of joint bases at certain ports and of a number of strategic airfields, perhaps coinciding with the ports of call of international civil aviation; and in this system of pooled security Germany, when ·she has at length served her term of penance and worked her passage back into the ranks of civilized nations, will be called on to cooperate with the other participants. Joint bases and joint contingents will thus remain on German soil, though with the title to their continuance amended. The occupation by victorious Powers of the territory of a defeated enemy—inevitably limited in time and, for this very reason, a wasting asset—will eventually be replaced by a comprehensive and permanent order, military and political, which alone can in the long run bring unity and peace to Europe.

'Once the issue of security is placed on this level, and treated as a matter not of negative measures of precaution and defence but of common organization for peace, familiar difficulties fall into a new perspective and become more readily soluble. Among them is the time-honoured problem of strategic frontiers: these cease to be relevant so soon as the instruments of security are maintained in the form of joint bases, whose location is determined under a common and accepted authority by considerations of strategic import, not of the national allegiance of the territory concerned. Nor can a system of organized military security be divorced from the economic organization which is a vital part of it. The control of "war potential" in the form of industrial power can perhaps be achieved in the initial stage by the unilateral action of the victorious Powers. But, like the more direct control of military occupation, such action will prove a wasting asset which cannot be effectively maintained over a long period through purely negative measures of destruction or prohibition. The security of joint military bases must be complemented and completed by the security of joint economic policies through which the German economy will be inseparably welded into a broader European framework. General de Gaulle had some such considerations in mind when he spoke recently of French interest in "a solution that combined the security of France and the Rhineland, the economic unity of the countries of the Rhine basin, and the future of the Ruhr as an arsenal for peace". The promotion of such far-sighted policies, particularly in relation to the European region which has become a main preoccupation of British security, is a prime responsibility of British statesmanship.'

On the 21st November *The Manchester Guardian* published an article called 'Western Europe',[1] which said: 'It is perfectly clear that no racehorse came out of the stable at Dumbarton Oaks. When at last the new organization is trotted out for our inspection we shall see a mule—a very strong mule, no doubt, with a good kick and a ready bite, but still a mule which by its very nature can not beget anything for the future.

'This result will not change the opinion of those in this and other countries who hold that in the long run peace cannot be secured until all nations, including the Great Powers, agree to limit their absolute sovereignty and accept some measure of international authority. This idea, of course, is not new. Before the war it was advocated by able writers like Mr. Brailsford in this country and Mr. Clarence Streit in the United States. The

[1] Reprinted from *The Manchester Guardian* 21st November 1944, by permission.

logic is, indeed, inescapable; the difficulty is how to achieve it. There is no hope that by some miracle of conversion all the Governments in the world will wake up one morning ready to abandon their independence and accept federal government. The idea, if it comes at all, will come slowly and will probably at first be limited to certain groups of nations in certain parts of the world. Dr. Mitrany has argued in his Chatham House booklet, "A Working Peace System", that progress should be made by nations combining to carry out particular tasks as they arise (as, for instance, the Allies are doing in this war), and the various international councils created for this purpose might then be ultimately merged into a supreme political organization. Mr. Lippmann has written of an "Atlantic community" which does not seem to exist in geography or politics. And in a recently published booklet, "The Way to Peace", Mr. Lionel Curtis makes the more practical proposal that the British democracies (by which he means the British Commonwealth) should join with those of Western Europe in a union for common security which would allow their national Governments to concentrate all their time and attention on social reform.

'It is clear that we are still a good long way from this. Recently, however, the idea of a "closer association" of the Western democracies has been brought into the realm of current politics by the initiative of M. Spaak, the Belgian Foreign Minister, and Mr. Eden himself has hinted at the British Government's approval.'

The following dispatch from *The Times* correspondent in Canada also suggests that this trend of opinion is not confined to the British Press:

## 'BELGIAN DESIRE FOR PARTNERS
### THE BRITISH CONNEXION

On returning to Ottawa from a visit to Belgium, Baron Silvercruys, Belgian Ambassador to Canada, said that the so-called neutrality policy to which Belgium adhered before the war was now dead and could be resurrected only if there were a revival of isolationism among the allied Great Powers and a drift back to "collective insecurity". Although the Belgians upheld the ideal of an international peace organization, they also felt that a closer and more intimate partnership should be established with their immediate neighbours, and particularly with Holland; Belgians were keenly aware that the integrity of Belgium and the safety of Britain were interdependent, and that for military and defence purposes the two countries were but one.'

. CHAPTER XLI

# DEMOCRATIC AND AUTHORITARIAN STATES

WHY do I think that a union for defence must begin with democracies and democracies only? I am glad of this chance of giving my reasons more fully than I could in my outline of policy. Let me start with a leaf from my own experience.

People opposed to South African Union in the Transvaal, Natal, and the Orange Free State pointed to the fact that the population of the Cape Colony was larger than the populations of the three other colonies added together. The proposal to unite them all under one government was, they argued, just a plot to deprive the three smaller and younger democracies of their independence and reannex them to the Cape Colony; for in a Union parliament the Cape members would be able to outvote those from the Transvaal, Natal, and the Orange Free State.

That was the most formidable argument we had to meet. Meet it we did, and, when the Union was in being, this alarming prediction that one colony would outvote the other three was falsified in fact. The members from the Cape never voted *en bloc*, nor did those from the other colonies. The party divisions ran in varying proportions through all four.

That is what always happens in federations. In Congress at Washington the members from any one State seldom if ever vote in a block. Democrat members from New York vote one way and Republican members from New York another. And as this is true in varying proportions of every State of the U.S.A. so I think it would be in such an international union as I am suggesting.

In the union parliament the questions at issue would be those of defence and of foreign policy—how much should be spent to ensure the union against risk of war, and whether the policy adopted by ministers could be trusted to minimize those risks. Decisions would be made after full debate, and if the government case broke down in discussion, some government members, defying the government Whips, would give their votes to the opposition and throw the government out of power. This happened in our parliament in 1940, when the Chamberlain Government resigned.

If the union included an authoritarian state, the members sent to the union parliament from the state would not be elected by its citizens, but appointed by the authoritarian government. They would vote together in a block as ordered by their government, and would not be free like the members elected from democratic states to decide how to cast their votes after listening to the debate. In a crisis this solid authoritarian block would often hold the balance between the parties drawn from the democratic states. The fate of governments would thus be determined by the government of the one authoritarian state. In actual practice the system would not be based on the principle of democracy, on government by public discussion.

The fathers of the American Union in their wisdom provided against this danger, when they laid it down that only states founded on democracy might join the Union.

Not long after the assassination of Huey Long, the Governor of Louisiana, I was staying with President Lowell of Harvard, whom I had long regarded as a master in the science of politics. When I asked him what it was all about he explained that Governor Long was establishing a dictatorship in Louisiana and would have done so had not his autocracy been tempered by assassination. I then referred to the constitutional provision which purports to exclude from the Union states which are not democracies, and asked, 'What would the United States have done if Governor Long had survived to create a dictatorship in Louisiana?' With a worried look on his face the President shrugged his shoulders and said, 'Search me'.

In my youth, when free institutions were regarded as invulnerable, everyone thought that it was only a matter of time before Germany, Russia, and even Japan and China would adopt and practise constitutional government. They were all moving in that direction, until at the close of the last century a feeling grew up that free institutions were no longer invulnerable. Very soon the movement towards democracy in all these countries was reversed. And that will go on unless and until democracies have united to make the principle for which they stand too firmly established and too deeply entrenched for any aggressor to think of attacking. When that has happened the authoritarian countries will again move in the same direction, learn to adopt systems of government responsible to the people themselves, and so qualify for membership in a union for the common defence of free institutions. It will happen all the more quickly if, in a League of Nations, authoritarian states are in constant touch with a union of democracies.

Such a union cannot hope to succeed unless the first experiment is confined to the most experienced democracies, as it was in America. That experiment only succeeded because it began with thirteen states experienced in democracy. Even so, their adoption of the federal constitution was the greatest miracle in history. But even the miracle wrought by Washington and Hamilton would not have sufficed unless those two statesmen had seen to it that their novel contrivance would work in practice. It was the devoted work of Washington as President and of Hamilton as Treasurer which, more than any other single factor, convinced the people of America that the new Constitution was a practical means, and the only practical means, of preserving the national freedom they had won in the fight for their independence. This page of history is indeed worth a volume of Logic.

## CHAPTER XLII

# PARTING WORDS

THE policy outlined in these talks is not submitted as a panacea to solve all the problems by which we are faced in these difficult times. It is simply the best answer I can give to the question foremost in all our minds: How can the fear of war which overshadows mankind be removed? No practical answer to a question like that can be found which is free from possible danger and difficulty. But is the possible danger of the change proposed really so great as the actual danger of world war if things remain as they are? And as to difficulties, they are sometimes found to be not so great in reality as they seemed when figured in our minds. Let me give you a case from my own experience.

A banquet was given in Cape Town to the delegates who were going to attend the National Convention at Durban to consider the project of South African Union. The leading speech was made by the Prime Minister of the Cape, Mr. John X. Merriman, a brilliant and cynical politician. From first to last his speech was a warning to his listeners to expect nothing from the Convention. He dwelt at length on the difficulties to be faced, and referred to them as lions in the path. His hearers were obviously discouraged and depressed, and I had to follow him. In the few minutes that were left I said that no doubt the Prime Minister was referring to the scene in the *Pilgrim's Progress* when Christian and Faithful encountered two lions in the path. He had, however, forgotten to add that when Christian and Faithful boldly faced the lions they found that both of them were chained.

Now this was exactly what happened at the National Convention. It faced the difficulties and found a way of surmounting them all—even the question of where the capital should be. Within two years the Union of South Africa was an accomplished fact. And so it will be when political leaders are found who will face the difficulties of merging states into one international union.

I have spoken frankly in these talks because the feeling has

grown upon me that the men and women who are winning
the war must also see to it that we win the peace. If not, the
peace will be lost a second time and you yourselves may live
to see your sons and daughters facing an ordeal more terrible
even than you and your fathers have had to face in this century. For that reason I hope that as many as possible of those
now serving will try to enter political life after this war.
Please do not infer from what I have said that I share the
vulgar opinion that politicians are unworthy people to whose
failings are due all the ills that our flesh is heir to. From my
own experience I should say that politicians as a class are not
worse but better, much better than the average run of human
beings. The more I see of Members of Parliament and the
lives they lead, the more am I seized with admiration of the
public spirit and devotion with which they face a tiresome
and tedious routine which deprives them of privacy and
leisure until they fall ill and their doctors have cancelled all
their engagements. As I see the drudgery they face year
after year (which I myself have never faced) I salute politicians as men to whom the public interest owes far more than
it does to their arm-chair critics, of whom I am one. There
is, I believe, no body of men, except those who fight for their
country, more deserving of public gratitude. But this would
cease to be true if once they claimed to be free from the
criticism of people outside their ranks, and that claim were
allowed. For there are in the practice of every profession
tendencies which unless recognized and watched impair the
value of those who follow it.

Politics in peace is the noblest of callings, as service in the
field is the noblest in war. It is just for that reason that I
urge the importance of watching the effects which political
life has on the minds of those who follow that noble profession, effects which tend to impair their value. To avoid
a disease you must know what causes it. A man whose job
lies in a tropical country may avoid malaria if knowing its
cause he takes a mosquito-proof net to sleep in and a plentiful
stock of quinine. So you in political life may escape its
endemic diseases if from the outset you realize your danger

in following public opinion instead of trying to lead it, of regarding the machinery to which you grow used as a framework too sacred to change, and of shutting your eyes and mouths to facts which clearly point to the need for change.

Disraeli, a great Conservative leader, realized how slow politicians are to see when a revolution is overtaking them. In his novel *Coningsby* he depicts a gathering of Tories in a country house after the Reform Bill had been passed into law. After long discussion they reach the conclusion that public opinion can still be frustrated and their ancient privileges preserved by skilful management of the new electoral machinery. Their host then turns to the gifted Jew Sidonia who has listened in silence, and asks his opinion. Sidonia briefly replies, 'You cannot evade a revolution.'

It is not this country only but the whole world that is now facing a revolution. In an article in *Foreign Affairs*, the Journal published by the Council on Foreign Relations in New York,[1] Count Carlo Sforza wrote as follows:

'We need not be astonished at the length of the crisis precipitated by the generation of 1914. The war of 1914–18 and the uneasy armistice which lasted until 1939 were stages of a revolution, and revolutions go on for a long while. The nature of the revolution is now plain. We are witnessing, and enduring, the breakup of nationalism. . . . On the day when the excesses of nationalism have been finally buried in disgrace and ruin we shall move with more speed towards the next stage of man's political development. The "realists" who can see no future less bloodstained than the past forget that problems can come to a head in certain periods and be disposed of. During long periods of history the "best people" believed that slavery was a law of nature. But the idea of slavery has been totally discredited; and more was done to wipe out slavery during the forty years which followed the American Civil War than during ten preceding centuries. . . . Our revolution, then, is the breakup of the dogma of nationalism.'

It is this revolution that political leaders are still hoping to evade.

Sir Edward Grigg, in his recent book *British Foreign*

[1] Vol. xxii, No. 1, Oct. 1943.

*Policy*, writes (p. 9): 'I find it impossible in retrospect to evade a growing conviction that even by that date (1921–2) within but three or four years of a struggle which had bound them very close, the major allies had already abandoned themselves to courses which were bound to end, if they remained unchecked, in the ruin of their common ideals and hopes.'

These ominous words exactly apply to the course of least resistance to which the major allies are now committed, not after the war, but while their forces are still fighting and dying in the field. With one voice they are telling their peoples that war can now be prevented by a league of sovereign nations in which the major responsibility is to be carried by the four or five leading states. 'Leagues of Governments are necessarily concerned with making the world safe for national sovereignty and not either for democracy or the people.' So Lothian had written in 1939.[1] He was the only man in our public life who has dared to say that the maintenance of national sovereignties is no longer compatible with the maintenance of our civilization. In February 1940, speaking as British Ambassador to the House of Delegates and Senate of Virginia, he said:

'As Mr. Elihu Root said a few years ago, mankind is confronted with almost the same fundamental problems as confronted the fathers of the American Constitution. If they are to be solved they must be diagnosed and answered as convincingly as were the problems of 1776 in the Federalist papers and the American Constitution. To-day as then an anarchy of sovereign States cannot escape chronic war or preserve individual liberty or create the conditions of prosperity and employment within their own boundaries unless, in some way, they can bring themselves collectively under the reign of a single constitutional law.'

I remarked on the growing doubt in the public mind as to whether world wars can in fact be prevented. I believe that men in the mass have realized by a kind of intuition what Lothian saw (though not in such definite terms as he did) that lasting peace can never exist in a world split up into

[1] *The Ending of Armageddon.*

sovereign states, with anarchy between them. When all their leaders insist that this must remain unchanged, men feel in their hearts that the peace they are promised is a house built upon sand. While their instinct tells them that sooner or later the nations must choose whether to maintain their sovereignties or their peace, their leaders continue to offer them volumes of logic to prove that the page of history, which records the failure of the League to bring peace to mankind, can be disregarded.

Lothian is dead, but his message lives on, a resounding challenge to the shop-soiled assumption on which the British and Allied plan for securing peace to the world is based. That message will rank, I believe, as the paramount truth for want of which whole nations fare the worse. Sooner or later events will give their inexorable judgement and decide whether or no Lothian was a false alarmist or a wakeful watchman who uttered his warnings in vain to ears that were deaf. If the structure of peace, built upon league and alliance, should again collapse, the error of those who have founded it so will appear great beyond measure, to be liquidated in millions of lives and in anguish untold. They will bear a responsibility heavier than human shoulders have ever assumed. They will live in history as men who had planned and achieved for freedom the crowning victory of all time—and then, having a pearl richer than all his tribe, threw it away; who, holding the fate of mankind in their hands, knew not the day of their visitation. Believing this, let me say it now, on the chance that my words may reach and convince some to whose voices the multitude listens, who can raise a standard to which the wise and honest can repair. Then, having told the world the only alternative to another such dreadful conflict, they can, like Washington, entrust the event to the hands of God.

## CHAPTER XLIII

# CONCLUSION

IN an earlier chapter I stated my faith that the personality of which we are each conscious (though not through our senses) is more real than the bodies we touch and see. I argued that the final reality within the material and visible universe is of that nature—personality freed from all limitations, the Holy Spirit of God—and so creative that He must bring into existence other creators to join as partners with Himself in the endless work of creation. To that end He gave men free-will and intelligence to learn from experience what action would make, and what destroy, what was in practice right or wrong. But He could not then by supernatural means reveal to us what was right or wrong, still less relieve us of the consequences wrought by our own mistakes. For to do so would destroy that very quality of free-will which admits us to partnership with Him in the work of creation. He does not intervene in matters subject to human control, but leaves us to learn the truth from experience—by trial and error.[1]

But where then does the partnership of God with man in the work of creation come in, if God, having given us free-will, must then stand aside and leave us to judge from our own experience what makes or un-makes, what is right or wrong? My answer is that there are things beyond human control. We can never determine how or when men of genius, that is to say, men of exceptional power to create, will be born. I cannot believe that such men as Moses and the Prophets, as St. Paul, Caesar, Edward I, Wycliffe, Hus, Luther or Milton, Washington, Napoleon, Lincoln, Mazzini, Marx, and above all Christ Himself, appeared on this earth at the moment they did by the mere operation of chance. Chance is, indeed, no more than a word we use to cover our own inability to trace an effect to its complex of causes. From time to time creation is brought to a standstill by obsessions, fixed ideas in the

---

[1] Since I wrote this paragraph the point it makes has been convincingly argued by Lord Samuel in Chapter XXI of *An Unknown Land*, published by Allen & Unwin, Ltd.

minds of men which no longer apply to the changing conditions of life. I think that when this happens the Master Creator Himself sees to it that some man has been born great enough to release the deadlock by lifting the minds of men out of the ruts, the deepening channels worn by the wheels of custom. Napoleons and Hitlers may be needed to shatter obsolete systems. Others far greater, like Washington and Lincoln, are sent at the right moment to show how the work of creation can be renewed on a higher plane.

When national sovereignty had done its work a Hitler was needed to shatter a social structure based on that principle. In God's own time some outstanding figure will emerge from the ranks of the publicists themselves, some leader whose voice can reach millions of listeners, who will tell them how they can really establish a 'peace which will afford to all nations the means of dwelling in safety within their own boundaries and which will afford assurance that all men in all lands may live out their lives in freedom from fear and want'. Millions will follow that leader's call to begin merging their sovereignties into one international state, and when that happens publicists in thousands will follow suit and come to think that that was what they themselves have always believed and said.

Such a leader must, I think, come from the ranks of the publicists themselves. When the Jewish hierarchy had destroyed Jesus, the leader who shattered the restrictions of Judaism was a Pharisee of the Pharisees. Wycliffe, Hus, and Luther, who challenged the authority of a hierarchy which was stifling true religion, were priests themselves. It needed a politician to convince the majority of his people that America could not remain half slave and half free. When Lincoln, their elected President, began to utter this truth, he quickly convinced a majority that had scarcely listened to Garrison, and slavery was abolished at the cost of a civil war, countless dollars, and a million American lives.

No wiser word has been spoken in this war than by Captain Cyril Falls when he said 'Let us stop saying "Hitler cannot win" and begin saying "Hitler shall not win."' Let us face the fact that Hitler might win. So he might, unless free men put into this struggle their last ounce of nerve and strength. Failing that the world may be plunged into chaos, as in the Dark Ages, a chaos in which nothing but brute force and the will of the stronger prevail. But no permanent order can be founded on Hitlerism, on mere physical force, on denial that right differs from wrong.

'And, behold, the Lord passed by, and a great and strong wind rent the mountains, and brake in pieces the rocks before the Lord; but the Lord was not in the wind: and after wind an earthquake; but the Lord was not in the earthquake: and after the earthquake a fire; but the Lord was not in the fire: and after the fire a still small voice. And it was so, when Elijah heard it, that he wrapped his face in his mantle, and went out, and stood in the entering in of the cave.'

How long this era of storm will last in which nothing but violence can count, whether for months, for years, or centuries, no man living can say. But of this I am sure, that sooner or later the 'still small voice' which bids men pursue the interests of others before their own, the voice of God Himself in their hearts, will be heard again, and will move them to create 'a wider and permanent system of general security'. And that system will, I believe, be shaped on lines not very different from those here sketched, by virtue of facts which cannot be changed. Nothing will greatly alter the fact that the limit of intelligent life and experience accorded to men is somewhere about 70 years for each. Still less can anything alter the fact that in each of those years there are but 365 days and in each of those days but 24 hours. When we think what men like Moses, the Prophets, Plato, and Pericles were, thousands of years ago, we can scarcely expect any great enlargement of human capacities within measurable time. Facts like these will always limit the amount of business which any one government can transact. They will mean that the tasks of maintaining peace in the world, and keeping pace with social reform, must be assigned to different governments, the task of maintaining peace to an international government, while the tasks of social reform are reserved to national governments. For the reasons explained in these pages the functions assigned to an international government must be closely restricted, and national governments must be left to control the composition and structure of the nations they rule. My belief is that that invisible force which the Greeks personified as ἀνάγκη, necessity, immutable facts, will impose that division. And whether it comes soon or late depends upon when from the ranks of the publicists the world is given a leader who, like Washington or Lincoln, can surmount the obsession of national sovereignty which binds the publicist mind, and bring the great issue before the people themselves.

Some twenty-six years ago I vainly hoped that the brilliant leadership that nerved our peoples to endure the sufferings which brought them to victory would also be used to secure their sons from facing those sufferings once more. That hope was expressed in words that fell on ears that were deaf, or more likely never reached them at all. I then little thought in the span of my own lifetime to see such another war, or to cherish that hope once more. Again I revive that unconquerable hope and can find no words in which to express it other than those which were then written.

In all these Dominions, so remote from each other, so diverse in character, and yet so closely united by a freedom wide and single as the ocean which connects them, are leaders whose words can reach to all their coasts. The attack, by which that freedom is menaced, was fostered and invited by the weakness of the Commonwealth, a weakness caused by failure to mould its growth in accordance with the necessary principle of its being. Self-government has not been applied to the first and greatest of public interests. The burden of controlling the issues of national life and death has not been placed, where alone it can rest with safety, on every citizen of the Commonwealth able to bear it. Its own internal disorganization is a primary cause of this war, and the chasm in its foundation must now be filled with the flower of its youth. Yet for all this failure it remains the hope of freedom, the essential system through which men can acquire and practise the art of governing themselves; and therefore it is that thousands have risen from every part of it to oppose with their own bodies the blows which are battering its walls. Never in the history of free states have men offered themselves so freely for the public cause. For many of them danger was easier to face than the discipline of military life, but they have made themselves subject to its rule that others might continue to govern themselves. There was little to draw them in the hope of personal distinction, which is hard to come by where the company of valour is so vast and every day calls for deeds daring as any for which men have been noted in lesser times. From the uttermost parts of the Commonwealth they have come to honour their uncovenanted bond, obedient to one uncalculating purpose; and the fields of their final achievement, where they lie in a fellowship too close and a peace too deep to be broken, are the image and epitome of the cause for which they fell. They have not feared to enter the darkness, because they walk by a light that is in themselves, which burns and shall burn unquenched wherever their ashes lie mingled by land or sea. From that fervent dust the breath of one man might kindle a flame whereby these nations might find and follow the print of their feet. So might a new birth of freedom be raised from their seed. So might these severed threads be caught up and woven into the stuff of other men's lives.

PRINTED IN
GREAT BRITAIN
AT THE
UNIVERSITY PRESS
OXFORD
BY
JOHN JOHNSON
PRINTER
TO THE
UNIVERSITY